...

TAIJI CHIN NA

(Qin Na)

太極擒拿

The Seizing Art of Taijiquan

...

Disclaimer

The author(s) and publisher of this material are NOT RESPONSIBLE in any manner whatsoever for any injury which may occur through reading or following the instructions in this manual.

The activities, physical or otherwise, described in this material may be too strenuous or dangerous for some people, and the reader(s) should consult a physician before engaging in them.

Publisher's Cataloging in Publication
(Prepared by Quality Books, Inc.)

Yang, Jwing-Ming, 1946-
    Taiji chin na / Yang Jwing-Ming.
    p. cm
    Preassigned LCCN: 95-60266
    ISBN 0-940871-37-8
    1. T'ai chi ch'uan. 2. Hand-to-hand fighting, Oriental. I.
Title.

GV504.Y36 1995   796.8'155
                                 QBI95-20097

ISBN: 0-940871-37-8

Library of Congress Card Catalog Number: 95-60266

Printed in Canada

Anatomical Drawings Copyright © 1994, TechPool Studios Corp. USA

YMAA Publication Center 楊氏武藝協會

38 Hyde Park Avenue • Jamaica Plain, MA 02130
1-800-669-8892 • email: ymaa@aol.com
Please see inside back cover for a complete listing of YMAA books and video-

太極擒拿

法賀

To My First Taiji Teacher

Kao Tao

謹奉獻給高濤老師

PROVERBS:

———————

"The Taller the Bamboo Grows, the Lower It Bows."

———————

"The Truly Humble Always Know Others,
and Do Not Care If Other People Know Them."

———————

"Those Who Have to Criticize Others are
Those Whose Minds are Void."

———————

"The Yin Side of Dignity is False Pride and Self-Spite."

———————

"Those Who Despise Themselves are Always
Concerned With Their Dignity."

ACKNOWLEDGMENTS

Thanks to Tim Comrie for his photography, Jerry Leake for design and layout, and James B. Philips for the cover drawing. Thanks also to Yang Mei-Ling, Ramel Rones, and Craig McConnell for general help, to Ray Ahles, David W. Grantham, Andrew Murray, Jeffrey Pratt, David Ripianzi, and many other YMAA members for proofing the manuscript and for contributing many valuable suggestions and discussions. Special thanks to James O'Leary for his editing. And a very special thanks to Liang Dexing (Jeffrey D. S, Liang) for his beautiful calligraphy on the front pages of this volume.

ABOUT THE AUTHOR

DR. YANG JWING-MING, PH.D.

Dr. Yang Jwing-Ming

Dr. Yang Jwing-Ming was born on August 11th, 1946, in *Xinzhu Xian, Taiwan,* Republic of China. He started his *Wushu* (*Gongfu* or *Kung Fu*) training at the age of fifteen under the *Shaolin* White Crane (*Bai He*) Master Cheng Gin-Gsao. Master Cheng originally learned Taizuquan from his grandfather when he was a child. When Master Cheng was fifteen years old, he started learning White Crane from Master Jin Shao-Feng, and he followed him for twenty-three years until Master Jin's death.

In thirteen years of study (1961-1974 A.D.) under Master Cheng, Dr. Yang became an expert in the White Crane Style of Chinese martial arts, which includes both the use of barehands and of various weapons such as saber, staff, spear, trident, two short rods, and many other weapons. With the same master he also studied White Crane *Qin Na* (or *Chin Na*), *Tui Na* and *Dian Xue* massages, and herbal treatment.

At the age of sixteen, Dr. Yang began the study of *Taijiquan* (*Yang* Style) under Master Kao Tao. After learning from Master Kao, Dr. Yang continued his study and research of *Taijiquan* with several masters and senior practitioners such as Master Li Mao-Ching and Mr. Wilson Chen in *Taipei*. Master Li learned his *Taijiquan* from the well-known Master Han Ching-Tang, and Mr. Chen learned his *Taijiquan* from Master Chang Xiang-San. Dr. Yang has mastered the Taiji barehand sequence, pushing hands, the two-man fighting sequence, *Taiji* sword, *Taiji* saber, and *Taiji Qigong*.

When Dr. Yang was eighteen years old he entered Tamkang College in *Taipei Xian* to study Physics. In college he began the study of traditional *Shaolin* Long Fist (*Changquan* or *Chang Chuan*) with Master Li Mao-Ching at the Tamkang College *Guoshu* Club (1964-1968 A.D.), and eventually became an assistant instructor under Master Li. In 1971 he completed his M.S. degree in Physics at the National Taiwan University, and then served in the Chinese Air Force from 1971 to 1972. In the service, Dr. Yang taught Physics at the Junior Academy of the Chinese Air Force while also teaching *Wushu*. After being honorably discharged in 1972, he returned to Tamkang College to teach Physics and resume study under Master Li Mao-Ching. From Master Li, Dr. Yang learned Northern Style *Wushu*, which includes both barehand (especially kicking) techniques and numerous weapons.

In 1974, Dr. Yang came to the United States to study Mechanical Engineering at Purdue University. At the request of a few students, Dr. Yang began to teach *Gongfu* (*Kung Fu*), which resulted in the foundation of the Purdue University Chinese Kung Fu Research Club in the spring of 1975. While at Purdue, Dr. Yang also taught college-credited courses in *Taijiquan*. In May of 1978 he was awarded a Ph.D. in Mechanical Engineering by Purdue.

In 1980, Dr. Yang moved to Houston to work for Texas Instruments. While in Houston he founded Yang's Shaolin Kung Fu Academy, which was eventually taken over by his student Mr. Jeffery Bolt after he moved to Boston in 1982. Dr. Yang founded Yang's Martial Arts Academy (YMAA) in Boston on October 1, 1982.

In January of 1984 he gave up his engineering career to devote more time to research, writing, and teaching. In March of 1986 he purchased property in the Jamaica Plain area of Boston to be used as the headquarters of the new organization, Yang's Martial Arts Association. The organization has continued to expand, and, as of July 1st 1989, YMAA has become just one division of Yang's Oriental Arts Association, Inc. (YOAA, Inc).

In summary, Dr. Yang has been involved in Chinese *Wushu* since 1961. During this time, he has spent thirteen years learning *Shaolin* White Crane (*Bai He*), Shaolin Long Fist (*Changquan*), and *Taijiquan*. Dr. Yang has more than twenty-six years of instructional experience: seven years in Taiwan, five years at Purdue University, two years in Houston, Texas, and twelve years in Boston, Massachusetts.

In addition, Dr. Yang has also been invited to offer seminars around the world to share his knowledge of Chinese martial arts and *Qigong*. The countries he has visited include Canada, Mexico, France, Italy, Poland, England, Ireland, Portugal, Switzerland, Germany, Hungary, and Saudi Arabia.

Dr. Yang has published nineteen other volumes on the martial arts and *Qigong*:

1. ***Shaolin Chin Na***; Unique Publications, Inc., 1980.
2. ***Shaolin Long Fist Kung Fu***; Unique Publications, Inc., 1981.
3. ***Yang Style Tai Chi Chuan***; Unique Publications, Inc., 1981.
4. ***Introduction to Ancient Chinese Weapons***; Unique Publications, Inc., 1985.
5. ***Chi Kung – Health and Martial Arts***; YMAA Publication Center, 1985.
6. ***Northern Shaolin Sword***; YMAA Publication Center, 1985.
7. ***Advanced Yang Style Tai Chi Chuan, Vol.1, Tai Chi Theory and Tai Chi Jing***; YMAA Publication Center, 1986.
8. ***Advanced Yang Style Tai Chi Chuan, Vol.2, Martial Applications***; YMAA Publication Center, 1986.
9. ***Analysis of Shaolin Chin Na***; YMAA Publication Center, 1987.
10. ***The Eight Pieces of Brocade***; YMAA Publication Center, 1988.
11. ***The Root of Chinese Chi Kung – The Secrets of Chi Kung Training***; YMAA Publication Center, 1989.
12. ***Muscle/Tendon Changing and Marrow/Brain Washing Chi Kung - The Secret of Youth***; YMAA Publication Center, 1989.

13. *Hsing Yi Chuan – Theory and Applications*; YMAA Publication Center, 1990.
14. *The Essence of Tai Chi Chi Kung – Health and Martial Arts*;
    YMAA Publication Center, 1990.
15. *Qigong for Arthritis*; YMAA Publication Center, 1991.
16. *Chinese Qigong Massage - General Massage*; YMAA Publication Center, 1992.
17. *How to Defend Yourself*; YMAA Publication Center, 1992.
18. *Baguazhang – Emei Baguazhang*; YMAA Publication Center, 1994.
19. *Comprehensive Applications of Shaolin Chin Na – The Practical Defense
    of Chinese Seizing Arts*; YMAA Publication Center, 1995.

Dr. Yang has also published the following videotapes:

1. *Yang Style Tai Chi Chuan and Its Applications*;
   YMAA Publication Center, 1984.
2. *Shaolin Long Fist Kung Fu – Lien Bu Chuan and Its Applications*;
   YMAA Publication Center, 1985.
3. *Shaolin Long Fist Kung Fu – Gung Li Chuan and Its Applications*;
   YMAA Publication Center, 1986.
4. *Shaolin Chin Na*; YMAA Publication Center, 1987.
5. *Wai Dan Chi Kung, Vol. 1 – The Eight Pieces of Brocade*;
   YMAA Publication Center, 1987.
6. *Chi Kung for Tai Chi Chuan*; YMAA Publication Center, 1990.
7. *Qigong for Arthritis*; YMAA Publication Center, 1991.
8. *Qigong Massage – Self Massage*; YMAA Publication Center, 1992.
9. *Qigong Massage – With a Partner*; YMAA Publication Center, 1992.
10. *Defend Yourself 1 – Unarmed Attack*; YMAA Publication Center, 1992.
11. *Defend Yourself 2 – Knife Attack*; YMAA Publication Center, 1992.
12. *Comprehensive Applications of Shaolin Chin Na 1*;
    YMAA Publication Center, 1995.
13. *Comprehensive Applications of Shaolin Chin Na 2*;
    YMAA Publication Center, 1995.
14. *Shaolin Long Fist Kung Fu – Yi Lu Mai Fu, Er Lu Mai Fu, and Their
    Applications*; YMAA Publication Center, 1995.
15. *Shaolin Long Fist Kung Fu – Shi Zi Tang and Its Applications*;
    YMAA Publication Center, 1995.

FOREWORD

GRANDMASTER LI MAO-CHING

The origin of *Taiji* is misty and turbid; we call it *Wuji* (no extremity). When it is extremely calm, it appears condensed and peaceful externally. However, concealed within it there exists both *Yin* and *Yang*. These two, *Yin* and *Yang,* mutually transport, vary, advance and withdraw. Consequently, there is neither void nor defect. The name we give to this hidden movement of *Yin* and *Yang* is *Taiji*.

Application of this theory to two person *Taiji* pushing hands practice reveals the same twin virtues of Yin and Yang. You and your partner mutually harmonize and coordinate with each other, and thereby improve both your own and each other's health. *Taiji* is used not only for defensive purposes. It says in the Yi Jing, or Book of Changes, that "The (hidden) beginning of the misty origin (i.e., *Wuji*) is called *Taiji*. From the nourishment of the two poles (i.e., *Yin* and *Yang*), ten thousand objects were born."[1]

The word "*Taiji*" was first seen in the **Yi Jing**. Though the word "*Taiji*" was also mentioned in the **Han** book, it recognized that this word originated from the **Yi Jing**. In the **Yi Jing**, it says: "*Taiji* is the key which dominates the generations and variations. (It) is the mother of the million objects between heaven and earth. (If we) trace the beginning of the world, it is certain that it originated from this — the sole misty *Qi*." It also says: "*Taiji*, the master of the *Qi*, is the order (i.e., rule), and the great foundation of the generations and variations is the origin of the sole *Qi*. Therefore, it is called 'the grand ultimate.' "Fu Xi's one day is *Taiji*, which are the same. It is the mother of the beginning. The origin of the million (objects) and the source of the sole *Qi*, therefore it is called 'grand ultimate.' (Which is) able to generate, originate, and transport without stop."[2 & 3]

It is said: "Knowing the origin, it is easy to figure out the root. Consequently, it is easy to explore the branches and leaves."[4] Therefore, the ultimate holy man (i.e., Confucius) said: "The gentleman keeps the origin. When the origin is firmly established, the Dao can then be begotten."[5] This is to encourage people. It means that the importance of education is in its origin. *Taiji* is the mother of the million objects between heaven and earth. This origin from *Taiji* begets countless generations. All of these vary from the sole *Qi*. That is why heaven and earth also reside within *Taiji* and are able to move ceaselessly. The birth of *Taiji* is the origin of the beginning. When this origin is applied to humanity, it is called Original *Qi*.

The million objects originated from Original *Qi*. It then derived into *Yin* and *Yang*, and followed with the four natural variations of the seasons. From this, we can see that *Qi* is the mother of the million objects. Therefore, when a human wishes to strengthen his or her body, he or she must first regulate his or her *Qi*. If the *Qi* is smooth and uniform, then the foundation of health can be established. This is the real meaning of variation in Taiji.

Among the five internal Yin organs in the human body, the kidneys acquire the Pre-birth *Qi*. This Pre-birth *Qi* is also called Original *Qi* or the Real *Qi*. The stomach area (i.e., Middle *Dan Tian*) stores the Post-birth *Qi*. In order to establish smooth and uniform *Qi*, a healthy condition of the kidneys and stomach are the main goals of Qigong practice.

Externally, you should train the fist techniques, and internally you should cultivate and regulate the *Qi* to nourish life. When *Qi* is circulated smoothly, then the muscles/tendons (i.e., physical body) will be comfortable and the blood circulation can be free. Naturally, hundreds of sicknesses will not occur.

When we apply *Taiji* into the origins of humanity, it is like a miniature heaven and earth. Before it is discriminated, it is calmness. Once it is divided, then *Yin* and *Yang* are discriminated (i.e., male and female). When this *Yin* and *Yang* are manifest in this world, the four seasons are derived and the five elements of *Qi* are generated. These five *Qi* are: metal, wood, water, fire, and the dust. When these five *Qi* are applied to humanity, they correspond to the lungs, liver, kidneys, heart, and spleen, which are the five *Yin* internal organs. These five *Qi* can also be applied to the East, West, South, North, and center.

The five elements have natural patterns of mutual generation and conquest following *Yin* and *Yang* theory. From the patterns of the five elements and the theory of *Yin* and *Yang*, millions of lives are derived and endure. When these patterns and theories are applied to the human body, it can become very strong. Among all of the Chinese martial arts, *Taijiquan* holds the first place, for it carries these five patterns and *Yin* and *Yang* theory. Therefore, a *Taijiquan* practitioner's ability to reach a profound level depends on how much he or she is able to ponder and understand the above theory.

When *Tiajiquan* is practiced, it is as soft as the falling leaves blown by autumn wind. But internally, it is storing the *Yang* and can assume shape as a sharp sword which is able to cut the vine and branches easily. The theory is simple, because you must know how to be relaxed, and then be able to tense at the correct instant. When you are relaxed, your mind is calm, neutral, and empty, until you feel you are transparent and invisible. It is like clouds at dawn or dusk, peaceful, calm and utterly still. Once the stored Jin is manifested, it is like a hurricane, whirlwind fast and powerful.

If a *Taijiquan* practitioner understands the theory of *Yin Yang*, and the mutual relations of the five elements, then he or she can be calm and round. He or she can also be strong internally, and manifest it externally. Naturally, the means of reaching this goal are through ceaseless study and practice.

When *Taijiquan* is applied externally, it is manifested into the four fighting categories: kicking (*Ti*, 踢), striking (*Da*, 打), wrestling (*Shuai*, 摔), and *Qin Na* (*Na*, 拿). This book will introduce the applications of *Qin Na* in *Taijiquan*.

The two words "*Qin Na*" were first used by the *Zejiang* Police Academy before World War II, in 1937. At that time, the principal of this academy, Mr. Zhao Long-Wen (趙龍文) was known as an excellent scholar. He was also a lover and promoter of the Chinese martial arts. At that time, all of the students, male or female, were required to learn and practice *Qin Na*, wrestling, and defense against both the dagger and the gun. The teacher was Mr. Han Ching-Tang (韓慶堂), and the assistants were Mrs. Jiang Tang-Zhu (江溏珠) and her husband. Mrs. Jiang was the daughter of a well known, retired Qing martial officer at that time. Later, Mr. Han's martial arts brother, Mr. Liu Jin-Sheng (劉錦昇) was also appointed as a coach, in order to satisfy the great demand for teaching. When they had time, they got together and mutually studied the techniques of Dividing the Muscle/Tendon and Misplacing the Bone (分筋搓骨手法). If they felt less than smooth or had difficulty, they would ask for the answer from Mrs. Jiang's father. From these efforts, they compiled a complete record of the postures used both in solo practice and also in mutual matching *Qin Na*. This compilation was then named the "Police *Qin Na* Applications"(分筋搓骨手法), or simply "*Qin Na* Techniques" (擒拿術). All of this history has been recounted in Dr. Yang's book: **Comprehensive Applications of Shaolin Chin Na**. I will not repeat it here. I will only conclude this foreword with some of the important points for *Qin Na* applications, and the requirements of success. This will enable you to reach a stage of "applying the techniques as you wish" (順心應手) and achieve effective control of your opponent. From my accumulation of more than fifty years of martial arts experience, I understand that a practitioner must have a firm foundation in Chinese *Gongfu*. Only then can he or she unify body and hands. Under these conditions, his or her legs will be able to coordinate the techniques naturally and smoothly. This is the key to winning and making the techniques effective.

Qin Na and *Taiji* have close relations which cannot be separated. When *Qin Na* is applied into the Eight Trigrams derived from *Taiji*, it occupies the word "thunder" (雷). This has the meaning of "thunder" in the Eight Trigrams. Among all *Taijiquan* techniques, *Cai* (pluck, 採), *Le* (pulling, 挒), *Lu* (capture, 擄), *An* (press down, 按), *Zhou* (elbow, 肘), and *Kao* (bump, 靠) are commonly adopted in *Qin Na*. When *Qin Na* is applied in *Taijiquan*, the defensive theory remains the same, using the soft against the hard. The only difference is that once *Qin Na* is used, in order to lock the opponent in position, the final control must be firm and hard. Though the result is different, the original theory remains the same.

When a practitioner learns Chinese *Gongfu* (i.e., imply external styles) and has a strong foundation, then he or she will be able to unify the hands, eyes (i.e., reaction), body (i.e., body movements), techniques, and stepping (手、眼、身、法、步). This will let you reach a stage of emitting power from the hands with speed like thunder, which allows nobody time to cover their ears. You attack the opponent without his or her expectation or preparation. In addition, you will be able to maneuver your strategies and vary your plan as you wish. In this case, you will have an advantage in catching the right timing and emitting your thunder strength. But remember, once you are delayed, you will have lost the opportunity. In *Taiji* it is said: "Once movement, ten thousand variations."

Again, I am very happy to hear that Dr. Yang Jwing-Ming has completed this book: ***Taiji Chin Na***, to share his knowledge with the public. I am so delighted that I have summarized the lessons and experience which I have accumulated from my teacher about *Qin Na*. This can be used as your reference.

Li Mao-Ching
Research Member
Guoshu Promoting Committee
Republic of China
February 15, 1995

---

1. 易:"渾元之始,是曰太極。二象所資,萬品之所生。"(孔子家語)

2. 易註:"太極者,主生化之樞,爲天地萬物之母,而溯世界之初始,則固來之,渾然一氣也。";"太極者,氣之主宰,其生化之序 生成變化之大本,一氣之源也,故曰太極。";"伏羲之一畫,即太極,爲一體,是太初之母,萬有之宗,一氣之源,故曰太極 能生,有始,運行不息。"(伏羲)

3. Fu Xi was the Chinese emperor during the legendary period (2852-2737 B.C.).

4. 易經:"所謂知其源,則流易測得其本,則枝葉易探。"

5. 聖曰:"君子務本,本立而道生。"

FOREWORD

GRANDMASTER JOU TSUNG HWA

After finishing this book, Master Yang Jwing-Ming shared it with me. I feel that this book is of great quality and I would like to offer some words about it.

First of all, the book is written by a very credible author, because Dr. Yang has a very high level of education in the Chinese martial arts. Most Chinese martial artists only have a background in either theory or practice, but Dr. Yang has a solid background in **both**. He also has a high level of western education, having graduated with a Ph.D. from Purdue University. He exhibits a fervent desire to share the wonders of Chinese martial arts with westerners, and his broad background in both eastern and western knowledge makes him a fine teacher.

Traditional Chin Na (Qin Na) books are mostly theoretical in nature, which makes learning from them difficult and incomplete. But because Dr. Yang makes such explicit use of pictures to show the techniques of Chin Na step by step, this book serves very well as a self-teaching guide. Also, because of his popular school (YMAA) in Massachusetts, and his many world-wide workshops, this book makes a fine lesson accompaniment as well, especially for those who find it otherwise difficult to learn by books alone.

I am sure the readers will find this Chin Na book to be informative as well as interesting.

Jou, Tsung Hwa
January 12, 1995

FOREWORD

MASTER LIANG SHOU-YU

I am very happy to see this book, ***Taiji Chin Na***, available in publication. This again is a great contribution made by Dr. Yang to the world martial arts society. He has constantly introduced and contributed the knowledge which he has obtained from Chinese culture, and also from his personal intelligent study and research. This kind of spirit is precious and difficult to find.

The contents of *Taijiquan* are very wide and profound. People always know that *Taiji* can maintain health, strengthen the physical and *Qi* bodies, relax the mind and spirit, culti-vate an individual's personality, and regulate the emotional and wisdom minds. However, many people are not aware that it can also offer a practitioner a great foundation for self-defense. From the drills of Pushing Hands and *Taiji* Sparring, a practitioner is able to com-prehend the keys of Leading *Jin* (*Yin Jin*, 引 勁), Neutralizing *Jin* (*Hua Jin*, 化 勁), Coiling *Jin* (*Chan Jin*, 纏 勁), Emitting Jin (*Fa Jin*, 發 勁), Understanding *Jin* (*Dong Jin*, 懂 勁), and many other skills for using the soft against the hard.

To Chinese martial arts society, *Taijiquan* is a widely accepted martial skill which can by used for health and self-defense. It contains the four required and necessary fighting skills and categories: kicking (*Ti*, 踢), striking (*Da*, 打), wrestling (*Shuai*, 摔), and *Qin Na* (*Na*, 拿). This book, *Taiji Chin Na*, is to introduce the correct and accurate *Qin Na* applications and tricks which can be used in the *Taiji* eight basic technical patterns or *Jins: Peng* (ward-off, 掤), *Lu* (rollback, 糉), *Ji* (squeeze or press, 擠), An (press or push down, 按), *Cai* (pluck, 採), *Lie* (rend or split, 挒), *Zhou* (elbow, 肘), and *Kao* (lean or press against, 靠). This book also introduces the *Qin Na* applications which can be applied from the 37 basic *Taijiquan* movements. Although *Taijiquan* develops many *Qin Na* skills, there has never been any-one who could compile and introduce them to the general public.

Dr. Yang has performed deep and profound research in *Qin Na*. His knowledge is the widest and the most profound among those *Qin Na* experts whom I have known. He has written many other *Qin Na* books; all have been widely welcomed and appreciated. He has introduced and shared his more than thirty years of personal *Taiji* and *Qin Na* experi-ence to western martial society. To the best of my knowledge, this is the first written book on *Taiji Qin Na* available in the world. I deeply believe that the publication of this book will enable reader to enhance their understanding of how to apply *Qin Na* in *Taijiquan*.

Canada
Liang Shou-Yu
December 1, 1994

PREFACE

DR. YANG JWING-MING

Even though *Qin Na* (*Chin Na*) has been popularly practiced in Chinese martial arts for hundreds of years, it was not until the 1982 publication of my first *Qin Na* book, **Shaolin Chin Na**, by Unique Publications, that these secret techniques of the Chinese martial arts were widely revealed to the western world. Since then, this art has grown so rapidly that my book has been translated into several different languages, making its way all over the world in less than ten years.

Later, due to the tremendous number of requests, I decided to write another volume which could discuss *Qin Na* theory and techniques in a more in-depth and profound manner. Therefore, the second volume, **The Analysis of Shaolin Chin Na – Instructor's Manual**, was published in 1987. It is beyond my belief that from 1982 until now, in such a short time, this art has grown so wide and popular that I have to travel to more than thirteen countries around the world at least twice a year to teach this art. I believe that the main reason for this is simply because this art can be adopted easily by almost all martial arts styles and blend into their own techniques. In addition to this, the *Qin Na* art has been proven to be one of the most effective defensive techniques, and it can be learned easily, even by a martial arts beginner.

From my experience teaching seminars, I realize that the hardest aspect of the art is not learning the techniques themselves, but in applying those techniques to dynamic situations. Usually, a practitioner can pick up a technique easily and make it effective only when his partner is cooperative. However, as we already know, when you encounter an enemy in real life, his cooperation is unlikely. Any success in executing a technique depends on how **accurate**, **fast**, **natural**, and **automatic** your reactions are, and the only way to develop skills in these areas is to practice. For this reason, I decided to write my third *Qin Na* book, **Comprehensive Applications of Shaolin Chin Na**, by YMAA, 1994, making this "seizing and controlling" art more complete.

As is well known in Chinese martial arts society, *Qin Na* techniques have been an integral part of every Chinese martial art style. It is not like Japanese *Jujitsu*, which is considered a style in itself. It is my understanding that there is no known "*Qin Na* Style" in Chinese martial arts. The reason for this is very simple. It is well known that there are four main fighting categories which exist in every Chinese martial style. These four categories are: Striking by Hands (*Da*, 打), Kicking with Legs (*Ti*, 踢), Wrestling (*Shuai*, 摔), and *Qin Na* (*Na*, 拿). It is also a fact that a substantial portion of Japanese culture was imported from China, beginning in the Chinese *Han* dynasty (206 B.C.-221 A.D.). It is further believed that the martial techniques which exist in Japan have been heavily influenced by the Chinese martial arts. When striking and kicking techniques passed to Japan and were derived into the *Karate* styles, Chinese wrestling became *Judo*, and *Qin Na* techniques were transformed into the art of *Jujitsu*. Many Japanese martial artists believe that the *Aikido* martial arts were actually developed from the theories of Chinese *Taijiquan* and *Qin Na*. From this, you can see that why *Qin Na* is not, in itself, considered to be a style in China.

There are also many *Qin Na* techniques in *Taijiquan*. In fact, due to the emphasis on sticking and adhering techniques in *Taijiquan's* close range fighting strategy, *Qin Na* techniques have always been a very important part of the art. In this book, I will try my best to introduce to the reader those *Qin Na* techniques which I know can be applied into Taijiquan fighting. In truth, many of these techniques actually originated in my White Crane Style. The reason that I can apply White Crane *Qin Na* into *Taijiqu*an easily is very simple. *Taijiquan* is known as a soft style and White Crane as a soft-hard style. It does not matter externally; the theory behind the soft side of White Crane remains the same as that of *Taijiquan*. Many non-proficient Chinese martial artists believe that if *Taijiquan* is interpreted by another style's theory or its theories have been blended with another style, then it is not pure *Taijiquan*. They do not know that *Taijiquan* actually originated from *Shaolin* styles, and therefore that it was built and evolved over the same theoretical root. For example, it is well known that the first routine of *Chen* Style *Taijiquan* is called *Changquan* (i.e., long fist), and that the second routine, called *Pao Chui* (i.e., cannon fist) all originated from the *Shaolin temple*. In fact, from a historical perspective, those profound *Taiji* masters of the past are all known to have learned many other different styles. For example, Sun Lu-Tang, Zhang Zhao-Dong, Wang Shu-Tian, Han Ching-Tang and many others are all experts in many different styles. The Chinese martial arts grew and developed in the same cultural environment as the *Yin* and *Yang* theory. From learning different styles, you are afforded different angles of viewing the same techniques. This is the way of "*Dao*."

Finally, you should understand one important fact: like many other Chinese martial arts, though a great portion of basic *Qin Na* techniques can simply be learned from books and videotapes, very often a qualified master is still necessary to lead you to a deep and profound level. Books can offer you the theory of the techniques while videotapes can offer you the continuous movements of the techniques. However, neither of these two can offer you the correct "**feeling**" of the locking and a clear concept of how an angle is set up. Because of this, if you are sincere in becoming a proficient *Qin Na* expert, you should also participate in seminars offered by qualified *Qin Na* masters. Very often, only a few minutes in a *Qin Na* seminar can solve the confusion and questions which might have taken you months or even years to figure out.

Other than merely reading this book, an interested reader should refer to the book **Shaolin Chin Na**, published by Unique Publications, as well as **Analysis of Shaolin Chin Na – Instructor's Manual** and **Comprehensive Applications of Shaolin Chin Na** by YMAA. These three books will help you build a firm foundation, both in theory and in routine practice. In addition, these three books — especially the second one — will teach you how to train the power required for *Qin Na* techniques and the theory and methods of how to treat common injuries. In the Appendix of the second volume, some secret herbal prescriptions for injuries, taught to me by my White Crane master, are also included. In order to avoid replication, we will not repeat these subjects in this volume.

In this volume, you may notice that **all of the Chinese pronunciations are spelled according to the *Pinyin* system**. The reason for this is simply that the *Pinyin* system has become more popular than any other system in the last fifteen years. It is believed that this system will become the most common and popular system in the next few decades.

Dr. Yang Jwing-Ming

CONTENTS

CHAPTER 1. GENERAL CONCEPTS

CHAPTER 2. BASIC THEORY AND TRAINING

CHAPTER 3. QIN NA IN PENG, LU, JI, AND AN

CHAPTER 4. QIN NA IN CAI, LIE, ZHOU, AND KAO

Chapter 5. Qin Na Applications in Taijiquan Postures

Chapter 6. Qin Na in Taiji Pushing Hands

Chapter 7. Conclusion

■ **Chapter 1** ■

GENERAL CONCEPTS

1-1. Introduction

T *aijiquan* was originally developed for combat in ancient times. Its fighting theory is to use the soft against the hard, and to use the round to neutralize the straight or square. In order to achieve this goal, the body must be soft and the movements must be smooth and natural. *Taijiquan* also emphasizes the cultivation of *Qi*, or internal energy. The concentrated mind leads the *Qi* to circulate in the body. Because of this, *Taijiquan* can be used for maintaining health and improving longevity.

It is because of this that, since the 1940's, *Taijiquan* has become publicly accepted as one of the best *Qigong* practices for health. Unfortunately, due to the over emphasis of its health aspects, the essence of *Taijiquan's* creation—martial applications—has gradually been ignored. It is very upsetting to see that, even in modern China, most *Taijiquan* practitioners do not understand this martial essence of *Taijiquan*. Naturally, they do not understand martial power (*Jin*) and the theory of using the mind to lead the *Qi* to energize muscular power to its maximum. Consequently, the martial applications of each movement have begun to slowly disappear.

In order to make the art of *Taijiquan* complete, I believe that it is our responsibility and obligation to again study its martial applications. Only from this study will we be able to recover its lost essence and find the root of its creation. Only then can its health benefits be completely comprehended. In this book, one type of *Taijiquan* martial applications, *Qin Na*, will be introduced to you. I hope that, through this introduction, general *Taijiquan* practitioners will be inspired and encouraged to discuss and find the real essence of their art.

What is Qin Na:

"*Qin*" (*Chin*) in Chinese means "to seize or catch," in the way an eagle seizes a rabbit or a policeman catches a murderer (*Qin Xiong*). "*Na*" means "to hold and control." Therefore, *Qin Na* can be translated as "seize and control."

1

Generally speaking, in order to have effective and efficient fighting capability, almost all Chinese martial styles include four categories of techniques. The first category is comprised of the techniques of striking, punching, pushing, pressing, etc. The second category is using the leg to kick, sweep, step, or to trip. In these techniques, contact time between you and your opponent must be very short, and the power for attacking is usually explosive and harmful. The third category is called "*Shuai Jiao*" (wrestling), and contains the skills of destroying the opponent's root and balance, consequently throwing him down. Often these techniques are mixed with the leg's sweeping or tripping, and the body's swinging or even throwing. The last category is *Qin Na*, containing grabbing techniques which specialize in controlling or locking the opponent's joints, muscles, or tendons.

However, you should understand an important fact. In a combat situation, the above three categories are often applied together, and cannot really be separated. For example, while one of your hands is grabbing and controlling your opponent, the other hand is used to strike a vital cavity. Another example of this is that often, you use grabbing to lock your opponent's joints while throwing him down for further attack. Because of this, sometimes it is very difficult to discriminate clearly between them in a real situation. As a matter of fact, many Chinese martial artists believe that since there are many other non-grabbing techniques, such as pressing or striking the cavities or nerves, which can make the opponent numb in part of the body (or even render him unconscious), thereby providing control of the opponent, these techniques should also be recognized as *Qin Na*. You can see that, as long as the techniques are able to immobilize an opponent, it does not matter if the cause is a joint lock, numbness, or unconsciousness - all of them can be classified as *Qin Na*.

In summary, grabbing *Qin Na* techniques control and lock the opponent's joints or muscles/tendons so he cannot move, thus neutralizing his fighting ability. Pressing *Qin Na* techniques are used to numb the opponent's limbs, causing him to lose consciousness, or even die. Pressing *Qin Na* is usually applied to the *Qi* cavities to disrupt normal *Qi* circulation to the organs or the brain. Pressing techniques are also frequently used on nerve endings to cause extreme pain and unconsciousness. *Qin Na* striking techniques are applied to vital points, and can be very deadly. Cavities on the *Qi* channels can be attacked, or certain vital areas struck to rupture arteries. All of these techniques serve to "seize and control" the opponent. Therefore, *Qin Na* techniques can be generally categorized as: [1]

1. "*Fen Jin*" (dividing the muscle/tendon) 分筋
2. "*Cuo Gu*" (misplacing the bone) 錯骨
3. "*Bi Qi*" (sealing the breath) 閉氣
4. "*Dian Mai*" (*Dim Mak*, in Cantonese)(pressing a vein/artery) or "*Duan Mai*" (sealing or blocking the vein/artery) [2] 點脈
5. "*Dian Xue*" (cavity press) or "*Dian Mai*" (*Dim Mak*, in Cantonese) (pressing a primary *Qi* channel) [3] 點穴，點脈

---

1. Throwing down *Qin Na* is often also classified as a part of the Chinese wrestling (*Shuai Jiao*).
2. "*Mai*" here means "*Xue Mai*" and translates to "Blood vessels."
3. "*Mai*" here means "*Qi Mai*" and translates to "Primary *Qi* channels."

Within these categories, *Fen Jin* also includes "Zhua *Jin*" (grabbing the muscle/tendon) and *Dian Xue* also includes "*Na Xue*" (grabbing or pressing the cavities).

Generally, dividing the muscle/tendon, misplacing the bone, and some techniques of sealing the breath are relatively easy to learn, and the theory behind them is easy to understand. They usually require only muscular strength and practice to make the control effective. When these same techniques are used to break bones or injure joints or tendons, you usually need to use *Jin* (martial power). (For a discussion of *Jin*, see the author's book ***Advanced Yang Style Tai Chi Chuan, Vol. 1, Tai Chi Theory and Tai Chi Jing***). Sealing the vein/artery and pressing the cavities requires detailed knowledge of the location and depth, of the cavities; the timing of the *Qi* circulation; development of Yi (mind), *Qi* (internal energy), and *Jin* (martial power); and special hand forms and techniques. This usually requires formal instruction by a qualified master, not only because the knowledge is deep, but also because most of the techniques are learned from sensing and feeling. Many of the techniques can easily cause death, and for this reason a master will normally only pass this knowledge down to students who are moral and trustworthy.

Qin Na in Chinese Martial Arts:

Nobody can tell exactly when *Qin Na* was first used. It probably began the first time one person grabbed another with the intention of controlling him. Grabbing the opponent's limbs or weapon is one of the most basic and instinctive means of immobilizing him or controlling his actions.

Because of their practicality, *Qin Na* techniques have been trained right along with other fighting techniques since the beginning of Chinese martial arts, many thousands of years ago. Although no system has sprung up which practices only *Qin Na*, almost every martial style has *Qin Na* mixed in with its other techniques. Even in Japan, Korea, and other oriental countries which have been significantly influenced by Chinese culture, the indigenous martial styles have *Qin Na* techniques mixed in to some degree.

Generally speaking, since martial styles in southern China specialize in hand techniques and close range fighting, they tend to have better developed *Qin Na* techniques, and they tend to rely more upon them than do the northern styles. Also, because southern martial styles emphasize hand conditioning more than the northern styles, they tend to use more muscles for grabbing and cavity press. Southern styles' emphasis on short range fighting causes them to train more for sticking and adhering. The techniques are usually applied with a circular motion, which can set up the opponent for a *Qin Na* control without his feeling the preparation. Footwork is also considered a very important part of *Qin Na* training for a southern martial artist. Remember that these statements are only generalizations; there are northern styles which also emphasize these things.

In Chinese internal styles such as *Taiji* and *Liu He Ba Fa*, neutralization is usually done with a circular motion, and so the *Qin Na* techniques tend to be smooth and round. Often the opponent will be controlled before he realizes that a technique is being applied. In coordination with circular stepping, circular *Qin Na* can be used to pull the opponent's root and throw him away.

Japanese *Jujitsu* and *Aikido* are based on the same principles as *Qin Na* and Taiji. Since these countries were significantly influenced by Chinese culture, it seems probable that Chinese *Qin Na* also influenced their indigenous martial arts.

Since fundamental *Qin Na* techniques can be used to seize and control a criminal without injuring or killing him, they have been an important part of training for constables, government officers, and modern policemen. Around 527 A.D., the *Shaolin temple* became heavily involved in the martial arts. Since many non-lethal *Qin Na* techniques are very effective, the martial artists at the temple extensively researched, developed, and trained them. In the late Qing dynasty in the 19th century, *Shaolin* techniques were taught to people in the general population, and *Qin Na* techniques were passed down along with the different martial styles which were developed in the *Shaolin* temple. Many *Qin Na* techniques were also developed for use with weapons specially designed to seize the opponent's weapon. If your opponent is disarmed, he is automatically in a disadvantageous situation. For example, the hook of the hook sword or the hand guard of a *Chai* (*Sai*) were designed for this purpose.

1-2. Qin Na Categories and Theory

Although *Qin Na* techniques from one *Gongfu* style may seem quite different from the techniques of another style, the theories and principles of application remain the same. These theories and principles form the root of all *Qin Na* techniques. If you adhere to these roots, your *Qin Na* will continue to grow and improve, but if you ignore these roots, your *Qin Na* will always remain undeveloped. In this section we will discuss these general theories and principles.

Before we discuss each *Qin Na* category, you should understand that there is no technique which is perfect for all situations. What you do depends upon what your opponent does, and since your opponent will not stand still and just let you control him, you must be able to adapt your *Qin Na* to fit the circumstances. Like all martial arts techniques, your **Qin Na must respond to and follow the situation**; techniques must be **skillful, alive, fast**, and **powerful**. You should further understand that **Qin Na must take the opponent by surprise**. In grabbing *Qin Na* you have to grasp your opponent's body, and so if your opponent is aware of your intention it will be extremely difficult for you to successfully apply the technique. In such a case you may be obliged to use a cavity strike *Qin Na* instead of a grabbing technique.

It is usually much easier to strike the opponent than to control him. Subduing an opponent through a *Qin Na* controlling technique is a way to show mercy to someone you do not want to injure. To successfully apply a grabbing *Qin Na*, you often need to fake or strike the opponent first to set him up for your controlling technique. For example, you can use a punch to cause your opponent to block, and when he blocks, you quickly grab his hand and use *Qin Na* to control him. Alternatively, you might kick his shin first to draw his attention to his leg, and immediately grab his hand and control him.

As mentioned, there are five categories of *Qin Na*: 1. *Fen Jin* or Zhua *Jin* (dividing the muscle/tendon or grabbing the muscle/tendon); 2. *Cuo Gu* (misplacing the bone); 3. *Bi Qi* (sealing the breath); 4. *Dian Mai* or *Duan Mai* (vein/artery press or sealing the vein/artery); 5. *Dian Mai* or *Dian Xue* (pressing primary *Qi* channel or cavity press). This book will discuss all of these categories in detail except the last two, which will be dis-

| *Figure 1–1* | *Figure 1–2* | *Figure 1–3* |

cussed only on an introductory level, because they require an in-depth understanding of *Qi* circulation, acupuncture, and specialized training techniques.

One additional point needs to be mentioned here. Very often *Qin Na* techniques make use of principles from several categories at once. For example, many techniques simultaneously use the principles of dividing the muscle/tendon and misplacing the bone.

1. Fen Jin or Zhua Jin (dividing the muscle/tendon or grabbing the muscle/tendon): 分筋，抓筋

"*Fen*" in Chinese means "to divide," "*Zhua*" means "to grab" and "*Jin*" means "tendon, sinew, or muscle." *Fen Jin* or *Zhua Jin Qin Na* refer to techniques which tear apart the opponent's muscles or tendons. Muscles contain nerves and many *Qi* branch channels, so when you tear a muscle or tendon, not only do you cause sensations of pain to travel to the brain, you also directly or indirectly affect the *Qi* and interfere with the normal functioning of the organs. If the pain is great enough, it can disturb the *Qi* and seriously damage the organs, and in extreme cases even cause death. For this reason, when you are in extreme pain your brain may "give the order" for you to pass out. Once you are unconscious, the *Qi* circulation will significantly decrease, which will limit damage to the organs and perhaps save your life.

Fen Jin Qin Na uses two main ways to divide the muscle/tendon. One way is to **twist** the opponent's joint and then **bend** (Figures 1-1 and 1-2). Twisting the joint also twists the muscles/tendons. If you bend the joint at the same time, you can tear the tendons off the bone. The other method is to split and tear the muscle/tendon apart without twisting. The most common place to do this is the fingers (Figure 1-3).

Zhua Jin (grabbing the muscle/tendon) relies upon the strength of the fingers to grab, press, and then pull the opponent's large muscles or tendons. This causes pain by overextending the muscles and tendons. Common targets for *Zhua Jin Qin Na* are the tendon on the shoulder (Figure 1-4), under the armpit (Figures 1-5 and 1-6), on the neck (Figure 1-7), and on the sides of the waist (Figure 1-8). *Zhua Jin Qin Na* is used particularly by the Eagle

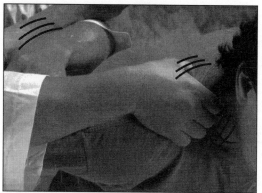

Figure 1–4

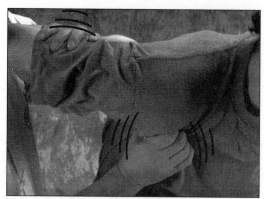

Figure 1–5

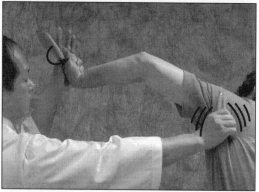

Figure 1–6

Figure 1–7

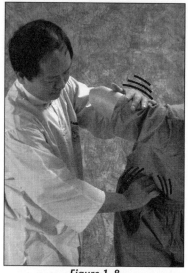

Figure 1–8

Claw and Tiger Claw Styles. Although *Zhua Jin* is usually classified with *Fen Jin Qin Na*, many Chinese martial artists separate the two categories because the principle used to divide the muscle/tendon is different.

2. Cuo Gu (misplacing the bone): 錯骨

"*Cuo*" means "wrong, disorder, or to place wrongly," and "*Gu*" means "bone." *Cuo Gu* therefore are *Qin Na* techniques which put bones in the wrong positions. These techniques are usually applied to the joints. If you examine the structure of a joint, you will see that the bones are connected to each other by ligaments, and that the muscles around and over the joints are connected to the bones by tendons (Figure 1-9). When a joint is bent backward (Figure 1-10) or **twisted** and **bent** in the wrong direction (Figure 1-11), it can cause extreme pain, the ligament can be torn off the bone, and the bones can be pulled apart. Strictly speaking, it is very difficult to use dividing the muscle/tendon and misplacing the bone techniques separately. When one is used, generally the other one is also more or less simultaneously applied.

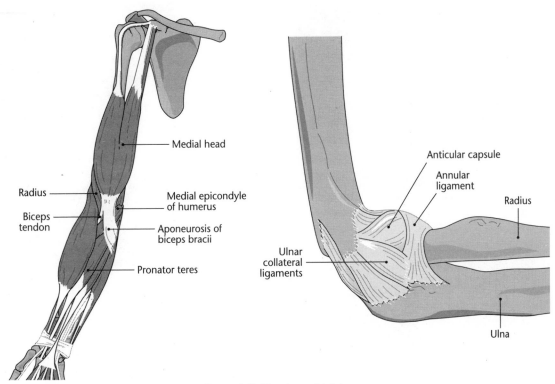

Figure 1–9. Structure of Joint

Medial head

Radius

Biceps tendon

Medial epicondyle of humerus

Aponeurosis of biceps bracii

Pronator teres

Anticular capsule

Annular ligament

Radius

Ulnar collateral ligaments

Ulna

Figure 1–10

Figure 1–11

3. Bi Qi (sealing the breath): 閉氣

"*Bi*" in Chinese means "to close, seal, or shut," and "*Qi*" (more specifically *Kong Qi*) means "air"[4]. *Bi Qi* is the technique of preventing the opponent from inhaling, thereby causing him to pass out. There are three categories of *Bi Qi*, differing in their approach to sealing.

---

4. The word "*Qi*" in Chinese can mean two things, depending on its context. The first meaning is air (*Kong Qi*) and the second is the energy which circulates in the human body. Unless otherwise noted, "*Qi*" in this book denotes this second meaning.

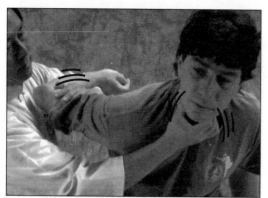

Figure 1–12

Figure 1–13

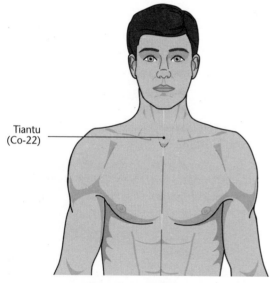

Tiantu
(Co-22)

Figure 1–14. Tiantu Cavity (Co-22)

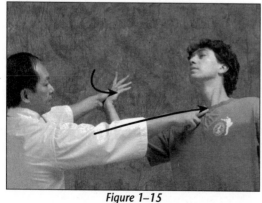

Figure 1–15

The first category is the direct sealing of the windpipe. You can grab your opponent's throat with your fingers (Figure 1-12), or compress his throat with your arm, and prevent him from inhaling (Figure 1-13). Alternatively, you can use your fingers to press or strike the *Tiantu* cavity (Co-22) on the base of his throat (Figures 1-14 and 1-15) to stop him from inhaling. Attacking this area causes the muscles around the windpipe to contract and close the windpipe.

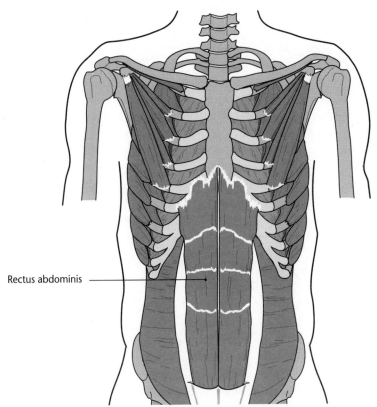

Rectus abdominis

Figure 1–16. Muscles can be used to seal the breath

The second category of *Bi Qi* is striking the muscles which surround the lungs. Because of the protection which the ribs afford, it is very difficult to strike the muscles around the lungs directly. However, some of these muscles extend beyond the ribs. When they are attacked, they contract in pain and compress the lungs, preventing inhalation. Two muscle groups in the stomach are commonly used in this way (Figure 1-16).

Finally, the last category of sealing the breath is cavity press or nerve ending strike. The principle of this category is very similar to that of the muscle strikes, the only difference being that cavities are struck rather than muscle groups. This category is normally much more difficult both in principle and technique. However, when it is done correctly it is more effective than striking the muscles.

If you take a look at the structure of the chest area, you will see that the lungs are well protected by the ribs, which prevent outside forces from damaging the lungs and other organs. You will notice also that each rib is not a single piece of bone wrapping around your body, but rather two pieces of bone, connected by strong ligaments and cartilage (Figure 1-17). When an outside force strikes the chest, the ribs act like a spring or an elastic ball to bounce the attacking force away or bounce yourself backward in order to protect the lungs and heart. This construction makes it very hard to cause the lungs to compress by striking the chest. You should also understand that the muscles which are outside the ribs will not compress the lungs when they contract, because the ribs will protect the lungs. Therefore, in order to cause contraction of the lungs you must strike particular acupuncture cavities or the ends of the nerves which emerge from the lung area under-

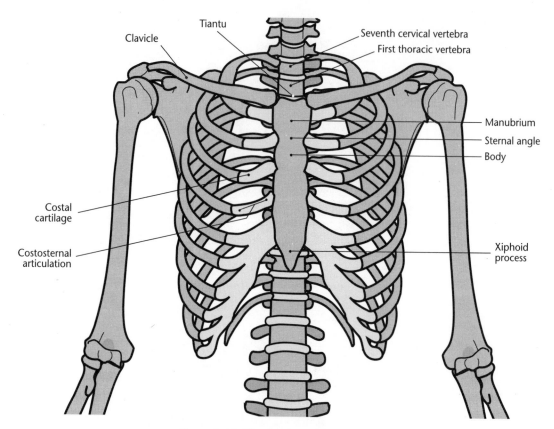

Figure 1–17. Ribs structure on the chest area

neath the ribs (Figure 1-18). Striking these cavities accurately and at the right depth will affect the *Qi* in the muscles around the lungs, causing them to contract. Alternatively, you can strike the nerve endings. This causes pain to penetrate the ribs and shock the internal muscles surrounding the lungs into contraction, thus sealing the breath.

4. *Dian Mai or Duan Mai (vein/artery press or sealing the vein/artery):* 點脈 ，斷脈

"*Dian Mai*" is also known as "*Dim Mak*," which is simply the same words spoken in a different dialect. "*Dian*" in Chinese means "to point or press" with a finger. "*Mai*" means "*Qi* channels" (*Qi Mai*), or "blood vessels" (*Xue Mai*). Therefore, *Dian Mai* means to strike or press either the *Qi* channels or the veins/arteries. When it means to strike or press the vein/artery, it is also called *Duan Mai* (sealing the vein/artery). "*Duan*" means "to break, seal, or stop." Sometimes it is also called *Tian Xue* (blood press), such as when the artery in the temple is struck and ruptured. When *Dian Mai* means to strike or press the cavities on the *Qi* channels, it is also called *Dian Xue* (cavity press). Here, we will discuss *Duan Mai* and leave the discussion of *Dian Xue* for later.

In principle, *Duan Mai* can be done either by striking or pressing. A striking *Duan Mai Qin Na* can rupture the blood vessel and stop the blood circulation, which usually causes death. For example, when the temple is struck, the muscles in that area will tighten up and rupture the artery (Figures 1-19 and 1-20). A pressing *Duan Mai Qin Na* can also stop or seal the blood circulation. For example, sealing the neck artery will stop the blood cir-

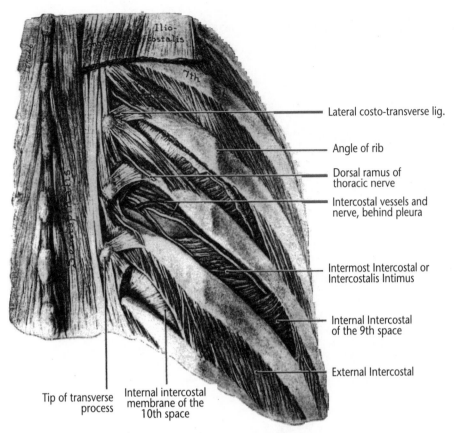

Lateral costo-transverse lig.

Angle of rib

Dorsal ramus of
thoracic nerve

Intercostal vessels and
nerve, behind pleura

Intermost Intercostal or
Intercostalis Intimus

Internal Intercostal
of the 9th space

External Intercostal

Tip of transverse
process

Internal intercostal
membrane of the
10th space

Figure 1–18. Nerves emerge from underneath the ribs

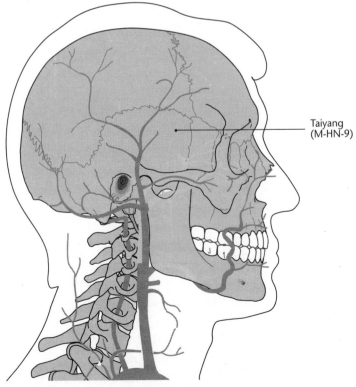

Taiyang
(M-HN-9)

Figure 1–19. Taiyang cavity (M-HN-9) on temple

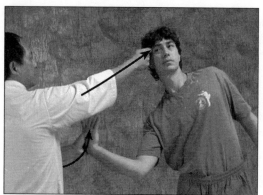

Figure 1–20

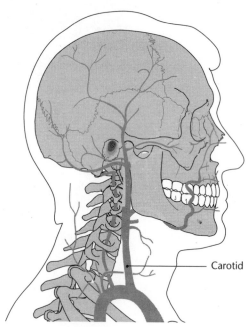

Figure 1–21. Artery (carotid) on the side of neck

Figure 1–22

culation to your head and thus cut down the oxygen supply to the brain. This will cause unconsciousness or even death. There are two major arteries, one on either side of your neck, which supply oxygen to your brain (Figure 1-21). When either or both of these are struck or pressed, the flow of blood to the brain can be stopped (Figure 1-22). Sometimes, the muscles on the side of the neck remain tensed. If you do not know how to revive the victim, he will die from the lack of oxygen. Therefore, you must be careful in using sealing the vein/artery techniques. If you are not absolutely sure how to revive the person, do not use these techniques.

5. *Dian Mai or Dian Xue (pressing Qi channel or pressing cavity):* 點脈，點穴

As mentioned, the other type of *Dian Mai* strikes or presses cavities on *Qi* channels, and is also called *Dian Xue* (pressing cavity). "*Dian*" means "to press with a finger" and "*Xue*" refers to the acupuncture cavities. The human body has more than 800 *Qi* cavities, mostly on the paths of the eight vessels and 12 channels. Two of the eight vessels are called the Governing and Conception Vessels (*Du Mai* and *Ren Mai*). The *Qi* in these two vessels circulates in a 24 hour cycle. The other 12 *Qi* channels are related to the 12 internal organs. The flow of *Qi* in these 12 channels is also related to the time of the day, with emphasis switching from one channel to the next gradually every 2 hours. Furthermore, these eight vessels and 12 channels also have seasonal and annual cycles. When the *Qi* circulation in these vessels and channels is stagnant or stopped, the person will sicken or die. Acupuncture is a way to readjust the *Qi* circulation and cure illness.

Cavity press is a method to disturb or affect the opponent's *Qi* circulation. There are about 108 cavities which can be struck or pressed to affect the *Qi* flow. Among these 108 cavities, 36 can cause death and the other 72 can cause numbness or unconsciousness. In order to make a strike effective, you must know the time of the major *Qi* flow (*Zi Wu Liu Zhu*) in that channel, the appropriate striking technique, and the depth of the cavity. We will not go into greater detail in this book, both because it is a very complicated subject, and because it can be very dangerous for a person to learn without supervision. In traditional Chinese martial society, a master will usually not pass these secrets on until he feels he can really trust a student. However, some techniques can be taught without too much danger. These cavities will not cause death, and most are attacked through the method called *Zhua Xue* (grabbing the cavity). If you are interested in some information about *Qi* flow and its timing, please refer to **Chi Kung—Health and Martial Arts** by YMAA.

Often when cavities are pressed, it is accomplished by both striking and pressing. When pressing is used, normally it gets involved in the grabbing. Therefore, some Chinese martial artists again divide cavity attack into "Cavity Striking" (*Da Xue*) and "Cavity Grabbing or Pressing" (*Na Xue* or *Dian Xue*). "Cavity Striking" is classified in the category of Striking, while "Cavity Grabbing or Pressing" belongs to the category of *Qin Na*.

There is another category which may make you confused. Often, the nerves near the joint areas are grabbed to numb or to immobilize joint movements. However, the areas in which the nerves are commonly exposed for grabbing are also located in the same locations as the cavities. In other words, the cavities and the nerve grabbing are in the same spot. Because of this, it is misrepresented that this kind of grabbing is Cavity Pressing or Nerve Grabbing. Strictly speaking, this kind of grabbing should be classified as Cavity Pressing.

Before we finish this section, you should understand that in Chinese martial arts you must have *Jin* to make your techniques effective. *Jin* is a way of expressing power which makes the power stronger and more penetrating. When *Jin* is expressed, the muscles and tendons are supported by the *Qi* in the body, so that the muscles and tendons reach their highest efficiency. *Jin* can be categorized as hard, soft-hard, or soft. When you apply a *Qin Na*, regardless of which category it falls into, if you do not know how to use your *Jin* in the technique your *Qin Na* will be ineffective. For example, if you do not use *Jin* in "Dividing the Muscle/Tendon" (*Fen Jin*) *Qin Na*, your opponent will have an opportunity to use his muscles to resist your muscles. If you do not use a jerking *Jin* in "Misplacing the Bone" (*Cuo Gu*) *Qin Na*, you will not be able to break or misplace the opponent's joint. In the same way, in a sealing the breath or cavity press technique, if no *Jin* is used, the power will not penetrate to the right depth and the technique will be ineffective. For a greater understanding of *Jin*, refer to the author's book: **Advanced Yang Style Tai Chi Chuan, Vol. 1; Tai Chi Theory and Tai Chi Jing.**

1-3. Different Levels of Qin Na Techniques

As with most Chinese martial arts, *Qin Na* is comprised of many different levels, according to different criteria or standards. In this section we would like to define these standards according to several different systems of categorization.

First, the levels of *Qin Na* techniques can be divided according to how much a person understands the technique and the technical difficulty of the technique executed. The same techniques—based on the same theory and principle—can generate very different results according to an individual's expertise. Normally, this can be judged according to a few common criteria. First, a beginner's power is usually dull and stagnant, and therefore the technique is executed slowly and poorly. When an expert is performing the same technique, his power is soft and gentle, and therefore his technique is fast and effective. Second, a beginner usually cannot catch the correct angle of locking through the feel of the contact, while an expert can usually grasp the correct angle instinctively. Usually, this instinct will take many months of diligent practice for each technique, until they become natural and smooth. This is also the reason why a beginner needs to use more muscular, slow power.

Third, when a technique is applied by a beginner, the victim can feel the angle as it occurs, but when done by a *Qin Na* expert, he will feel nothing until he is locked in place. The reason for this is that an expert will use a flowing, circular motion. When this circular motion is used, usually you will not realize you are being locked and therefore your reaction will not be as instinctive and automatic as when someone tries to lock you at an obvious angle. Finally, when a beginner is executing a technique, usually he does not know how to coordinate with his breathing and mind, and therefore the technique is not executed as effectively as would be an expert. This is like when you use an ax to chop a piece of wood. If you know how to place your mind on the bottom of the wood that you would like to chop, coordinating with your exhalation, you will soon find that you can break the wood much more easily than you would without such mental concentration.

Next, the levels of *Qin Na* techniques can be very different according to different martial styles. For example, "Small Wrap Hand" wrist *Qin Na* is one of the most common techniques based on the theory of "Dividing the Muscle/Tendon." However, because of different understanding and training methods in various martial styles, it can be used to accomplish distinctly different results, and its effectiveness can also vary. Although ostensibly the same technique, some martial styles will execute it with good speed and an accurate locking angle, while others go slowly and remain on the surface. This means that even the same technique can vary in its effectiveness, depending on the styles, the teacher and the student.

Next, the levels of *Qin Na* techniques can be distinguished according to different *Qin Na* categories discussed in the previous sections. Generally speaking, the theory and the techniques of the "Dividing Muscle/Tendon" and "Misplacing the Bone" *Qin Na* techniques are the easiest to learn and apply. "Grabbing the Tendon" *Qin Na* is harder since it needs more strength, accuracy, and the concentration of the mind to make it work. In some advanced level "Grabbing Tendon" *Qin Na*, the *Qi* and the coordination of the breathing are required. "Sealing the Vein/Artery" are the third most difficult techniques to learn.

Although some of the "Sealing the Vein/Artery" *Qin Na* techniques applied to the neck are pretty easy to learn, most of the others are much more difficult, and require special training. Finally, "Pressing Cavity" *Qin Na* is the hardest, since it requires in-depth knowledge about the locations of cavities, the application of specific hand forms and techniques, the time window of vulnerability associated with each cavity, and the depth of penetration required for your power to properly affect the cavity. According to Chinese medicine, *Qi* circulates in the body's *Qi* channels, and is affected and significantly influenced by the time of day and the seasons of the year. Furthermore, in order to effectively use even a small number of "Pressing Cavity" techniques, *Jin* training is required. Normally, it will take a person more than ten years of vigorous practice to understand these theories and reach the final mastery of "Pressing Cavity" *Qin Na*.

Remember, a good *Qin Na* is not necessarily complicated. Soon, you will realize that the **simple techniques are usually faster and easier to apply**. Very often, this helps make them more effective than those techniques which look fancy but take a lot of time to apply. The key to judging a good technique is to decide both how **fast** and **effective** the technique is when it is applied. Also, you should remember that almost all of the *Qin Na* techniques are related to the mutual angle between you and your opponent. When you set up an angle for locking, if your opponent is experienced, he can sense it and remove the angle you have set up. Furthermore, he may mount a counter-attack *Qin Na* technique to lock you. Therefore, the longer the time you take when you execute a technique, the greater the chance your opponent will be able to escape or even counterattack. When two *Qin Na* experts are practicing *Qin Na*, it is continuous, without an end. The reason for this is simply because every *Qin Na* can be countered, and again every Counter-*Qin Na* can be countered. Therefore, if both practitioners are able to **feel** or **sense** the attacks clearly and accurately, either side will be able to change the locking angle to free himself and immediately execute another *Qin Na* on his opponent. Naturally, to reach this stage, you will need many years of practice and accumulation of experience.

Finally, you should understand that in order to reach an in-depth level of *Qin Na*, you should follow the training procedures which have been used in the past. First, you should **regulate your body** until all of the physical positions are accurate. This includes the mutual angle for locking, the positioning of your body, and the correct posture for controlling. After you have mastered all of these factors, you should then **regulate your breathing**. Correct breathing helps to manifest your power to a stronger stage. You will also need to **regulate your mind**. Remember, your mind leads the *Qi* (or bioelectricity) to the muscles and tendons to activate them for action. The more your mind can be concentrated, the more *Qi* can be led, and the more power you can generate. It is said: "*Yi* arrives, *Qi* also arrives" (*Yi Dao, Qi Yi Dao*) [5]. Once you have regulated your body, breathing, mind, and *Qi*, then you can raise up your spirit of controlling. This will lead you to the final level of perfect technique execution. If you are interested in knowing more about this external and internal training, please refer to ***The Root of Chinese Chi Kung***, published by YMAA.

---

5. 意到，氣亦到。

1-4. Qin Na and Health

If a person has never practiced *Qin Na* before, the painful feeling he or she gets through practice may cause him or her to jump to the conclusion that *Qin Na* is only for martial arts. In fact, only those people who have practiced *Qin Na* for some time realize that through practicing *Qin Na*, they can gain many health benefits, both physical and mental. In this section, let us review some of the health benefits which we are able to gain from practicing *Qin Na*.

Mental Health:

1. **Increase mental awareness.** The first benefit which a *Qin Na* practitioner is able to learn is building up the sense of awareness. This begins with an awareness of the wrong angles which can be harmful to the joints, tendons, and muscles. The reason for this is that *Qin Na* specializes in locking the joints through the angles one sets up, especially affecting the tendons and ligaments. Through training, a practitioner will be able to learn the angles which can be harmful to the body. Naturally, he or she will also build up an awareness to avoid the wrong angles which can cause injury to the joints. You should remember that most bodily injury is to the joints, caused by using the wrong angle of force or postures.

2. **Build up the mental endurance and establish a strong will.** After only five minutes of practice, every *Qin Na* beginner will realize that practicing *Qin Na* is a painful process. This pain is not only from the physical twisting and locking of the joints. It is also from mental struggling. We should understand that our life is painful, and that our minds are always in conflict. According to Chinese philosophy and understanding, a human has two minds: the emotional mind (*Xin*) and the wisdom mind (*Yi*). These two minds often conflict with each other. On one hand, the wisdom mind knows what we should or shouldn't do. But on the other hand, the emotional mind makes a person always end up on the path to sensory satisfaction. Everybody knows that their wisdom mind is clear and has wise judgment. Unfortunately, we often surrender to our emotional mind, and suppress our wisdom mind.

   One of the main purposes of training Chinese martial arts is to establish a discipline that trains you how to use your wisdom mind to govern your emotional mind. Only then will you have a strong will. Both physical and mental hardships are necessary to accomplish this goal. When you practice *Qin Na*, you know both that it will be painful and that you must build up your endurance to deal with this pain in order to learn. As a matter of fact, learning *Qin Na* is just like any other traditional martial art; a method of self-challenge. Through this challenge, you will be able to understand yourself better and more capable of comprehending the meaning of your life.

3. **Understand the human *Qi* body.** In order to control your opponents effectively, along with understanding the structure of the human physical body, you should also understand the human *Qi* body. For example, in order to make Cavity Press *Qin Na* effective, which uses grabbing, striking or finger pressing to affect the body's *Qi* circulation, you must have a good understanding of the distribution of *Qi* in your opponent's body, and the correct depth and timing of your attack.

According to Chinese medicine and *Qigong* practice, a person has two bodies, the physical body and the *Qi* body. Western medicine has reached a very high level in understanding the physical body. However, its understanding of the *Qi* body is still in its infancy. If you are able to understand both your physical body and your *Qi* body, you will be able to regulate your bodies to a healthier state. If you are interested in understanding more about the *Qi* body, please refer to the book: ***The Root of Chinese Chi Kung*** by YMAA.

4. **Train mental balance, stability, center, and root.** According to Chinese medicine and martial arts, in order to have good physical balance, stability, and centering, you must first have mental balance, stability, and centering. You should understand that the mind is the master that governs and controls the actions of your physical body. If your mind is confused and scattered, this will not only affect your decisions, but will also destroy the feeling of your physical balance and center. In addition, when you have firm mental balance, stability, centering, and rooting, you will also be able to build up your spirit of vitality.

   One *Qin Na* training consists of "take down" techniques. In this category of training, you learn how to firm your center and root while at the same time finding your opponent's center and root to destroy them. By understanding the relationship between your own mental state and root, you will better be able to attack your enemy's spirit, and consequently disrupt his physical coordination.

5. **Make friends.** One of the invisible benefits of *Qin Na* training, like all other sports, is that through practice you can make so many friends. I am amazed at how often I rediscover this benefit. I have traveled to more than twelve countries in the last eight years, and have made thousands of friends. This has filled my life with more love and meaning.

Physical Health:

1. **Stretching the physical body.** Two of the *Qin Na* categories are "Misplacing the Bone" and "Dividing the Muscle/Tendon." These two categories specialize in locking the joints through twisting and bending. Unless you are using *Qin Na* against an enemy, when you practice with your partner, you will usually not twist and bend the ligaments or tendons beyond the limit which can cause injury. Because of this, *Qin Na* training has become one the best ways to stretch the joints.

   According to Chinese medicine and *Qigong*, the more we stimulate our physical body properly, the more the blood and *Qi* circulation can be improved. A healthy condition can be improved and strength and endurance can be increased. In fact, this is the basic theory behind *Yoga*. Through twisting and stretching, the deep places in the joints can be stimulated and strength can be maintained. Like *Yoga*, from countless practitioners' experience, *Qin Na* has been proven one of the best methods of stretching of the joints.

2. **Understanding the structure of the physical body.** In order to make *Qin Na* effective, you must also know the structure of the joints, and how the muscles and tendons relate to the action or movement of the body. Through practicing *Qin Na*, you will be able to gain a clearer picture of this structure. Only through understanding this physical structure may you reduce or prevent physical damage or injury to your body.

3. **Learning how to heal yourself.** Truly speaking, it does not matter how carefully both you and your partner pay attention, you will eventually experience some sort of minor injury during the learning process. The reasons for this are, first, you and your partner are excited in learning and are expecting some painful reaction from each other. Understanding this condition, you both may use power which is beyond the limits you can endure. Second, since both you and your partner are beginners, you do not yet have enough experience to see how much power you should apply to each other. This can result in injury. Normally, injury does not occur with experienced practitioners.

Once you have an injury, you will learn how to move it correctly, how to massage it, how to relax it, and how to apply herbs to expedite the healing process.

4. **Firming physical balance, stability, centering, and root.** We have discussed earlier the importance of mental and physical balance, stability, centering, and root, and how they relate to each other. Here, I would like to remind you that through practicing *Qin Na*, you will be able to coordinate your mental and physical centers smoothly and comfortably.

1-5. Differences of Shaolin Qin Na and Taiji Qin Na

Strictly speaking, it is very hard to distinguish the differences in *Qin Na* as applied from within external martial styles and internal martial styles. The reason for this is simply because it does not matter how or from what the *Qin Na* is created and applied, it is all based on the same theories of locking (Dividing the Muscle/Tendon and Misplacing the Bone), sealing (Sealing the Vein or Artery), and pressing (striking or pressing the cavities). In addition, it does not matter which style a martial artist has practiced, when he has reached a high level of *Qin Na* expertise, he should be so skillful that all techniques can be executed **softly** and **circularly**.

This is similar to the differences between external martial styles and internal martial styles. Many people think that the techniques in the external styles are hard and that only muscular power is used to execute the techniques. They also believe that external stylists do not train the cultivation of *Qi*. In fact, this is not true. In Chinese martial society, it is said: "External styles from external to internal, and internal style from internal to external; though the path is opposite, the final goal is the same."[6] This means that external martial artists start with external, training to use muscular power to execute their techniques first, then gradually they will minimize the usage of the muscles and train to cultivate the internal *Qi* to energize the muscles to their maximum usage. This is exactly the opposite approach from the internal stylists, who start with the cultivation of *Qi* first and gradually apply the *Qi* to the muscles to execute their techniques. There is a well known proverb which says: "Externally train tendons, bones, and skin; internally train a mouthful of *Qi*."[7] This means a martial artist should learn how to train the physical body to be strong, and that he should also train internal *Qi*. The proverb refers to the mouthful of *Qi* because breathing is closely related to the cultivation of *Qi*.

---

6. 外家由外而內，內家由內而外，其途雖異，其終的卻一致。

7. 外練筋骨皮，內練一口氣。

From this, you can see that, when a martial artist reaches a high level of training, it does not matter if he or she is an internal or external stylist, the final goal of training is the same. However, if we take a detailed look at the differences in the external styles' *Qin Na* and the internal styles' *Qin Na*, we can reach several general conclusions.

1. ***Shaolin Qin Na* is harder, while *Taiji Qin Na* is softer.** Because the different training methods for the beginner in both Taiji and *Shaolin*, generally speaking the applications of *Shaolin Qin Na* are harder, while Taiji *Qin Na* is softer. This implies that *Shaolin Qin Na* uses more muscles while Taiji *Qin Na* uses more *Qi*.

2. ***Shaolin Qin Na* emphasizes both straight and round movements, while *Taiji Qin Na* is usually more round.** This distinction is again caused by the differences between the basic training principles which *Shaolin* emphasizes—both straight and round actions - while Taiji focuses mainly on round movements.

3. **Relatively speaking, *Shaolin Qin Na* is more offensive and aggressive, while *Taiji Qin Na* is more defensive and passive.** Since the strategy of *Shaolin* martial arts emphasizes both defense and offense, while Taiji specializes in using defense as offense, relatively speaking *Shaolin Qin Na* is more offensive while Taiji *Qin Na* is more defensive.

Even though we have examined the differences between *Shaolin* and *Taiji Qin Na*, you should not be restricted by these differences. A good martial artist and *Qin Na* expert should master both hard and soft techniques. This means that when it is necessary to be soft, you are able to be soft, and when it is necessary to be hard, you can also be hard. Only then can you say you are really a *Qin Na* expert.

1-6. About This Book

Before continuing to read this book, you should understand a few important points:

1. This book can only offer you some *Qin Na* techniques with which I am familiar. To tell the truth, **many of these *Qin Na* techniques originated from my White Crane and Long Fist background.** The reason for this is simply that the martial applications of *Taijiquan* have been ignored in the last fifty years. Many of the martial techniques have been lost. *Qin Na* is one of the typical examples. Even though *Taijiquan* greatly emphasizes *Qin Na*, it is nearly impossible to find a master, even in China today, who is an expert in it. Naturally, there is no book available. Fortunately, since *Qin Na* theory and its basic principles of application remains the same, this allows me to trace back some of the possible *Qin Na* applications in *Taijiquan*. I hope from the publication of this book that sincere study and research of this subject can be conducted. If you are interested in knowing more about the martial applications of *Taijiquan*, you may read the book: ***Advanced Yang Style Tai Chi Chuan, Vol. 2, Martial Applications.***

2. Behind every joint-locking *Qin Na* technique, there is always one or more hidden striking techniques which can be used to injure or kill your opponent. This was necessary, especially in ancient times when guns were not available. Often in battle, due to slippage from sweat or the exceptional strength of an opponent, joint locking *Qin Na* becomes ineffective. When this happens, you will be forced to injure or kill your oppo-

nent instead of mercifully controlling him. In fact, **Qin Na techniques often served only for temporarily locking the opponent, which can therefore create a safe opportunity for your further attacking or taking down.**

3. In the same fighting situation, there can be many possible *Qin Na* techniques and options. Some techniques may be more effective and powerful for some opponents, while others may be easier to apply for some other opponents. Some techniques emphasize speed more than strength, while others may rely on physical strength. The most important point is that you should **treat all of the techniques as alive, and adapt them wisely and skillfully depending on the situation.** This means that when you apply your techniques, you must consider your size, power, height, and skill.

4. If you apply them **skillfully and circularly**, techniques from other styles can be adapted and be made soft. When they are soft and round, it will be harder for your opponent to sense his danger. Actually, in the higher levels of *Qin Na*, techniques can be applied so softly that muscular usage is reduced to a minimum. Naturally, the thought of execution is stronger and more focused, and this enables the *Qi* to circulate smoothly and abundantly to energize the muscles to a state of higher efficiency.

5. In order to effectively control your opponent and immediately put him into an awkward and submissive situation, **jerking martial power (*Fa Jin*) is often necessary.** Once you have locked your opponent into an accurate angle, if you apply jerking martial power, you may immediately lock or injure him efficiently. Naturally, if you practice with your friends, you should not do this, since it can detach the ligaments from the bones, tear the tendons off, disconnect the joints, or even break the bones. If you are interested in knowing more about martial power (*Jin*), you may refer to the book: ***Advanced Yang Style Tai Chi Chuan, Vol. 1—Theory and Jing***, by YMAA.

6. Though some Cavity Press *Qin Nas* are also included in this book, **these techniques only serve as a reference.** From the discussion of these techniques, you may obtain some idea of how and why Cavity press *Qin Na* works. Cavity Press techniques are considered to be one of the highest skills in Chinese martial arts. Naturally, it will take you many years of learning and practice under a proficient master. To discuss this subject in a few pages is not possible. In fact, it is very difficult to write about this subject clearly in book form, since a great deal of information about training and applications are from the master's experience.

7. In **every *Qin Na* technique, there are always one or more counter techniques.** Again, in every one of these counter techniques, there are also one or more counter-counter techniques. That means that if your *Qin Na* techniques are very skillful and you are able to achieve the right timing, you will be able to counter any *Qin Na*. Since most of the counter attack *Qin Nas* have been discussed in the book: ***Analysis of Shaolin Chin Na—Instructor's Manual***, we will not repeat them here.

In order to have a better foundation, other than reading this book, you should also read ***Analysis of Shaolin Chin Na—Instructor's Manual***, published by YMAA. This book will help you build up a firm theoretical foundation and classify all of the different techniques. In addition, if you are interested in knowing how *Qin Na* be applied in an actual combat situation, you may refer to the book: ***Comprehensive Applications of Shaolin Chin Na.***

Although this book can offer you theory and pictures, it cannot offer you the continuous movement of the action. With the help of the companion videotape, you will be able to see the action, and this will lead you to a better understanding of how a technique can be executed. Finally, even if you have books and videotapes, if you do not have the correct feeling, you will often miss the key angles and points for effective locking. Participating in *Qin Na* seminars offered by qualified masters is also highly recommended. From seminars, you can be led on to the right path in just a few days or even a few hours. This could save you a lot of confusion and wondering.

Next, you should always have a humble and appreciative mind. Those who are humble and appreciative will continue to absorb knowledge, while those who become satisfied will become impervious to it. It is said in Chinese society: "Satisfaction loses and humility gains." [8]

In the second chapter, basic *Taiji* technical moving patterns and their martial application theories will be discussed. Only after you have understood these basic moving patterns will you be able to understand how they can be used in *Qin Na*, and how *Qin Na* can be used against these moving patterns. In the third and fourth chapters, *Qin Na* techniques which can be used both from and against these pattern will be introduced. Then, in Chapter 5, we will summarize those *Qin Na* techniques which can be used in 37 *Yang* Style *Taijiquan* postures. Finally, in Chapter 6, in order to help you understand how *Taiji Qin Na* can be applied in *Taiji* Pushing Hands situations, some examples will be highlighted.

Finally, Chinese masters always say: "Practice makes perfect." You should practice, practice, and then practice. The only trick to perfecting an art once you understand the basic theories and principles is through constant practice. From practice, your techniques will become ever more skillful, and your understanding will grow ever deeper. Remember, when you practice with a partner you should avoid hurting each other intentionally. Always control your power. **A good martial artist should always know how to control his power.** Some *Qin Na* injuries can be permanent. For example, once a ligament is detached from the bones in the joint, the damage will be permanent, and the only way to repair it is through surgery.

8. 滿招損，謙受益。

▪ Chapter 2 ▪

BASIC TAIJI THEORY

2-1. Introduction

If we desire to understand *Taiji* theory, then we must first trace back its origins and roots. Only then will we know how and where it came from. Although a great proportion of Chinese martial arts history is vague, we can still trace its history with some accuracy and in some detail.

If we trace Chinese martial arts history back, we can see a clear lineage beginning during the *Liang* dynasty (502-557 A.D.). There are no surviving martial documents from before this time which record or discuss *Qi* and how to correlate it with martial arts, even though at that time, Chinese *Qigong* practice had existed for more than two thousand years. It is understood that before the Chinese *Han* dynasty (206 B.C.-221 A.D.), there were only two schools of *Qigong* practice: the medical group and the scholarly group. It was not until the East *Han* dynasty (circa 58 A.D.) that Buddhist *Qigong* was imported to China from India. Still, even then very little training theory and methods were passed down. The many Buddhist holy writings or Chinese classics which a student could obtain were purely the doctrines of Buddhism, and talked very little about how to cultivate *Qi* internally.

This situation lasted until the Chinese *Liang* dynasty, when Da Mo was invited to China to preach in front of the emperor. However, because Emperor Liang Wu did not favor Da Mo's Buddhist theories and means of cultivation, Da Mo was forced to retire to the *Shaolin* Temple. Before Da Mo died in the Temple, he passed down two classics on the cultivation of *Qi*, which can help a practitioner to enter a state of enlightenment or Buddhahood.

From Da Mo's classics, the *Shaolin* monks trained the cultivation of *Qi*, and realized that from this cultivation, muscular power could be enhanced to a tremendous level, which could make martial techniques more powerful and effective. This was the beginning of internal cultivation in the martial arts. According to ancient records, it was only about 50 years later that internal styles based on Da Mo's internal *Qi* cultivation were created. Two of the best known of these styles are "Small Nine Heaven" (*Xiao Jiu Tian*) and "Post-Heaven Techniques" (*Hou Tian Fa*)[1]. All of these styles were created based on the same *Taiji* theories and principles known today. These theories and principles are: 1. *Qi* should be first cultivated and developed internally, then this *Qi* is slowly manifested as power through the physical body, and finally applied into the techniques; 2. In order to allow the *Qi* to circulate smoothly and freely in the body, the physical body must first be relaxed, and the movements must be soft; 3. The Yin and Yang theory and concepts are the foundations and root of *Qi* development. From this, we can see that the roots of *Taijiquan* have existed for at least 1300 years. Within this time, thousands of techniques have been discovered and hundreds of styles have been created. Moreover, the very theoretical underpinnings of *Taijiquan* have been studied and researched continuously. From the accumulation of thought, its theories have reached a very deep and profound level, even as its contents have expanded into an ever wider range.

The implication of this is that these two styles were probably the progenitors of *Taijiquan*. It is believed that *Taijiquan* was not actually named "*Taijiquan*" until the Chinese *Song* dynasty (circa 1101 A.D.). Chang San-Feng is widely credited as the creator of *Taijiquan*.

From surviving fragments of documents from this time, it can be surmised that the Shaolin temple was the major influence on the development of *Qi* cultivation in martial arts society. It is therefore valid to infer that substantial *Taijiquan* theory originated at the temple. In fact, if we look to contemporary *Chen* Style *Taijiquan*, similarities emerge between it and certain external Shaolin styles. For example, both the first and second routines—"*Changquan*" and "*Pao Chui*" (Cannon Fist)—originated at the *Shaolin* temple, yet they also exist in *Chen* Style (even the names were kept the same as those in the temple). Although the *Shaolin Changquan* and *Pao Chui* have been modified and revised in *Chen* Style *Taijiquan*, we can still trace back the root and origin of every movement clearly in today's *Chen* Style *Taijiquan*. This holds true for many of the *Taijiquan* weapons routines.

It is well known that *Yang* Style originated from *Chen* Style, and that they still share the same *Taiji* root and essence. *Wu* and *Sun* Styles originated from *Yang* Styles. From this, we can see that *Taijiquan* and *Shaolin* martial arts in fact share the same root. It is no wonder that many *Taijiquan* masters who have also learned *Shaolin* martial arts are more expert and proficient in the martial roots and applications of *Taijiquan*. The reason for this is simply because the "*Dao*" of Chinese martial arts remains the same in all Chinese styles. Different styles are only different variations and derivations (branches and flowers) from the same root. When you learn different styles, you will have different angles from which to view the same "*Dao*." Naturally, your mind can be more clear, and your understanding can be more profound.

Now, let us see what is "*Taijiquan*," as written down in the past. First, we must define what we mean by "*Taiji*." It is said:[1, 2]

---

1. 太極拳刀、劍、桿、散手合編。陳炎林。(Taijiquan, Saber, Sword, Staff, and Sparring, by Chen Yan-Lin, Reprinted in Taipei, Taiwan, 1943.)

2. Advanced Yang Style Tai Chi Chuan, V. 1, Tai Chi Theory and Tai Chi Jing, Dr. Yang Jwing-Ming, YMAA, 1987.

"What is *Taiji*? It is generated from *Wuji*. It is the mother of *Yin* and *Yang*. When it moves, it divides. At rest it reunites."

太極者，無極而生，陰陽之母也，動之則分，靜之則合。

Taiji can be translated as "Grand Ultimate" or "Grand Extremity." That refers to the most essential movements, or the very origin of motivation or force. *Wuji* means "No Extremity," and means "No Dividing" or "No Discrimination." *Wuji* is a state of formlessness, of staying in the center: calm, quiet, and peaceful. When you are in the Wuji state, there is no form or shape. Once you have generated a mind, or have formed the mental shape with which you will influence physical reality, the motivation of dividing or discriminating starts. When this dividing is happens, Wuji will be derived into *Yin* and *Yang*. From this, you can see what is *Taiji*: it is the motivation of distinguishment. When you have this motivation, the *Qi* will then be led, and *Yin* and *Yang* can be distinguished.

Once this motivation (i.e., *Taiji*) stops, the motivator of division stops, and the Yin and Yang will once again reunite and return back to Wuji. From this, you can see that *Taiji* is actually the motive force generated from the mind (*Yi*). From this force, the *Qi* is led and circulates throughout the body. We can therefore conclude that *Taijiquan* is the martial style which trains the practitioner to use the mind to lead the *Qi*, circulating it in the body and consequently generating the *Yin* and *Yang* states, either for health, fighting or otherwise.

Again, *Taijiquan* is also called "*Changquan*" (Long Fist). It is said:

What is Long Fist? (It is) like a long river and a large ocean, rolling ceaselessly.

長拳者，如長江大海滔滔不絕也。

Originally, the name "*Changquan*" came from the *Shaolin* Temple. "*Changquan*" means "Long Fist." It can also be translated as "Long Range" or "Long Sequence." Ancient documents suggest that the meaning of "*Changquan*" in *Taijiquan* means the "Long Sequence" like a long river that acts as a conduit to the open ocean. The *Qi* circulating in the body is rolling continuously, flowing and ebbing in natural cycles.

Taijiquan is also called "*Shi San Shi*" (Thirteen Postures). It is said:

What are the Thirteen Postures? *Peng, Lu, Ji, An, Cai, Lie, Zhou, Kou;* these are the eight trigrams. *Jin Bu, Tui Bu, Zuo Gu, You Pan, Zhong Ding;* these are the five elements. *Peng, Lu, Ji, An* are *Qian* (heaven), *Kun* (earth), *Kan* (water), *Li* (fire); the four main sides. *Cai, Lie, Zhou, Kou* are *Xun* (wind), *Zhen* (thunder), *Dui* (lake), and *Gen* (mountain); the four diagonal corners. *Jin Bu, Tui Bu, Zuo Gu, You Pan,* and *Zhong Ding* are *Jin* (metal) *Mu* (wood), *Shui* (water), *Fo* (fire), and *Tu* (earth). All together they are the Thirteen Postures.

十三勢者，掤、攦、擠、按、採、挒、肘、靠，此八卦也。進步、
退步、左顧、右盼、中定，此五行也。掤、攦、擠、按，即乾、
坤、坎、離，四正方也。採、挒、肘、靠，即巽、震、兌、艮，
四斜角也。進、退、顧、盼、定，即金、木、水、火、土也。合
之爲十三勢也。

Taijiquan includes eight basic moving or *Jin* (martial power) patterns which are considered the eight corners of the Eight Trigrams. *Peng, Lu, Ji,* and *An* are considered the four sides of the Eight Trigrams, while *Cai, Lie, Zhou,* and *Kao* are regarded as the four diagonal corners. *Taijiquan* also contains five basic strategic movements or steppings: *Jin Bu* (forward), *Tui Bu* (backward), *Zuo Gu* (see the left), *You Pan* (look to the right), and *Zhong Ding* (firm the center).

From this, you can see that these Thirteen Postures are actually the foundation of *Taijiquan*. From these Thirteen Postures, hundreds of techniques and strategic movements can be generated. As in a waltz, though there are only three steps in the basic movement, the variations can number in the hundreds. Therefore, in order to understand the *Qin Na* applications of *Taijiquan*, you must first become familiar with the *Qin Na* hidden in these Thirteen Postures, and you must also know the *Qin Na* which can be used against these Thirteen Postures.

Taijiquan has also been called *San Shi Qi* Shi which means "Thirty-Seven Postures." The reason for this is that, if you count the technique movements or postures of *Yang* Style *Taijiquan*, you will find that they number only thirty-seven. It is from these thirty-seven postures that more than 250 martial applications are derived. Naturally, these thirty-seven postures are also built upon the foundation of the "Thirteen Postures" or "Thirteen *Jin* Patterns and Strategies." In fact, many of these thirty-seven postures are constructed from two or more of the original thirteen *Jin* patterns. For example, "Wave Hands in the Clouds" and "Grasp the Sparrow's Tail" are the combinations of "*Peng Jin*" and "*Lie Jin*." From this, you can see that the original thirteen patterns first derive into thirty-seven basic postures or movements, and that these thirty-seven basic postures can themselves be derived into hundreds of techniques and variations.

2-2. The Three Different Fighting Ranges and Circles

Within Chinese martial arts, fighting ranges also differ according to style and strategy. Generally, fighting ranges can be divided into three categories: long, medium, and short. In the long range, the distance between you and your opponent is beyond the reach of your legs; you cannot reach each other without stepping forward (Figure 2-1). Normally, this is the safest range, since neither of you are at a distance from which any movement can be made without the other having a chance to react.

In the medium range, the distance between you and your opponent is closer. In this range either of you can reach the other with a kick. (Figure 2-2). Naturally, this is more dangerous for both sides; when you enter this range, both sides must be very alert. Whoever attacks first may have the advantage of timing, and can put his opponent into a defensive situation. Often, this range is used to execute a faking technique first, setting up

Figure 2–1

Figure 2–2

further attacks or creating an opportunity to move into the short range.

Finally, in the short range, the distance between you and your opponent is so close that either of you can reach the other simply by extending an arm (Figure 2-3). When you and your opponent are at such a short distance, both of you must be extremely alert, since either one of you can attack the other with great speed and surprise.

Therefore, when you fight you want to keep the distance between you and your opponent in the long range. Only when you have an opportunity should you enter the medium or short ranges. Once you are in the medium and short ranges, you must react immediately to any change. This strategy is the same in *Taijiquan* fighting. However, since *Taijiquan* strategy uses defense as offense, you usually must wait for your opponent's attack. Once your opponent attacks you, use your hands to intercept and stick to the attack. Then you can shorten the distance between you and your opponent from the long range into the medium and short ranges, and at the same time you can adhere your hands to his arms or body. From *Taiji* Pushing Hands training, you learn how to stick and adhere, and practice how to destroy your opponent's balance. Once your opponent loses his balance and his mind focuses on regaining it, immediately separate the adhering hands and attack. From this, you can see that *Taijiquan* fighting strategy and methods are different from most external styles, in which sticking and adhering are not the main training objectives.

After you know the three ranges, then you should learn about the three circles in *Taijiquan*: Large, Medium, and Small circles. When you initially intercept your opponent's attack, your arms are widely extended (Figure 2-4). If you fight in this long extended arm circle, it is called "Large Circle" (*Da Quan*). In this circle, realistically speaking, it is very hard to keep your hands adhered to your opponent's arm. However, if you immediately close into the "Medium Circle" (*Zhong Quan*), in which your arms are half bent, then the adhering maneuvers become much easier and more practical (Figure 2-5). This is simply because your arms have more extending and shortening range in which to move for the purpose of adhering at this distance. In this circle, you have to compete with your opponent to see who is more capable of destroying the other's balance, thus creating an opportunity for attack.

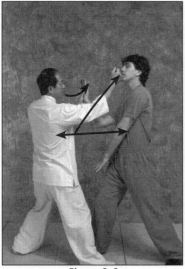

| Figure 2–3 | Figure 2–4 | Figure 2–5 |

When a proficient *Taiji* expert has reached a very high level of fighting skill, then he or she will gradually learn how to close still more and fight in the "Small Circle" (*Xiao Quan*) (Figure 2-6). Since your skills are much higher than your opponent in this circle, you are able to attack in such a short range without fail. The reason is that, in such a short range, the attack can be so fast that it is almost impossible to react to the attack successfully. This is why it is said: "The higher the skills are, the smaller the circle will be."[3]

Now that you understand the differences between the three ranges and the three circles, in the next section we would like to discuss the eight most important *Taiji* moving patterns, and the five strategic movements - together called the Thirteen Postures.

2-3. The Thirteen Postures

In this section, we will define the eight basic *Taiji* technical moving patterns: *Peng, Lu, Ji, An, Cai, Lie, Zhou,* and *Kao.* We will also discuss the five important *Taiji* strategic directional movements: forward, backward, left, right, and center. Since these eight technical patterns and five strategic movements are the main body of *Taijiquan*, before we discuss the *Qin Na* applications of *Taijiquan*, you should first clearly understand the meaning of these Thirteen Postures.

I. EIGHT BASIC TECHNICAL MOVING PATTERNS

1. *Peng* 掤

Peng can be translated as "wardoff." *Peng* has the feeling of roundness and expansion. Generally, this round and expanding feeling is formed and generated from the chest and the arm(s). For example, when you use your arm to push people away with the support of the arcing chest (Figure 2-7), it is called "*Peng Kai*," and means "Open with Wardoff." The expanding force can be either upward, forward, or sideways (Figure 2-8). The force gener-

---

3. 技高圈小。

28

Figure 2–6

Figure 2–7

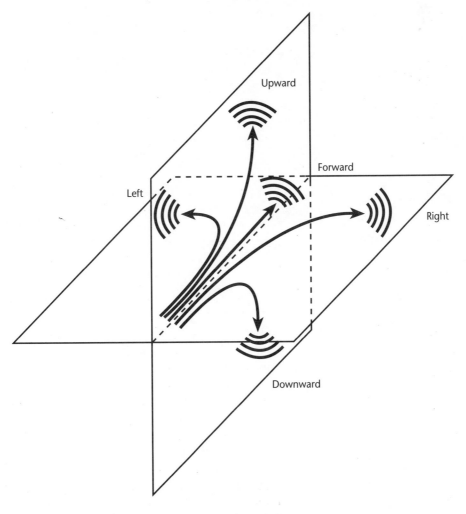

Figure 2–8

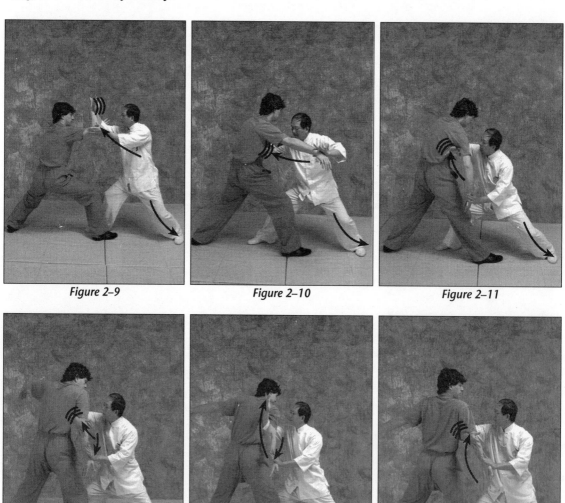

Figure 2–9   Figure 2–10   Figure 2–11

Figure 2–12   Figure 2–13   Figure 2–14

ated from *Peng* is very offensive and forceful, just like a beach ball bouncing you away. *Peng* is often used to generate a round, circular defensive force by the chest and the arms. This allows you a chance to ward off the opponent's power upward, and thereby neutralize his attacking force (Figure 2-9). The typical examples in *Taijiquan* postures are Peng (wardoff forward or slightly upward)(Figures 2-10, 2-11, and 2-12), Grasp Sparrow's Tail (upward)(Figure 2-13), Wave Hands in the Clouds (sideways)(Figure 2-14), and Crane Spreads Its Wings (upward diagonally)(Figure 2-15).

2. *Lu* 掤

Lu means to yield, lead and neutralize; it is commonly translated as "rollback." The main purpose of this movement is to yield the force first, then to lead it backward and to the side for neutralizing (Figure 2-16). Theoretically, *Lu* is a defensive strategic movement. However, occasionally *Lu* can be aggressive when the timing and situation allows. For example, when you yield and lead, you may also lock or break the opponent's arm (Figure 2-17).

Figure 2–15

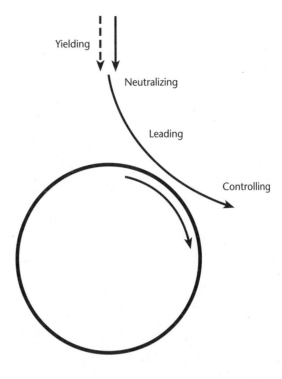

Figure 2–16

Figure 2–17

Figure 2–18

Figure 2–19

In Chinese martial arts, *Lu* can be applied in two ways. One is to first wardoff the opponent's arm with your arm (Figures 2-18 and 2-19), and then to rollback his arm backward and to your side (Figures 2-20 and 2-21). This rollback action is also called "*Xiao Lu*" (small rollback). The other case is to use one of your hands to grab your opponent's wrist while using the forearm of the other arm to press and lock the rear side of his post-arm (upper-arm) (Figure 2-22). This kind of rollback is called "*Da Lu*" (large rollback).

Figure 2–20

Figure 2–21

Figure 2–22

Figure 2–23

Figure 2–24

Figure 2–25

3. Ji 擠

Ji means to "squeeze" or to "press." This action can be performed with two hands, where the palms face and then press against each other (Figures 2-23 and 2-24). Alternatively, the *Ji* action can also be done by "pressing forward" with both hands (Figures 2-25 and 2-26), forearms (Figures 2-27 and 2-28), or one hand to the other arm (Figures 2-29 and 2-30).

4. An 按

An means to "stamp," or to "press down, forward, or upward." *An* can be done with both hands (Figure 2-31) or with a single hand (Figure 2-32). The *An* action is generally done with the fingers pointing forward first (Figure 2-33) and then, right before reaching the target, the wrist is angled downward (Figure 2-34), forward (Figure 2-35), or upward (Figure 2-36). This kind of action is called "*Zuo Wan*" (settling the wrist).

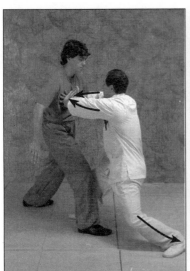

Figure 2–26

Figure 2–27

Figure 2–28

Figure 2–29

Figure 2–30

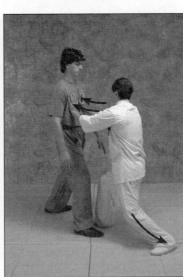

Figure 2–31

Figure 2–32

Figure 2–33

Figure 2–34

Figure 2–35

Figure 2–36

Figure 2–37

An is commonly used to seal the opponent's arm or joints (Figure 2-37), or for attacking his abdominal area (Figure 2-38) by "pressing downward." It is also often used to attack the opponent's chest by "pressing forward" (Figure 2-39) or "pressing upward" (Figure 2-40).

5. Cai 採

Cai means to "pluck" or to "grab." This is the action of locking the opponent's joints, such as the elbow (Figure 2-41) or wrist (Figure 2-42). Normally, after plucking or grabbing, the motion then leads either downward (e.g., Pick Up Needle from Sea Bottom)(Figure 2-43), sideward (e.g., Wave Hands in Clouds)(Figure 2-44), downward diagonally (e.g., Diagonal Flying)(Figure 2-45), or upward (e.g., Stand High to Search Out the Horse)(Figure 2-46). The main purpose of Cai is to forcibly lead the opponent's arm in the desired direction. From this action, the opponent's balance can be destroyed, or the arm can be immobilized for further attack.

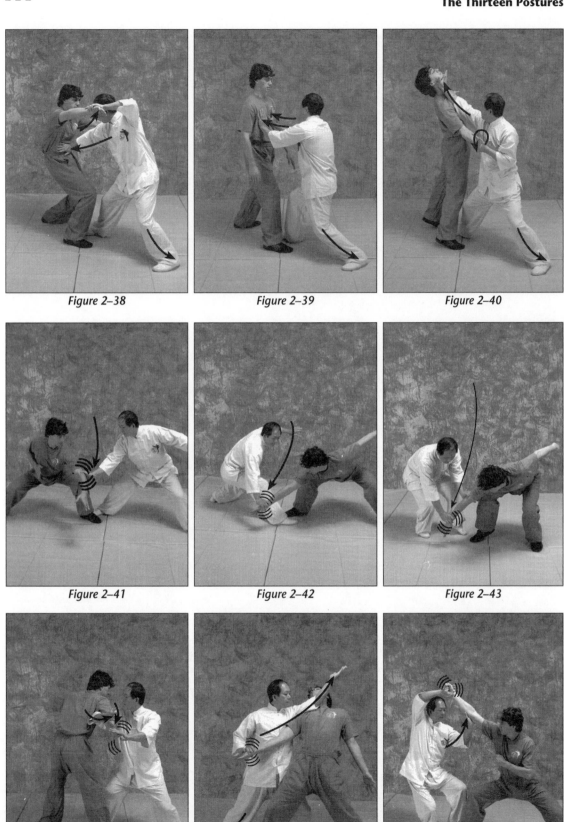

Figure 2–38

Figure 2–39

Figure 2–40

Figure 2–41

Figure 2–42

Figure 2–43

Figure 2–44

Figure 2–45

Figure 2–46

Figure 2–47 Figure 2–48 Figure 2–49

Figure 2–50 Figure 2–51 Figure 2–52

6. *Lie* 挒

Lie means to "rend" or to "split." This movement has the feeling of splitting a bamboo shaft or a piece of wood into two parts. Therefore, the action is forward and to the side (Figure 2-47). *Lie* is the action of using the arm to split or rend so as to put your opponent into a locked position or to make him fall. Very often it is considered a sideward *Peng*. can be used to lock the arm (e.g., Wild Horses Share the Mane)(Figure 2-48) or to bounce the opponent off balance (e.g., Grasp the Sparrow's Tail or Diagonal Flying) (Figures 2-49 and 2-50).

7. *Zhou* 肘

Zhou means to "elbow," and implies the use of the elbow to attack, or to neutralize a lock of the elbow. It includes both offensive and defensive purposes. When the elbow is used to attack through striking (*Da*) or pressing (*Ji*), the chest area is the main target

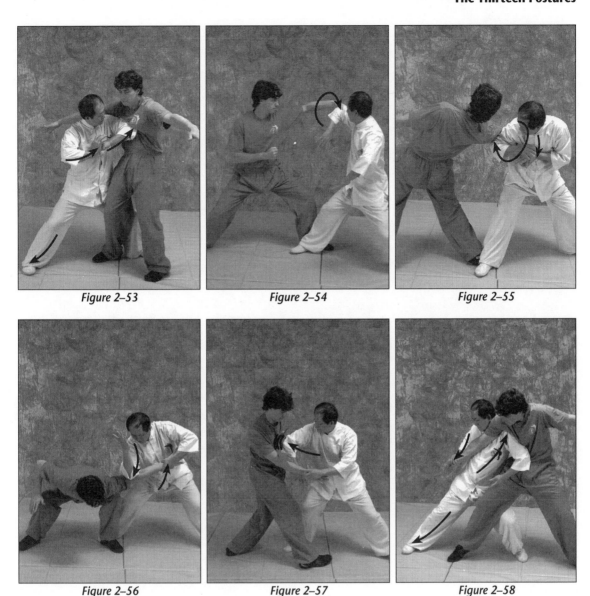

Figure 2–53   Figure 2–54   Figure 2–55

Figure 2–56   Figure 2–57   Figure 2–58

(Figures 2-51 to 2-53). When the elbow is used to neutralize a lock, a circular yielding motion is generally applied. From the circular yielding motion, the elbow can neutralize the attack (*Hua*) (Figure 2-54) to wrap or coil your opponent's arm (*Chan*) (Figure 2-55), or to seal the opponent's arm from further attack (*Feng*) (Figures 2-56 and 2-57). The elbow is like a steering wheel which directs its arm's movement. Therefore, it is very common that, in order to immobilize your arm movement, your opponent will lock or grab your elbow, and consequently your arm will be controlled. When this happens, you must know how to circle your elbow and how coil your forearm to reverse the situation. From this, you can see that for defensive purposes, knowing how to maneuver your elbow is very important.

8. *Kao* 靠

Kao means to "bump," and implies using part of your body, such as your shoulder (*Jian Kao*) (Figure 2-58), back (*Bei Kao*) (Figure 2-59), hip (*Tun Kao*) (Figure 2-60), thigh

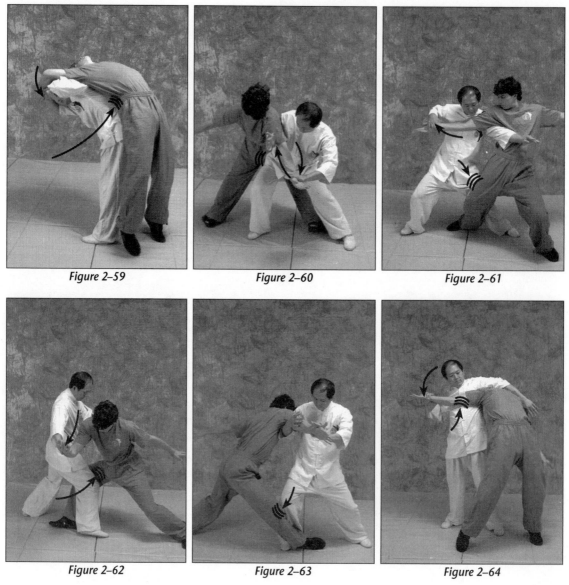

Figure 2–59

Figure 2–60

Figure 2–61

Figure 2–62

Figure 2–63

Figure 2–64

(*Tui Kao*) (Figures 2-61 and 2-62), knee (*Xi Kao*) (Figure 2-63), and Chest (*Xiong Kao*) (Figure 2-64) to bump the opponent's body. From the direction of *Kao*, it can be classified as: Forward *Kao* (*Qian Kao*) (Figure 2-65), Downward *Kao* (*Xia Kao*) (Figure 2-66), Sideways *Kao* (*Ce Kao*) (Figure 2-67), and Upward *Kao* (*Shang Kao*) (Figure 2-68). *Kao* is especially important in very close range situations with your opponent. If you apply *Kao* skillfully, you can destroy your opponent's rooting and balance, and are therefore able to prevent him from further attack. Alternatively, whenever your opponent is attempting to regain his balance, you can take the opportunity to execute further action, such as kicking or striking. Naturally, you can also use *Kao* to make your opponent fall when applied correctly. *Kao* is extremely powerful and destructive in some circumstances; you should be very careful in you training, and avoid using it on your opponents vital areas, such as the solar plexus, unless you desire to cause serious injury.

Figure 2–65

Figure 2–66

Figure 2–67

Figure 2–68

II. THE FIVE STRATEGIC DIRECTIONAL MOVEMENTS

In a battle, it is very important to keep an advantageous distance between you and your opponent for your attack or defense. Because of this, all of the Chinese martial arts styles train students how to move forward, backward, and sideways for advancing, retreating, and dodging. It is the same in *Taijiquan*. In order to apply the techniques correctly, you must know how to set up a correct distance and angle which will allow you to have the most advantageous maneuvering. Therefore, how you step and direct your body naturally and automatically in a battle is an important factor in winning.

However, in *Taijiquan*, due to the sticking and adhering strategy and techniques, you and your opponent are often in a stationary and urgent position. At that moment, you may not be able to step and move, since it could offer your opponent an opportunity to destroy your balance and rooting. Therefore, in *Taijiquan* pushing hands training, stationary pushing hands has always been the first priority. In order to help you move beyond such limited training, here we will summarize the basic strategic movements in *Taijiquan*.

Figure 2–69

Figure 2–70

Figure 2–71

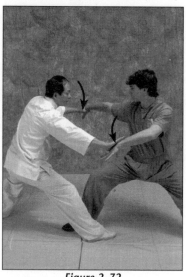

Figure 2–72

Figure 2–73

1. *Jin Bu* (Step Forward) 進步

Step Forward (*Jin Bu*) is normally used to maintain distance when your opponent is retreating. In order to stick and adhere, you must keep a good distance. Often, when your opponent realizes that your techniques are better than his, he will try to retreat and free himself from your sticking and adhering. Therefore, in order to keep him in the same awkward situation, you must know how to step forward skillfully (Figure 2-69).

Step Forward is also often used to close the distance between you and your opponent from the long range into the medium or short ranges, or from the medium range into the short range. For example, once your have neutralized your opponent's punch with sticking (Figure 2-70), in order to adhere to his arm, you must close from the medium range into the short range, which allows you to have better control for your *Taijiquan* techniques (Figure 2-71). Naturally, when the opportunity allows, after you control your opponent's arms (Figure 2-72), you may step forward to gain advancing power for your striking (Figure 2-73).

| *Figure 2–74* | *Figure 2–75* | *Figure 2–76* |

2. *Tui Bu* (Step Backward) 退步

The strategy of "Step Backward" is exactly opposite from that of "Step Forward." With stepping backward, you can retreat from an urgent situation (Figure 2-74). Often, stepping backward is used to yield to oncoming power, providing you more time to lead and neutralize an attack. For example, when your opponent is pressing your chest with his palms, you may step backward to yield and at the same time squeeze both his arms inward (Figure 2-75). From this, you can see that generally speaking, "Step Backward" is a defensive maneuver.

3. *Zuo Gu* (See the Left) 左顧

Zuo means left and *Gu* means to "see" or to "look for." Therefore, *Zuo Gu* means to see or to look for the opportunity on your left. While you are in a fighting situation, you should always be looking for an opportunity to step to your sides. Stepping to the side will offer you an advantageous opportunity to enter your opponent's empty door (Figure 2-76). Often, stepping to the left is part of a technique which could put your opponent into an awkward position. For example, when you apply the *Da Lu* (Large Rollback) technique, in order to make the technique effective, you must step your left leg to your left and put your opponent into a controlled position (Figures 2-77 to 2-79).

Naturally, stepping to the side is also commonly use to dodge or to avoid oncoming power. From sideways stepping, you may direct your opponent's power to the side and thereby stop him from further action. For example, in *Xiao Lu* (Small Rollback), once you have neutralized your opponent's power (Figure 2-80), you may step your right leg to his right (i.e., your left) and at the same time pull him off balance (Figure 2-81).

Often "*Zuo Gu*" is also translated as "Beware of the Left." This means to "beware" of the left hand side attack from your opponent. This can also be interpreted as "beware of" an opportunity on your left.

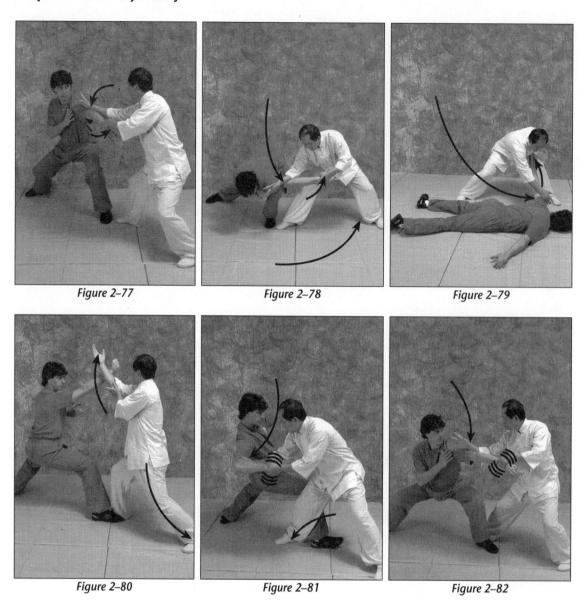

Figure 2–77   Figure 2–78   Figure 2–79

Figure 2–80   Figure 2–81   Figure 2–82

4. *You Pan* (Look to the Right) 右 盼

This is the same strategic movement as the "See the Left.." This time, you should keep looking for an opportunity for you to step to your right. The purposes are the same as those of "See the Left," and it serves for dodging and setting up advantageous angles for your attack. For example, in the *Da Lu* (Large Rollback) technique, once you have performed rollback on your opponent's arm (Figure 2-82), you may step both your legs to your right; this will offer you a good angle for your *Ji* (Pressing) (Figure 2-83). Also, in the Wave Hands in the Cloud (*Yun Shou*) technique, if your opponent's left leg is forward, once you have controlled his right arm (Figure 2-84), you may step your left leg to the side of his left leg (i.e., to your right)(Figure 2-85);this will offer you an advantageous angle to take him down (Figure 2-86).

| Figure 2–83 | Figure 2–84 | Figure 2–85 |

| Figure 2–86 | Figure 2–87 |

5. *Zhong Ding* (Firm the Center) 中 定

Zhong means "center" and *Ding* means to "stabilize" or to "firm." In *Taijiquan* practice, "*Zhong Ding*" is probably one of the most important trainings on which a beginner should concentrate. In order to stabilize your center, you must first have firm root. In order to have a firm root, you must first have firmed your center. In order to firm your center, you must first have good balance. In order to balance yourself, you must first know how to relax yourself and to allow the *Qi* to move smoothly and naturally in your body. This will offer you an accurate sensation of your balance. Only when you have a firm root, then your spirit can be raised (Figure 2-87).

From this, you can see that to firm the center and root is not an easy task, especially for a beginner. Generally, "*Zhong Ding*" is learned from standing *Qigong* and stationary pushing hands practice. In stationary pushing hands drills, you and your partner are looking for each other's center and rooting, and trying to destroy it. Naturally, you must also learn how to protect your center and rooting from being destroyed by your partner.

2-4. Yi, Qi, and Action

When there is an action, we generate *Yi* (idea or mind) first, and from this *Yi*, the *Qi* is led to the muscles and nerves to activate or energize the muscles for contraction and relaxation. From this, you can see that the origin of any action is the Yi.

Yi, or the mind, is generated within the brain. It is generally believed that we understand the functioning of only about 10% of the brain. From this, you can see that we still cannot completely rely on modern science to explain all of the functioning or the behavior of the brain. That means our science is still in its infancy.

Except for some extraordinary people, such as Einstein or Hawking, we develop and utilize only about 33% of our brains. This means that about 67% of our brain is never even used as far as we know. Some Chinese Buddhist and Daoist *Qigong* practices learn how to lead the *Qi* to the brain to activate or energize the extra brain cells for functioning, and hopefully assist one to reach a stage of spiritual enlightenment.

According to the model adopted by YMAA, the *Qi* circulating in living organisms is a form of bioelectric energy. In our analysis of this bioelectricity, it is helpful to consider that a brain cell will consume at least 12 or more times the oxygen of regular cells. Oxygen and food are the original sources of bioelectricity in the cells through biochemical reaction in the body. The twelve-fold oxygen requirements of the brain cells leads us to conclude that these cells probably consume 12 times or more electricity than ordinary cells. This means that, in order to increase brain functioning to a higher level, we must learn how to charge the batteries in our body to a higher level. Only then can we hope to lead plenty of *Qi* to the brain to activate and maintain its higher level of functioning. According to past experience with *Qigong* practice in China, this battery is also called the "*Lower Dan Tian*," and is located approximately at our physical center of gravity (within the Large and Small Intestines). In order to charge the *Qi* to a higher level in the *Lower Dan Tian*, the methods of "Abdominal Breathing" and "Embryo Breathing" were discovered in the past. If you are interested in knowing more about these two breathing techniques, you should refer to **The Essence of Tai Chi Chi Kung** by YMAA.

To lead the *Qi* upward to the brain, concentration or meditation training is necessary. From concentration and meditation practice, the *Qi* or bioelectricity can be led by the mind to the brain to activate more brain cells for functioning. In addition, through mind concentration, the EMF (electromotive force) generated from the brain will be stronger. Naturally, the *Qi* or bioelectricity led or directed by the brain will be stronger.

Our physical body is like a living machine; its functioning depends on *Qi* or bioelectricity levels. When the *Qi* level is high, this machine can be enhanced to a higher efficiency, and when the *Qi* level is low, the operation of the machine will be stagnant. Unless they have special training like weight lifting or special sports, normally a person will only use less than half of his maximum physical strength for daily work. This means that unless it is necessary, most of us never demand peak functioning of our physical body.

From this, you can see that, in order for your body to have a higher functioning capability, **you must have a concentrated, meditative mind, an abundant *Qi* storage in the *Lower Dan Tian*, and knowledge of how to lead the *Qi* to the required body area to**

energize the physical body to a higher working efficiency. That is why, since 550 A.D., all Chinese martial styles have practiced Qigong.

Some martial styles believed that, since it would take a long time to develop the concentrated, meditative mind and to charge the *Qi* in the Lower Dan Tian to a higher level, we should first use the already available *Qi* in our bodies to energize the physical body for fighting. It was critical that you learned techniques first for your defense in ancient times. Only after you knew how to defend yourself could you begin to cultivate your *Qi* and train your concentrated, meditative mind. These styles are called "external styles."

However, other styles believed that, since the mind and the *Qi* are the origins of physical power, one should first learn how to cultivate the *Qi* and train the concentrated mind. Only when the *Qi* was strong could it be led by the concentrated mind to the physical body for techniques. In order to allow the *Qi* to circulate in the body smoothly, the body must be soft and relaxed. This was the origin of *Taijiquan*, known as one of the "internal styles."

From the above explanation, you can see that ***Taijiquan* emphasizes the soft and uses it against the hard. *Taijiquan* focuses more on internal training, such as the concentrated, meditative mind and the cultivation of *Qi*. Finally, in order to be relaxed physically for smooth *Qi* circulation, the movements are more round.** Not coincidentally, these same characteristics apply to *Qin Na* techniques. When you have reached the higher levels of *Qin Na*, the techniques become soft and round. The concentrated mind is the essential key to executing a technique.

▪ Chapter 3 ▪

Qin Na in Peng, Lu, Ji, and An

3-1. Introduction

As explained in the last chapter, *Peng*, *Lu*, *Ji*, *An*, *Cai*, *Lie*, *Zhou* and *Kao* are the eight fundamental methods or patterns of Jin manifestation in Taijiquan. From these eight patterns, hundreds of techniques can be derived and developed. Since these eight patterns are the most basic *Jin* patterns in *Taijiquan*, it would be wise first to understand those *Qin Na* techniques which can be applied and used against these patterns. Naturally, after you have mastered all of the *Qin Na* techniques from these eight *Jin* patterns, you will be able to apply them into *Taiji* Pushing Hands. This is because *Taiji* Pushing Hands techniques are all built upon the foundation of these eight basic patterns.

In this chapter, I would like to introduce the possible *Qin Na* applications for the first four patterns: *Peng*, *Lu*, *Ji*, and *An*, and in the next chapter, the remaining four patterns: *Cai*, *Lie*, *Zhou*, and *Kao*.

Again, I would like to remind you that the *Qin Na* introduced here are only some of the possible techniques with which I am familiar. Through practicing and pondering, you will soon discover that there are many other techniques which can be developed according to the same theory. You should also understand that since *Qin Na* theory remains the same for any style, it is not surprising that many techniques are very similar to Shaolin *Qin Na* or any other style. As a matter of fact, many *Qin Na* techniques introduced in this book are adapted from Shaolin White Crane *Qin Na*.

3-2. Qin Na in Peng

Peng is expanding the chest and using the chest's arcing power to extend the arm forward, upward or sideward. Few *Qin Na* techniques are executed using *Peng* itself. Often, it is mixed with other *Jin* patterns such as *Cai* (pluck) or *An* (press with wrist).

| *Figure 3–1* | *Figure 3–2* | *Figure 3–3* |

Normally, *Peng* is executed with the forearm or elbow. Therefore, when you use your forearm to wardoff for *Qin Na* control, you usually pay more attention to the locking of your opponent's elbow or post arm. However, if the distance between you and your opponent is so close that you can apply *Peng Jin* to his neck, then you have the option to control his neck as well. Naturally, the same theory applies when you use *Qin Na* against *Peng*.

I. QIN NA FOR PENG

Technique #1: The Forearm Wardsoff the Enemy's Elbow
(Bi Peng Di Zhou) 臂掤敵肘

This technique is used to lock your opponent's elbow with your forearm. For example, if your opponent punches you with his right hand (Figure 3-1) or adheres to your left arm with his right hand (Figure 3-2), use your left forearm to intercept or neutralize his right arm, while placing your right forearm under his elbow or on the rear side of his post-arm to press his tendons (Figure 3-3). Finally, using the leverage of your left hand and right forearm, you may lock him upward (Figure 3-4). You may also use this leverage and *Jin* to break his elbow. When you execute this technique, you should position yourself on your opponent's right hand side to avoid his left hand attack.

Theory:
Misplacing the Bone (elbow) and Pressing the Tendon (if post-arm tendons are pressed). When you use your left forearm to neutralize the attack, you are using **Upward** and **Sideways Wardoff (*Peng*)** to lead and direct your opponent's oncoming force to your left. Once you have locked your opponent in the final position, you are using **Downward Press (*An*)** for your left hand and **Upward Wardoff (*Peng*)** to lock his elbow joint.

Figure 3–4 Figure 3–5 Figure 3–6

Figure 3–7 Figure 3–8 Figure 3–9

Technique #2: The Crane Spreads Its Wings or Reverse Wrist Press

(Bai He Liang Chi or Fan Ya Wan) 白鶴亮翅 ，反壓腕

This technique can be used when your opponent's right hand is either punching you or adhering to your right forearm in a pushing hands situation. If your opponent punches you with his right fist, first you use your left forearm to cover his punching while at the same time clamping upward your right hand on his wrist (Figure 3-5). Immediately, twist his wrist counterclockwise to lock it (Figure 3-6). Finally, while using your left hand to continue the twisting on his right wrist, use your right forearm to push the right hand side of his neck (Figure 3-7).

However, if your opponent's right hand is adhering to your right forearm (Figure 3-8), use your left hand to grab his right hand and twist it counterclockwise with both of your hands (Figures 3-9 and 3-10). Once the position of his right arm is set, immediately use your right forearm to push the side of his neck (Figure 3-11). From the leverage of your left hand's twisting and right forearm's pushing, you can lock him up easily.

| Figure 3–10 | Figure 3–11 | Figure 3–12 |

Theory:

Misplacing the Bone (elbow and shoulder) and Dividing the Muscle/Tendon (wrist). When you grab your opponent's right wrist and twist it counterclockwise, it is a form of **Pluck (Cai)**. When you use your right forearm to push his neck, it is a **Sideways Peng**. In this technique, you should pay attention to the angle at which you lock his right arm. If his arm is either too straight or too bent, the technique will not be effective. Naturally, your right arm's Wardoff also plays a main role in the locking. With an accurate wardoff angle of your right arm, you may generate effective leverage for your locking.

Technique #3: Upward Elbow Wrap

(Shang Chan Zhou) 上纏肘

Although this technique is very similar to the last technique, the means of approaching and locking are somewhat different. This technique is used against the same situation as when your opponent's right hand is adhering to your right wrist (Figure 3-12). After you have neutralized his power to your right, again you use your left hand to grab his right hand (Figure 3-13) and twist it counterclockwise with both of your hands (Figure 3-14). Next, reposition yourself to his right hand side, continue twisting his right wrist with your left hand while coiling your right hand around his right arm, and reach to his elbow and lift it upward (Figure 3-15). In this case, you have used the leverage of your left and right hands to lock his right arm. In order to control him more effectively, you may lock his right arm with your right hand and right abdominal area while using your left forearm to push his neck or head sideways (Figure 3-16) or forward (Figure 3-17).

Theory:

Misplacing the Bone (elbow and shoulder). Again, the left hand's grabbing is a form of **Pluck (Cai)**. Your right hand's coiling and reaching to his elbow is a *Jin* of **Coiling (Chan)** and in the final position of locking, your left forearm's pushing and expanding is a form of **Sideways Wardoff** or **Forward Wardoff (Peng)**. To make this technique effective, you should raise his right elbow high with your right hand while pushing away his neck or head with your left forearm. Remember, when you apply your *Qin Na* technique to be soft, easy, and circular. This will prevent your opponent from feeling your intention before you lock him.

Figure 3–13   *Figure 3–14*   *Figure 3–15*

Figure 3–16   *Figure 3–17*   *Figure 3–18*

Technique #4: Prop Up Elbow

(Shang Jia Zhou) 上 架 肘

When your opponent's right hand is adhering to your right wrist (Figure 3-18), reposition yourself to his right hand side, coil your right hand counterclockwise around his forearm, and then either press it down or grab his wrist while placing your left hand on his elbow to stop him from elbowing you (Figure 3-19). Next, place your left elbow under his right elbow and use the leverage of your right hand and left elbow to straighten his right arm and lift him upward (Figure 3-20). His palm should face upward. Finally, use the right hand's pressing and the left post-arm's upward wardoff power to generate good leverage and lock him upward (Figure 3-21).

Theory:

Misplacing the Bone (elbow). When you circle your right hand around his forearm and finally reach his wrist, it is a form of **Coiling (Chan)**. In the final locking, if you use your right hand to press his wrist down, it is a **Downward Press (An)**, and if

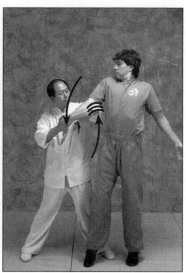

Figure 3–19   Figure 3–20   Figure 3–21

your right hand is used to lock or grab his wrist, then it is a **Pluck (Cai).** Naturally, your left post arm's upward lifting and expanding is an **Upward Wardoff (Peng)** generated from your left post-arm. In this technique, you may also use your post-arm to press the rear tendons of his post-arm upward. If you do so, then it is mixture of the body Misplacing the Bone (elbow) and Pressing the Tendon (post-arm) techniques.

Technique #5: The Crane Spreads Its Wings

(Bai He Liang Chi) 白鶴亮翅

When your opponent's left hand is adhering to your right wrist or forearm (Figure 3-22), first raise up your right arm and use your left hand to grab his left hand (Figure 3-23). Next, twist his left wrist with both of your hands by circling his arm downward clockwise (Figure 3-24). Finally, step both of your legs forward to shorten the distance between you and your opponent, while locking his left arm by your stomach and using your right forearm to push his chin upward and forward (Figure 3-25).

Theory:

Misplacing the Bone (elbow and shoulder) and Dividing the Muscle/Tendon (wrist). This is again an application of the *Taijiquan* posture "The Crane Spreads Its Wings." Your left hand's grabbing is a form of **Pluck (Cai)** and your right forearm's pushing and expanding is a form of **Sideways Wardoff (Peng).** The leverage generated from your left hand's twisting and your right forearm's expanding wardoff *Jin* is the key to the locking.

Technique #6: Arm Wardsoff the Enemy's Leg

(Bi Peng Di Tui) 臂掤敵腿

During pushing hands, when both of your arms are wide open (Figure 3-26), it is possible that your opponent will kick you. If your opponent kicks your middle body with his right leg, immediately use your left forearm to scoop his right leg upward (Figure 3-27). Finally, use your right hand to press his toes downward while lifting your left forearm on to the tendons of his calf (Figure 3-28).

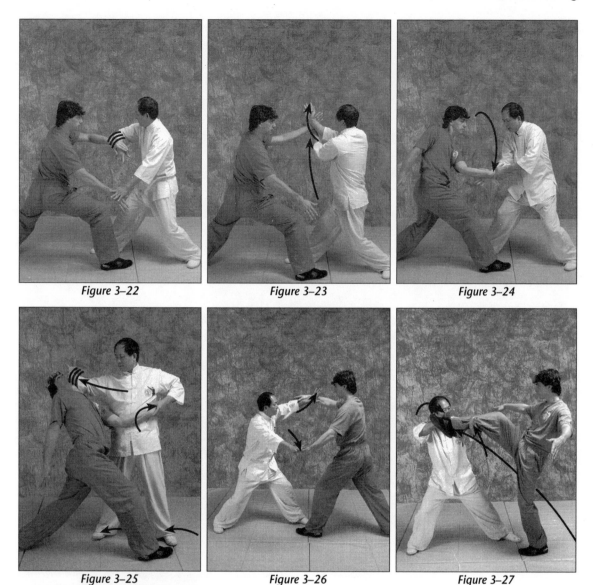

Figure 3–22   Figure 3–23   Figure 3–24

Figure 3–25   Figure 3–26   Figure 3–27

Figure 3–28

Theory:

Pressing the Tendon (calf). This is an example of **Upward Wardoff (Peng)** against a kick. After you have scooped his leg and trapped it, the upward wardoff *Jin* must be strong, simply because his leg is also strong. If your left arm is right on his calf tendons, with the leverage generated from your left forearm and right hand's **Downward Pressing (An)**, you can create great pain in his calf. You should keep his leg as straight as possible. That means you may have to raise his leg higher.

Figure 3–29   Figure 3–30   Figure 3–31

Figure 3–32   Figure 3–33   Figure 3–34

II. QIN NA AGAINST PENG

Technique #1: Small Elbow Wrap

(Xiao Chan Zhou) 小纏肘

When your opponent is using his forearm to perform upward or forward Wardoff agaist your chest (Figure 3-29), first use your right forearm to raise his right forearm up while placing your left hand on his elbow (Figure 3-30). Next, step your left leg to the front of his right leg, grab his right wrist with your right hand, and use the leverage of your left forearm and right hand to rotate his right arm (Figure 3-31). Then, bow your body forward and pull his body toward your front to destroy his balance (Figure 3-32). Finally, sweep

Figure 3–35   Figure 3–36   Figure 3–37

your left leg backward to take him down (Figure 3-33). If you like, you may use both of your legs to lock his arm behind him while using your hands to grab his hair to control him completely (Figure 3-34).

Theory:

Misplacing the Bone (shoulder). The first movement in which you use your right forearm to lead his arm upward is an **Upward Wardoff (Peng)**. When you circle his arm downward is it a **Downward Rollback (Lu)**. Naturally, your right hand's grabbing is a **Pluck (Cai)**. The trick to making this technique successful is to lead your opponent to your front; this will destroy his balance for your sweeping.

Technique #2: The Old Man Carries the Fish on his Back

(Lao Han Bei Yu) 老漢背魚

Again, if your opponent is using his right forearm to perform wardoff against your chest either forward or upward (Figure 3-35), immediately use your left forearm to push his elbow downward while using your right hand to raise his forearm upward to bend his arm (Figure 3-36). Finally, step your left leg behind him, turn your body to your right, and then bow forward to lock his right arm behind your back (Figure 3-37).

Theory:

Misplacing the Bone (shoulder and elbow). When you use both of your arms to bend his elbow, it is an action of **Squeezing (Ji)** like the posture of Play the Guitar in *Taijiquan*. In the final position of locking, it is using the **Back Upward Pressing (Kao)** to set up a locking angle. To make this technique effective, your opponent's arm should not be too bent or too straight.

  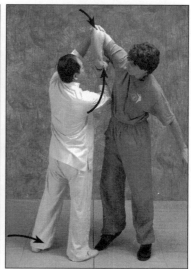

| *Figure 3–38* | *Figure 3–39* | *Figure 3–40* |

Technique #3: Upward Wrist Press

(Shang Ya Wan) 上壓腕

If your opponent uses his right arm to perform wardoff against your chest either forward or upward (Figure 3-38), immediately use your right hand to grab his right wrist while placing your left hand on his elbow and pushing it upward (Figure 3-39). Finally, move your left leg closer to your right leg, pressing your right hand upward to generate strain on his wrist while pressing your left hand downward to his elbow (Figure 3-40). This will generate good leverage for the locking. You should increase your squeezing pressure until his heels are off the ground.

Theory:

Dividing the Muscle/Tendon (wrist). Again, when using both of your hands to control his wrist and elbow, it is an action of **Squeeze (Ji).** This kind of squeezing motion is also called **Close (He)** in *Taijiquan*. Naturally, the right hand grabbing is an action of **Pluck (Cai).** Once you have locked his arm upward, the final lock is generated from the **Squeeze (Ji)** of both hands.

Technique #4: Press Shoulder with Single Finger and Extending the Neck for Water

(Yi Zhi Ding Jian or *Yin Jing Qiu Shui)* 一指頂肩，引頸求水

Again, when your opponent uses his forearm to perform wardoff against your chest (Figure 3-41), first use your right hand to grab his wrist while using your left forearm to press his elbow upward (Figure 3-42). Next, step your left leg behind his right leg, coil your left hand around his right arm until your left hand reaches his post-arm near the elbow area, and lift your left elbow to lock his arm behind him (Figure 3-43). In this case, the ligaments on his shoulder area will be very tensed. If you use your index or middle finger to press his *Jianneiling* cavity (M-UE-48) upward, you will be able to generate great pain in his shoulder (Figures 3-44 and 3-45). Alternatively, you may use your hand to press his chin upward to generate good leverage for locking (Figure 3-46).

Figure 3–41

Figure 3–42

Figure 3–43

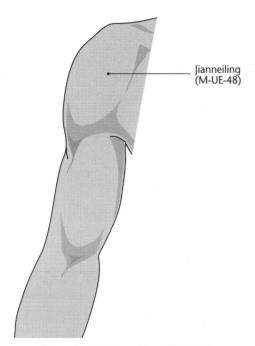

Jianneiling
(M-UE-48)

Figure 3–45

Figure 3–44. Jianneiling (M-UE-48)

Theory:

Misplacing the Bone (shoulder) and Cavity Press (*Jianneiling* cavity). Again, your right hand's grabbing is a **Pluck (*Cai*)**, and both hands' closing and rotating movement is an action of **Squeeze (*Ji*)** or **Close (*He*)**. Your circling your left hand around his right arm until the post-arm near the elbow area is an action of **Coil (*Chan*)**, and when you lift up your elbow while pressing your left hand on his post-arm, it is a Downward **Press (*An*)**. Naturally, in the final locking, your right hand's lifting is a Raise or **Lift (*Ti*)**, and when you use your finger to press his *Jianneiling* cavity (M-UE-48), it is a **Point** or **Press (*Dian*)**.

Figure 3–46

| Figure 3–47 | Figure 3–48 | Figure 3–49 |

Technique #5: Reverse Elbow Wrap

(Fan Chan Zhou) 反纏肘

Strictly speaking, this technique is an option of the last technique. Again, when your opponent uses his right forearm to perform wardoff against your chest (Figure 3-47), first step your left leg behind his right leg, grabbing his right wrist with your right hand while coiling your left hand around his arm until it reaches his post-arm near the elbow area (Figure 3-48). Next, lift his forearm upward with your left elbow while stepping your right leg backward (Figure 3-49). Finally, circle him down to the ground (Figure 3-50).

Theory:

Misplacing the Bone (shoulder). Again, your right hand's grabbing is a **Pluck (*Cai*)** and your left hand's circling around his right arm until the post-arm near the elbow area is an action of **Coil (*Chan*)**. When you lift up your elbow while pressing your left hand on his post-arm to generate strain on his shoulder, it is a **Downward Press (*An*)**. Finally, the action of leading him to the ground is a movement of **Rollback (*Lu*)**.

Technique #6: Upward Elbow Wrap

(Shang Chan Zhou) 上纏肘

When your opponent uses his right forearm to perform wardoff against your chest (Figure 3-51), again use your left forearm to press his elbow down, while using your right forearm to raise his right forearm (Figure 3-52). Next, circle his arm counterclockwise while grabbing his wrist with your left hand (Figure 3-53). Continue the circular motion of both of your hands, and then twist his wrist with your left hand while pressing his elbow upward with your right hand (Figure 3-54). To make the lock more effective, you should squeeze both of your hands toward each other. Alternatively, you may lock his right arm with your right hand and abdominal area while using your left hand to push his head either sideward (Figure 3-55) or forward (Figure 3-56).

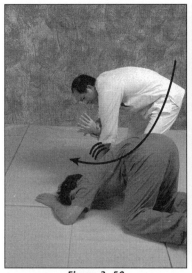

Figure 3–50

Figure 3–51

Figure 3–52

Figure 3–53

Figure 3–54

Figure 3–55

Figure 3–56

Theory:

Misplacing the Bone (shoulder and elbow). Your left hand's grabbing on his wrist is a **Pluck (Cai)**, and the circling of your right hand around his arm until his elbow is a **Coil (Chan)**. When you squeeze both hands toward each other, it is a **Squeeze (Ji)**, and your left forearm's pushing against his neck or head is a **Wardoff (Peng)**. Remember that the circular motions in *Taijiquan* are very important. It is the same in *Taiji Qin Na*. When you use circular motions, you are able to set up a *Qin Na* lock before your opponent feels it. A good *Qin Na* technique is soft, smooth, and round. The action should be natural, easy, and straightforward.

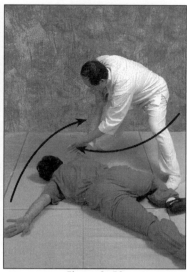

| *Figure 3–57* | *Figure 3–58* | *Figure 3–59* |

3-3. Qin Na in Lu

As explained in Chapter 2, *Lu* means to yield, lead and then neutralize to the side and backward; it is commonly translated as "rollback." *Lu* is generally used for defensive purposes. However, when the situation is right, *Lu* can be used to attack. In this section, we will introduce the offensive *Lu* which can be used for *Qin Na*. Then we will review some of the *Qin Na* which can be used against *Lu*.

I. QIN NA FOR LU

When you use *Lu* to yield, lead, control or neutralize the opponent's arm, normally you use one hand to grab or pluck your opponent's wrist while using the other hand to control his elbow or post-arm. *Lu* can be distinguished as "small rollback" and "large rollback."

Technique #1: Large Rollback

(Da Lu) 大擺

When your opponent's hands are on your right forearm either pushing it or pressing it downward (Figure 3-57), first step your right leg backward to yield and lead, neutralizing his power backward by grabbing his right wrist with your right hand and placing your left forearm on his post-arm or elbow (Figure 3-58). Finally, step your right leg back and use the leverage generated from both of your hands to lock his arm and lead it down to the ground (Figure 3-59).

Theory:

Misplacing the Bone (elbow) or Pressing the Tendon (post-arm). Your right hand's grabbing is a **Pluck (Cai)**. In fact, the entire motion is a **Large Rollback (Da Lu)**. If you use your left forearm to press the tendons in his post-arm, the location of pressing is important. The place to press is about three inches above the elbow.

Figure 3–60

Figure 3–61

Figure 3–62

Figure 3–63

Technique #2: Lead the Snake to Enter the Cave

(Yin She Ru Dong) 引 蛇 入 洞

When both of your opponent's hands are on your right forearm (Figure 3-60), first wardoff his power upward while using your left hand to grab his left wrist (Figure 3-61). Next, coil your right hand around his left arm until his elbow, and lock his arm straight (Figure 3-62). Finally, step your left leg backward and use the leverage of both of your hands to lead him down to the ground (Figure 3-63).

Theory:

Misplacing the Bone (elbow). The entire action is the technique of **Small Rollback (Xiao Lu)**. When you raise your right arm upward, it is an **Upward Wardoff (Peng)**, when you circle your right hand around his left arm until his elbow, it is a **Coil (Chan)**, the left hand's wrist grabbing is a **Pluck (Cai)**, and naturally, when you lead his power to the ground, it is **Rollback (Lu)**.

Figure 3-64

Figure 3-65

Figure 3-66

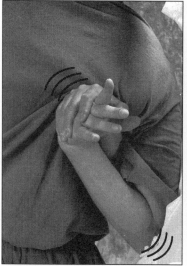

Figure 3-67

Figure 3-68

Technique #3: Hands Hold a Panda

(Shou Bao Wan Xiong) 手抱浣熊

Again, when both of your opponent's hands are on your right forearm, first wardoff the oncoming power upward (Figure 3-64). Next, coil your right hand around his right arm until it reaches the internal side of his elbow, while also using your left hand to grab his right wrist and circle his arm down (Figure 3-65). Then, step your right leg behind his right leg while pulling his right elbow in with your right hand and pushing his right wrist to his back with your left hand (Figure 3-66). Finally, use your right hand and your chest to lock his arm behind him (Figure 3-67) and use your left hand to push his chin away (Figure 3-68).

Theory:

Dividing the Muscle/Tendon (wrist). When you raise your right arm upward, it is an **Upward Wardoff (*Peng*)**. When you circle your right hand around his right arm, it is a **Coil (*Chan*)**. The left hand's grabbing is a **Pluck (*Cai*)**, and when you lead his power to your left and backward, it is a **Small Rollback (*Xiao Lu*)**. Finally, when you lock his right arm between your right hand and chest, it is a **Squeeze (*Ji*)**.

| *Figure 3–69* | *Figure 3–70* | *Figure 3–71* |

Technique #4: Small Elbow Wrap

(Xiao Chan Zhou) 小纏肘

When your opponent's hands are on your right forearm and are pressing it (Figure 3-69), first raise your right arm upward to wardoff his power and grab his right wrist while also placing your left forearm on his right elbow and circling his arm down (Figure 3-70). Right after you neutralize his power, you should immediately step your left leg behind his right leg. Finally, lead his arm and body to the front of your body while sweeping your left leg backward to make him fall (Figure 3-71).

Theory:

Misplacing the Bone (shoulder and elbow). Your right arm's raising is an **Upward Wardoff (*Peng*)** and its grabbing is a **Pluck (*Cai*)**. When you lead his body to your front and make him fall, it is **Rollback (*Lu*)**.

Technique #5: Reverse Elbow Wrap

(Reverse Elbow Wrap) 反纏肘

When both of your opponent's hands are on your right forearm to press it down (Figure 3-72), immediately step your left leg behind his right leg, raise your right arm up to wardoff the power, and grab his wrist while coiling your left hand around his right arm until it reaches his post-arm near the elbow area and lock his arm behind his back (Figure 3-73). Finally, step your right leg backward while leading him down to the ground (Figure 3-74). The locking leverage is generated from your left elbow and hand (Figure 3-75).

Theory:

Misplacing the Bone (shoulder and elbow). When you raise your right arm up to neutralize his pressing, it is an **Upward Wardoff (*Peng*)**, and then its grabbing on his right wrist is a **Pluck (*Cai*)**. When you circle your left hand around his right arm, it is a **Coil (*Chan*)**, and finally when you lead him down to the ground, it is a **Rollback (*Lu*)**.

Figure 3–72

Figure 3–73

Figure 3–74

Figure 3–75

Figure 3–76

Figure 3–77

Technique #6: Push the Boat to Follow the Stream

(Shun Shui Tui Zhou) 順水推舟

When your opponent's left hand is on your right wrist (Figure 3-76), immediately turn your right hand upward and circle around his wrist while using your left hand to grab his left wrist (Figure 3-77). Next, step your left leg backward and twist his wrist with your left hand while using your right hand, which is on his wrist, to control his left arm (Figure 3-78). Finally, lead him down to the ground (Figure 3-79). The control is generated from the left hand's wrist twisting (Figure 3-80).

Theory:

Dividing the Muscle/Tendon (wrist). Your right hand's circling around his left wrist is a **Coil (*Chan*)** and your left hand's grabbing is a **Pluck (*Cai*)**. When you lead his body down to the ground, it is a **Rollback (*Lu*)**. The key control of this technique is on the twisting of his wrist with your left hand. Your right hand is only to help you control his arm.

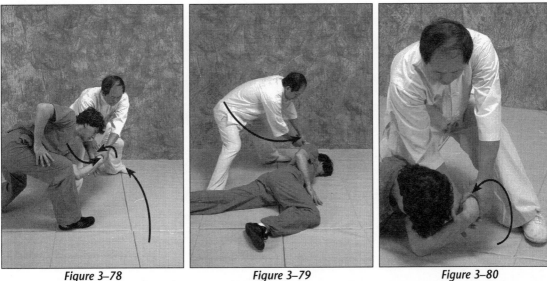

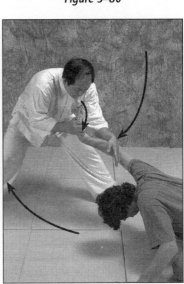

Figure 3–78   Figure 3–79   Figure 3–80

Figure 3–81   Figure 3–82   Figure 3–83

Technique #7: Wild Chicken Breaks Its Wings

(Ye Ji Yao Chi) 野雞拗翅

When your opponent's right hand is pressing or pushing your chest (Figure 3-81), immediately turn your body to your right, use your right hand to grab his right wrist and turn it 90 degrees clockwise while placing your left hand on his elbow (Figure 3-82). Then, step your right leg backward and at the same time use the leverage generated from both of your hands to press him down (Figure 3-83). You may continue your locking pressure and lead him until his entire body is on the ground (Figure 3-84).

Theory:

Dividing the Muscle/Tendon (Wrist). When you use your right hand to grab his right wrist, it is a **Pluck (Cai)**, and when you lead him down to the ground. it is a **Rollback (Lu)**. In this technique, when you control your opponent, his elbow should be lower than his wrist. The entire control is on the twisting and bending of his wrist by your right hand. Your left hand only serves to keep his elbow down.

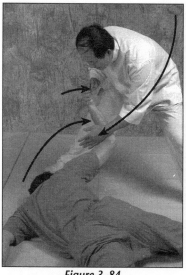

Figure 3–84

Figure 3–85

Figure 3–86

Figure 3–87

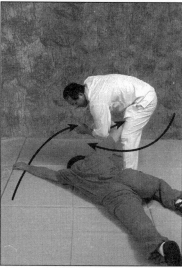

Figure 3–88

Technique #8: Arm Rollsback the Enemy's Elbow

(Bi Lu Di Zhou) 臂擺敵肘

When your opponent's right hand is on your left shoulder to control it, immediately turn your body to your right to yield (Figure 3-85). Next, use your right hand to grab his right wrist while placing your left forearm on his right elbow (Figure 3-86). Finally, step your right leg backward, bow toward him, and use the leverage of both of your hands to lead him down (Figure 3-87). You may continue to step your right leg backward to lead him down to the ground (Figure 3-88).

Theory:

Dividing the Muscle/Tendon (Wrist). When you use your right hand to grab his right wrist, it is a **Pluck (Cai)**, and when you lead him down to the ground. it is a **Rollback (Lu)**. In this technique, when you control your opponent, his elbow should be lower than his wrist. The entire control is on his wrist's twisting and bending by your right hand. Your left forearm only serves to keep his elbow down.

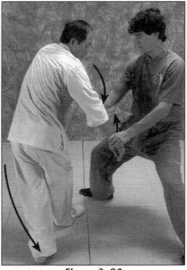

| Figure 3–89 | Figure 3–90 | Figure 3–91 |

II. QIN NA AGAINST LU

When your opponent uses "small rollback" against you, one of his hands will be grabbing your wrist while the other leads and controls your elbow joint to rollback. When your opponent uses the "large rollback," while one of his hands is grabbing you, the forearm of the other arm will be on your elbow or post arm area.

It is not easy to grab your opponent's forearm that is on your elbow or post arm. Therefore, there are not many *Qin Na* which you can use against his forearm's rollback. However, in order to make the rollback technique effective, your opponent must use the other hand to pluck your wrist. This will offer you many options for *Qin Na* techniques to use against his Pluck (*Cai*). We will examine the *Qin Na* against Pluck in the next chapter. In this section, we will introduce some of the possible *Qin Na* techniques which can be used against *Lu*.

Technique #1: Send the Devil to Heaven

(Song Mo Shang Tian) 送魔上天

When your opponent uses the Small Rollback technique to control your right arm and intends to lead it to his side, immediately use your left hand to grab his right hand (Figure 3-89). Next, step your left leg behind your right leg while twisting his right wrist with your left hand, and free your right arm through the gap of his thumb and index finger (Figure 3-90). Then, turn your body counterclockwise while lifting his right arm upward (Figure 3-91). Continue to turn your body and twist his wrist with both hands (Figure 3-92). Finally, lock his arm upward until his heels are off the ground (Figure 3-93).

Theory:

Dividing the Muscle/Tendon (wrist). Your left hand grabbing is a **Pluck (*Cai*)**, and the final twisting on his wrist is a **Turning (Zhuan)**. To make this technique most effective, you should use your left hand to twist his wrist while using your right hand to grab his fingers and bend them downward.

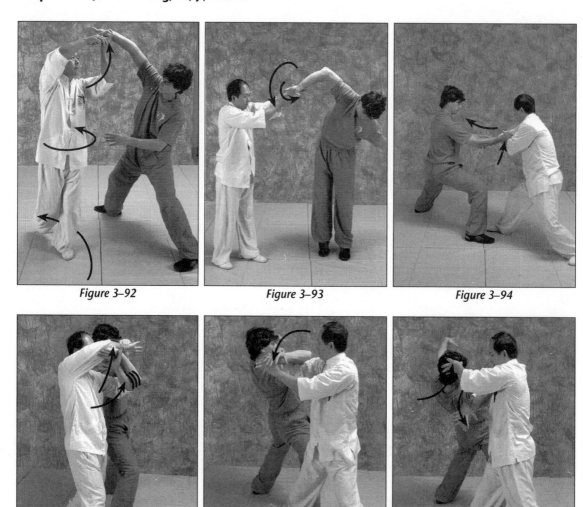

Figure 3–92   Figure 3–93   Figure 3–94

Figure 3–95   Figure 3–96   Figure 3–97

Technique #2: Forward Upward Turning

(Qian Shang Fan) 前上翻

When your opponent is leading your right arm to your right with a Small Rollback (Figure 3-94), immediately use your left hand to grab his right wrist and circle it up while stepping your left leg behind him (Figure 3-95). When you do this, you should use your left elbow to push his elbow to keep his arm bent. Next, reposition yourself and use both hands to bend his right arm backward (Figure 3-96). Finally, let your right hand take over the control and use your left hand to push the upper back of his head to lock him in place (Figure 3-97). If you wish, you may sweep your right leg backward while pulling his right arm backward to take him down (Figure 3-98).

Theory:

Misplacing the Bone (shoulder and elbow). At the beginning, your left hand grabbing is a **Pluck (Cai)**, when you step your left leg behind him and use your elbow to push his elbow to keep it bent, it is an **Elbow Leaning Against Push (Kao)**,

Figure 3–98

Figure 3–99

Figure 3–100

Figure 3–101

when you push both of your hands down against his forearm to keep it bent, it is a **Press Down (An)**, and the final position of control is a **Rend (Lie)**. You should remember that the stepping of your legs is coordinated with the technique, instead of the technique coordinating with the steppings. Therefore, you should always look for better stepping which offers you a better position for controlling.

Technique #3: The Old Man Carries the Fish on His Back

(Lao Han Bei Yu) 老漢背魚

This technique is again used against a Small Rollback. Though it is similar, the theory of locking is different.

When your opponent is leading your right arm to his left with both hands (Figure 3-99), again step your left leg behind his right leg, use your left hand to grab his right wrist and use your left elbow to push against his elbow to keep it bent (Figure 3-100). Finally, step your right leg again and pull his arm backward, while bowing forward and using your upper back to push against his upper back (Figure 3-101).

Theory:
Misplacing the Bone (shoulder and elbow). At the beginning, your left hand grabbing is a **Pluck (Cai)**, when you step your left leg behind him and use your elbow to push his elbow to keep it bent, it is an **Elbow Leaning Against Push (Kao)**. Finally, when using your upper back to push his upper back, it is a **Lean Against (Kao)**. When you control your opponent in the final position, his arm should not be too bent or too straight. A 90 degree angle in the elbow is the most effective setup.

Figure 3–102

Figure 3–103

Figure 3–104

Technique #4: Feudal Lord Lifts the Tripod

(Ba Wang Tai Ding) 霸王抬鼎

This is a technique against a Small Rollback in which your opponent is trying to lock your elbow.

When your opponent tries to lock your left arm with both of his hands (Figure 3-102). immediately scoop up your left elbow to prevent him from locking you, while using your right hand to grab his right wrist (Figure 3-103). Next, reposition yourself, free your left hand and then push his elbow to your right while twisting his right wrist to keep his arm bent (Figure 3-104). Finally, continue your right hand twisting on his wrist while lifting and squeezing his elbow toward your right hand with your left hand to lock him there (Figure 3-105).

Theory:

Dividing the Muscle/Tendon (wrist) and Misplacing the Bone (elbow). Your right hand's grabbing is a **Pluck (*Cai*)** and when you raise your left arm up to neutralize his grabbing, it is a **Wardoff (*Peng*)**. In the final lock, it is a **Squeeze (*Ji*)**. Remember, where you stand is very important. Your final position should be far beyond his left hand's reach.

Technique #5: The Crane Spreads Its Wings and Arm Wraps Around the Dragon's Neck

(Bai He Liang Chi and Bi Chan Long Jing) 白鶴亮翅，臂纏龍頸

This is again used against Small Rollback on you arm. When your opponent's two hands are leading your left arm to his left (Figure 3-106), again, you scoop your left arm upward to prevent your opponent from locking you, while also using your right hand to grab his right wrist (Figure 3-107). Next, reposition yourself, twist his left wrist with your right hand and lock his arm on your stomach, while placing your left elbow on his throat

Figure 3–105   Figure 3–106   Figure 3–107

Figure 3–108   Figure 3–109   Figure 3–110

(Figure 3-108). Finally, increase your right hand's twisting and pulling backward to generate pain in his left arm while expanding your left arm against his throat to lock him (Figure 3-109).

Alternatively, you may continue extending your left arm around his neck and lock his neck in place (Figure 3-110).

Theory:

Dividing the Muscle/Tendon (wrist), Misplacing the Bone (elbow), and Sealing the Breath (neck in alternative technique). Your left arm's upward scooping is an **Upward Wardoff (*Peng*)**, and your right hand's grabbing is a **Pluck (*Cai*)**. When you expand your left arm to lock his neck, it is also a **Wardoff (*Peng*)** while your locking of his arm with your stomach is a **Lean Against (*Kao*)** with the stomach area. When you circle your left arm around his neck, it is a **Coil (*Chan*)**.

| *Figure 3-111* | *Figure 3-112* | *Figure 3-113* |

Technique #6: White Crane Twists Its Neck

(Bai He Niu Jing) 白鶴扭頸

This technique is used against a Large Rollback. When your opponent's right hand is grabbing your right wrist while his left forearm is on your right post-arm getting ready to lead you down (Figure 3-111), immediately use your left hand to grab his left fingers (Figure 3-112). Next, twist his fingers toward him to generate pain in the base of his pinkie tendons (Figure 3-113). Finally, free your right hand and press his elbow upward while continuing the twisting of his fingers to lock his left arm (Figure 3-114). You should lead him down to the ground.

Theory:

Dividing the Muscle/Tendon (base of pinkie). Your left hand grabbing is a **Pluck (Cai)**, and the final twisting of his fingers is a **Turning (Zhuan)**. The force of squeezing from both hands is a **Squeeze (Ji)**. To make this technique most effective, you should place your mind and attention on the base of his pinkie. When your mind is there, you will be able to feel the locking easily.

Technique #7: Play the Guitar

(Shou Hui Pi Pa) 手揮琵琶

Again, this technique is used against the Large Rollback. When your opponent's right hand is grabbing your right wrist while his left forearm is on your post-arm (Figure 3-115), use your left hand to grab his left fingers (Figure 3-116). Next, twist his fingers toward him and then downward while using your right hand to push his elbow upward (Figure 3-117). Finally, raise your body up and use the leverage of both of your hands to lock him in place (Figure 3-118). It is very important you twist his fingers in the right angle which allows you to lock his pinkie's tendon on the base of finger (Figure 3-119).

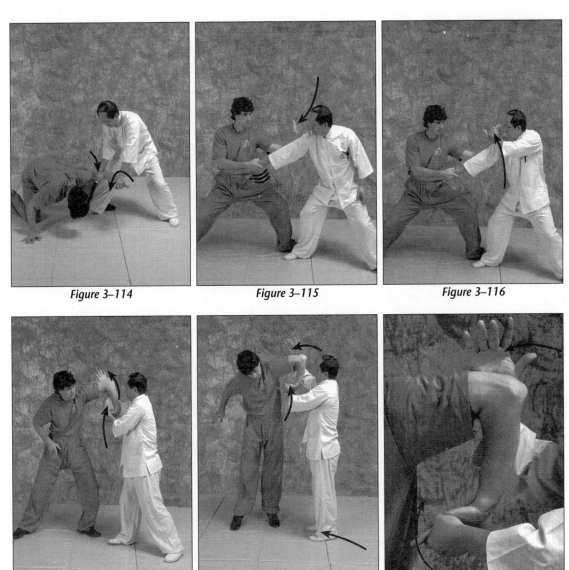

Figure 3–114

Figure 3–115

Figure 3–116

Figure 3–117

Figure 3–118

Figure 3–119

Theory:

Dividing the Muscle/Tendon (base of pinkie). Your left hand grabbing is a **Pluck (Cai)**, and the final twisting on his fingers is a **Turning (Zhuan)** and the force of squeezing from both hands is a **Squeeze (Ji)**. To make this technique most effective, you should place your mind and attention on the base of his pinkie. When your mind is there, you will be able to feel the locking easily.

Figure 3–120

Figure 3–121

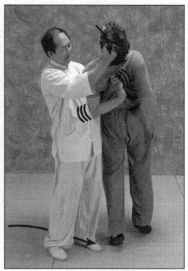
Figure 3–122

Technique #8: White Crane Bores the Bush

(Bai He Chuan Cong) 白鶴穿叢

This technique can be considered as an option to the last technique. However, the locking theory is different. Again, when your opponent uses his right hand to grab your right wrist while using his left forearm to press your post-arm, use your left hand to grab his left fingers (Finger 3-120), immediately twist his fingers to lock the tendons on the base of his pinkie while freeing your right hand, and push his left elbow upward (Figure 3-121). Finally, circle his arm to his back and sandwich his arm between your left hand and chest, while using your right hand to pull his hair backward (Figure 3-122).

Theory:

Dividing the Muscle/Tendon (base of pinkie). Your left hand grabbing is a **Pluck (Cai)**, and the final locking of his arm with your left hand and chest is a **Squeeze (Ji)**. To make this technique most effective, after you have locked his hand behind him, you should put more pressure toward his pinkie to generate pain in the pinkie's tendons. To prevent him from struggling, your right hand pulling of his hair is important. This action can destroy his balance and stability, which is necessary to prevent strong struggling.

Technique #9: Left Right Cross Elbow

(Zuo You Jiao Zhou) 左右交肘

When your opponent's right hand is grabbing your right wrist while his left forearm is on your post-arm, first use your left hand to grab his left wrist (Figure 3-123). Next bend your right elbow and grab his right wrist with your right hand while pulling his left hand toward his right (Figure 3-124). Finally, twist both of his arms and lock them in place (Figure 3-125). His left arm should be straight.

Theory:

Misplacing the Bone (elbow). Your left hand grabbing is a **Pluck (Cai)**, and the final twisting of his arms is a **Turning (Zhuan)**. To make this technique most effective, you should use his right arm to push against his left elbow and keep it straight.

Figure 3–123

Figure 3–124

Figure 3–125

Figure 3–126

Figure 3–127

3-4. Qin Na in Ji

As mentioned in Chapter 2, *Ji* means to "squeeze" or to "press," which can be done by two hands or the arms squeezing against each other. It can also be executed by pressing forward with two hands, one hand and one forearm, or even two forearms.

I. QIN NA FOR JI

Ji is normally used for offense. However, it can be used for defense when the situation is right. For example, when your opponent uses his two hands to "stamp" or "press" (*An*) your chest (Figure 3-126), you may use both of your hands to squeeze his elbows to the center and downward to neutralize his *An* (Figure 3-127). Honestly speaking, there are not too many *Qin Na* techniques which use forward *Ji*. However, there are many techniques where the *Ji* is done by pressing both hands against each other. In this section, we will introduce some of the possible *Ji Qin Na* in *Taijiquan*.

Figure 3–128

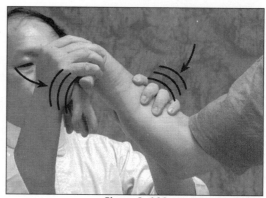

Figure 3–129

Figure 3–130

Technique #1: Two Hands Squeeze the Wrist

(Shuang Shou Ji Wan) 雙手擠腕

When both of your hands are on your opponent's wrist and elbow joints (Figure 3-128), immediately use your right hand to grab his right wrist and bend it downward while using your left hand to grab his right arm and squeeze it in to generate good leverage for your right hand's wrist locking (Figure 3-129). You should position yourself on his right hand side to avoid his left hand attack (Figure 3-130).

Theory:

Dividing the Muscle/Tendon (wrist). Your right hand grabbing is a **Pluck (Cai)**, and the final squeezing action is a **Squeeze (Ji)**. Occasionally, you will encounter an opponent who is double jointed. In this case, this technique will not be effective. If you realize this, immediately use your right leg or knee to kick his groin.

Technique #2: Upward, Horizontal, and Downward Wrist Press

(Shang, Zhong, Xia Ya Wan) 上，中，下壓腕

From the same situation, when both of your hands are on your opponent's wrist and elbow joints (Figure 3-131), immediately bend his wrist inward and then upward, while using your left hand to squeeze his elbow downward to generate good leverage for your right hand's wrist locking (Figure 3-132).

Alternatively, you may lock his arm in front of your chest (Figure 3-133) or even squeeze his arm in front of your abdominal area (Figure 3-134).

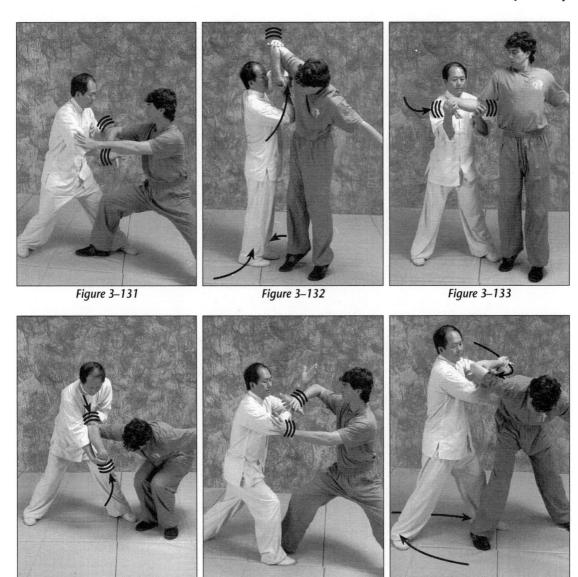

Figure 3–131 Figure 3–132 Figure 3–133

Figure 3–134 Figure 3–135 Figure 3–136

Theory:

Dividing the Muscle/Tendon (wrist). Your right hand grabbing is a **Pluck (Cai)**, and the final squeezing action is a **Squeeze (Ji)**. Occasionally, you will encounter an opponent who is double jointed. In this case, this technique will not be effective. If you realize this, immediately use your right leg or knee to kick his groin.

Technique #3: Both Hands Seize the Murderer

(Shuang Shou Qin Xiong) 雙手擒凶

When both of your opponent's hands are on your right forearm, first turn to your right to neutralize his pressing or pushing (Figure 3-135). Next, immediately reposition yourself and use your right hand to grab his right wrist while coiling your left hand around his right arm until it reaches his post-arm near the elbow and lock his arm behind him (Figure 3-136). Finally, use your right hand to push his shoulder upward while squeezing your left hand downward and lifting your left elbow upward to lock him there (Figure 3-137).

| *Figure 3–137* | *Figure 3–138* | *Figure 3–139* |

Theory:

Misplacing the Bone (shoulder). Your right hand grabbing is a **Pluck (*Cai*)**, your left hand's circling around his right arm up to his post-arm is a **Coil (*Chan*)**, finally the both hands' squeezing is a **Squeeze (*Ji*)**. In this technique, to prevent his right arm from straightening out, you must use your left elbow to lock his right forearm. In order to make the pain significant, you must raise his right arm up with your left arm.

Technique #4: Squeeze to Seal the Breath

(Ji Xiong Bi Qi) 擠胸閉氣

Again, in the same position, when both of your opponent's hands are on your right forearm (Figure 3-138), step your right leg back and your left leg behind him to neutralize his pressing or pushing, while covering your left forearm on his elbow (Figure 3-139). Next, continue to coil your left hand around his right arm. Finally, reach the back of his upper chest to squeeze foreword and at the same time squeeze your right hand toward his solar plexus to seal his breath (Figure 3-140).

Theory:

Sealing the Breath (solar plexus). Your left hand's circling around his right arm is a **Coil (*Chan*)** and the final both hand's pressing action is a **Squeeze (*Ji*)**.

Technique #5: Upward Elbow Wrap

(Shang Chan Zhou) 上纏肘

When both of your opponent's hands are on your right forearm (Figure 3-141), immediately step your right leg behind his right leg while using your left hand to grab his right wrist (Figure 3-142). Next, coil your right hand around his right arm until it reaches his elbow and finally use the leverage generated from both hands to lock him upward (Figure 3-143). In order to make this technique effective, you should strongly twist his right wrist with your left hand, while squeezing his post-arm toward you to generate good leverage for the locking (Figure 3-144).

Figure 3–140   Figure 3–141   Figure 3–142

   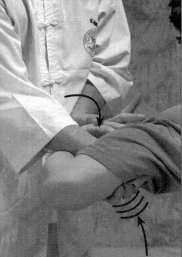

Figure 3–143   Figure 3–144

Theory:

Dividing the Muscle/Tendon (wrist). Your left hand grabbing is a **Pluck (*Cai*)**, the final twisting of his wrist is a **Turning (*Zhuan*)** and the locking generated from both hands' pressing is **Squeeze (*Ji*)**. To make this technique most effective, you should use your left hand to twist his wrist strongly while squeezing your right hand inward to generate good leverage.

II. QIN NA AGAINST JI

Other than *Qin Na*, in actual *Taijiquan* applications, there are not too many occasions in which *Ji* is executed by squeezing both hands against each other. *Ji* is done more often by pressing forward. In this section, we will focus on *Qin Na* which can be applied to this forward pressing.

| Figure 3–145 | Figure 3–146 | Figure 3–147 |

As mentioned earlier, when *Ji* is executed by pressing forward, normally your opponent uses both of his hands, one hand and one forearm, or both forearms to press forward. Generally speaking, the best option against these kinds of *Ji* is to lock his elbow or shoulder.

Technique #1: The Old Man Carries the Fish on His Back

(Lao Han Bei Yu) 老漢背魚

When your opponent uses both of his hands to press your chest (Figure 3-145), immediately use your right hand to raise his right forearm up while using your left forearm to press his right elbow downward (Figure 3-146). Next, use both of your hands to lock his right forearm while stepping your left leg behind his right leg (Figure 3-147). Finally, bow forward and pull his arm down to lock him behind your back (Figure 3-148).

Theory:

Misplacing the Bone (shoulder and elbow). Your both forearms' intercepting to his right arm is an action of **Squeeze (Ji)** and in the final position of locking, it is the **Back Lean Against (Kao)**. In order to make this technique effective, you must keep his arm bent. The best locking angle for his forearm and post-arm is at 90 degrees.

Technique #2: Press Shoulder with Single Finger and Extending the Neck for Water

(Yi Zhi Ding Jian or Yin Jing Qiu Shui) 一指頂肩，引頸求水

When your opponent presses your chest with both of his hands (Figure 3-149), immediately use your right hand to grab his right wrist, while pushing his right elbow upward with your left hand (Figure 3-150). Next, reposition yourself while coiling your left hand around his right arm until it reaches his post-arm near the elbow area to lock his arm behind him (Figure 3-151). Under these conditions, the tendon in his shoulder should be

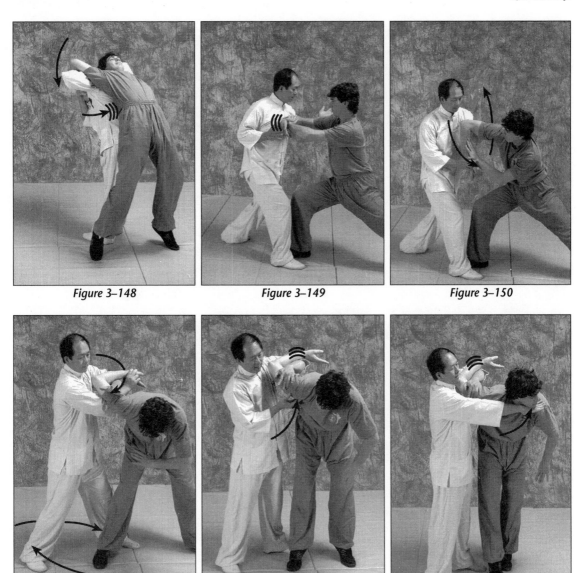

Figure 3–148   Figure 3–149   Figure 3–150

Figure 3–151   Figure 3–152   Figure 3–153

very tensed. If you press your index or middle finger upward into his *Jianneiling* cavity (M-UE-48), a significant pain can be generated (Figure 3-152). Alternatively, you may use your right hand to raise his chin up to generate good leverage for his arm's locking (Figure 3-153).

Theory:

Misplacing the Bone (shoulder) and Cavity Press (*Jianneiling* cavity). At the beginning, your right hand's grabbing is a **Pluck (*Cai*)**, your left hand's circling around his arm is a **Coil (*Chan*)**, and the final Cavity Press is a **Point (*Dian*)**. His arm locked behind him should be kept bent. The trick of doing this is to use your left elbow to prevent him from straightening his arm.

| Figure 3–154 | Figure 3–155 | Figure 3–156 |

Technique #3: Large Wrap Hand

(Da Chan Shou) 大纏手

When your opponent presses your chest with both of his hands (Figure 3-154), immediately scoop your right arm upward to neutralize his pressing while grabbing his right wrist with your left hand (Figure 3-155). Next, reposition yourself, coil your right hand around his right arm until it reaches his post-arm near the elbow and use the leverage generated from both hands to press him down (Figure 3-156). You may circle to your right to force him down (Figure 3-157).

Theory:

Misplacing the Bone (shoulder and elbow). Your right forearm's upward scooping is a **Wardoff (Peng)**, your left hand's grabbing is a **Pluck (Cai)**, your right hand's coiling is a **Coil (Chan)**, and your right hand's downward pressing is a **Press (An)**.

Technique #4: Feudal Lord Lifts the Tripod

(Ba Wang Tai Ding) 霸王抬鼎

When your opponent presses your chest with both of his hands (Figure 3-158), immediately turn your body to your right to neutralize the press, and grab his right wrist with your right hand while pushing his elbow to his left with your left hand (Figure 3-159). Finally, reposition yourself and use the leverage generated from both of your hands to lock his right arm (Figure 3-160).

Theory:

Misplacing the Bone (elbow). Your right hand's grabbing is a **Pluck (Cai)**. To prevent him from turning his body, you should push the left side of your body against his right shoulder area.

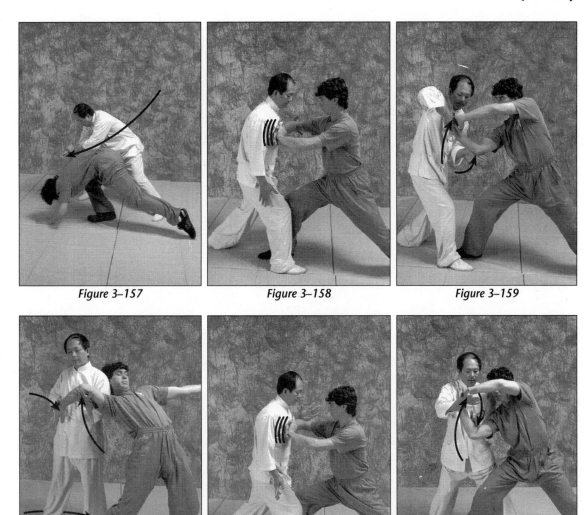

Figure 3–157   Figure 3–158   Figure 3–159

Figure 3–160   Figure 3–161   Figure 3–162

Technique #5: Arm Wraps Around the Dragon's Neck

(Bi Chan Long Jing) 臂纏龍頸

In the same situation, when your opponent presses your chest with both of his hands (Figure 3-161), immediately reposition yourself to his right hand side, and raise your right forearm up to lock his right forearm while pushing his elbow to his left with your left forearm (Figure 3-162). Next, lock his right arm in front of your chest while placing your left arm on his throat (Figure 3-163). Finally, circle your left arm around his neck to lock him up (Figure 3-164).

Theory:

Misplacing the Bone (elbow) and Sealing the Breath (neck). Your right hand's grabbing or locking is a **Pluck (*Cai*)**, your left arm's opening on this throat is a **Rend (*Lie*)**, and finally the arm wrapping around his neck is a **Coil (*Chan*)**. To make this technique effective, you should keep his right arm bent and lock it in front of your chest.

Figure 3–163   Figure 3–164   Figure 3–165

Figure 3–166

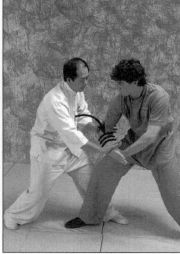

Figure 3–167

3-5. Qin Na in An

An means to "stamp" or to "press down, forward, or upward" by the hand or hands. Offensively, *An* is normally used to strike a cavity in the chest area (Figure 3-165) or to push the opponent off balance (Figure 3-166). Defensively, *An* is used to seal your opponent's wrists, arms, elbows, or even shoulder to immobilize the free movement of his upper limbs (Figure 3-167).

I. QIN NA FOR AN

Strictly speaking, the purpose of *An* is to strike or to seal. Therefore, there are not too many *Qin Na* techniques which can be used for *An*. Here, we can introduce only a few possible *Qin Na* for *An*.

Figure 3–168

Figure 3–169

Figure 3–170

Figure 3–171

Technique #1: Feudal Lord Pushes the Caldron

(Ba Wang Tui Ding) 霸王推鼎

When your opponent presses your right forearm with both of his hands (Figure 3-168), immediately step your left leg behind his right leg and turn your body to your right to neutralize the press, coil your left hand around his right arm until it reaches his sacrum while placing your right hand on his chin (Figure 3-169). Next, use the leverage of your right hand and left hand to push his upper body backward to lock his spine (Figure 1-170). If necessary, you may continue your pushing until he falls (Figure 3-171).

Theory:

Misplacing the Bone (spine). When you circle your left hand around his right arm and reach his sacrum, it is a **Coil (*Chan*)**, the final push from your right hand to his chin or upper body is a **Press Down (*An*)**. Your positioning is very important. A proper position offers you good leverage for pushing and safe distance from his left hand.

| Figure 3–172 | Figure 3–173 | Figure 3–174 |

Technique #2: Force the Bow

(Qiang Po Jiu Gong) 強迫鞠躬

When both of your opponent's hands are pressing your right forearm (Figure 3-172), immediately turn your body to your right, and step your left leg behind his right leg while grabbing his right wrist with your right hand (Figure 3-173). Next, insert your left hand under his left armpit and reach the upper back of his head (Figure 3-174). Finally, release your right hand and move it under his right armpit to reach the upper back of his head and press his head down with both hands to lock his neck (Figure 3-175). To avoid his kicking you, you should stand with one leg forward against his tailbone.

Theory:

Misplacing the Bone (neck) and Sealing the Breath (windpipe). Your right hand's grabbing is a **Pluck (*Cai*)** and both of your hands' pressing against the rear of his head is a **Press Down (*An*)**. To prevent him from straightening his arm and slipping down, you must press both of your hands on his upper head instead of his neck.

Technique #3: Repulse the Monkey

(Dao Nian Hou) 倒攆猴

When both of your opponent's hands are pressing on your right forearm, immediately turn your body to your right to neutralize his pushing or pressing, while using your left hand to grab his right wrist (Figure 3-176). Next, twist his left wrist counterclockwise while placing your right hand on his chin (Figure 3-177). Then, use the leverage generated from both of your hands to lock his left arm and head (Figure 3-178). To take him down, you may simply increase your twisting and pushing pressure while circling him to your left (Figure 3-179).

Alternatively, once you have locked his wrist and head, you may move your right leg behind his right leg (Figure 3-180), then sweep your right leg backward to take him down (Figure 3-181).

Figure 3–175

Figure 3–176

Figure 3–177

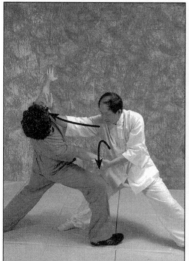

Figure 3–178

Figure 3–179

Figure 3–180

Figure 3–181

Theory:

Dividing the Muscle/Tendon (wrist) and Misplacing the Bone (neck). Your left hand's grabbing is a **Pluck (*Cai*)**, and your right hand's forward pushing is a **Forward Press (*An*)**. This technique is not too effective if you wish to lock him in place. The locking is only to put him into an awkward position for your taking down.

Figure 3–182

Figure 3–183

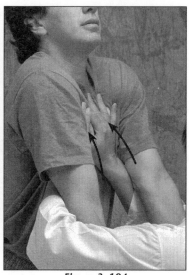

Figure 3–184

Figure 3–185

Technique #4: Double Hands Push the Mountain

(Shuang Shou Tui Shan) 雙手推山

When both of your opponent's hands are on your shoulders, immediately raise both of your arms up from the center (Figure 3-182). Next, coil both of your hands around both his arms until they reach his upper chest (Figure 3-183). Finally, push both of your hands forward and upward to his upper chest (Figure 3-184). This will allow you to lock both his arms in front of your chest (Figure 3-185). You should beware of his knee kicking. If you lock him properly, he will not be able to kick you.

Theory:

Pressing the Tendon (post-arm) and Misplacing the Bone (shoulder). When you raise both of your arms upward, it is an **Upward Wardoff (*Peng*)** and when you circle your hands around his arms until they reach the upper chest, it is a **Coil (*Chan*)**. Finally, the forward and upward pushing by both of your hands to his upper chest is a **Upward Pushing (*An*)**. This technique is useful only if both of your opponent's hands are grabbing you tightly. If he releases his grabbing while you are coiling your hands, you will not be able to lock his arm.

Figure 3–186

Figure 3–187

Figure 3–188

Figure 3–189

II. QIN NA AGAINST AN

Because the hand is opened when *An* is applied, almost all of the *Qin Na* techniques against open hands can be used against *An*. Truly speaking, there are more than twenty *Qin Na* techniques which can be used against the open hand. Here, we will introduce only some of them for your reference. If you are interested in learning more *Qin Na* against open hands, you should refer to ***Comprehensive Applications of Shaolin Chin Na***, by YMAA.

Technique #1: White Crane Twists Its Neck

(Bai He Niu Jing) 白鶴扭頸

This technique is used against your opponent when he is pressing or pushing your chest. When you discover your opponent's hand or hands are pressing or pushing toward your chest (Figure 3-186), immediately reposition yourself to his right hand side to avoid his pressing, while using your right hand to grab his right fingers and placing your left hand on his elbow (Figure 3-187). Next, twist his fingers clockwise while pressing your left hand on his elbow to generate good leverage for locking the base of his pinkie's tendons (Figure 3-188). Under this lock, your opponent will have to follow your will. Therefore, you may circle him down to the ground for better control (Figure 3-189).

Theory:

Dividing the Muscle/Tendon (base of pinkie's tendon). Your right hand's grabbing is a **Pluck (*Cai*)** and the final position of locking from both of your hands is a **Squeeze (*Ji*)**. When you control your opponent, you should pay more attention to the base of his pinkie. Only when your mind is there are you able to lock his tendons effectively. Your left hand is only to offer you good leverage for your control.

| Figure 3–190 | Figure 3–191 | Figure 3–192 |

Technique #2: White Crane Covers Its Wings

(Bai He Yan Chi) 白鶴掩翅

This technique is very similar to the last technique. Again, when your opponent uses his hand to push or press you, immediately reposition yourself to his right, while using your right hand to grab his right fingers and placing your left hand on his right elbow (Figure 3-190). Next, twist his fingers to generate pain in the base of his pinkie, and move your left hand under his right arm and reach his pinkie (Figure 3-191). Finally, use your left elbow to stop his right elbow from going down, while using your left middle finger to push the top of your right thumb to increase the twisting pressure on his pinkie's base tendons (Figure 3-192). This will allow you to lock his pinkie effectively.

Theory:

Dividing the Muscle/Tendon (base of pinkie's tendon). Your right hand's grabbing is a **Pluck (Cai)**, the final position of your right hand's twisting is a **Turning (Zhuan)** and your left middle finger's downward pressing is a **Downward Press (An)**. Again, when you control your opponent, you should pay more attention to the base of his pinkie. Only when your mind is there are you able to lock his tendons effectively. Your left hand is only to offer you good leverage for your control.

Technique #3: White Crane Bores the Bush

(Bai He Chuan Cong) 白鶴穿叢

In the same situation, when your opponent uses his right hand to press or push your chest, again use your right hand to grab his right fingers while placing your left hand on his right elbow (Figure 3-193). Naturally, you should again reposition yourself to his right hand side. Next, step your right leg behind his right leg, while twisting his pinkie's tendons with your right hand and rotating his arm downward with the help of your left hand (Figure 3-194). Finally, lock his right arm behind him, while pushing your left hand to his head to his left (Figure 3-195) or simply pulling his hair backward (Figure 3-196).

Figure 3–193

Figure 3–194

Figure 3–195

Figure 3–196

Figure 3–197

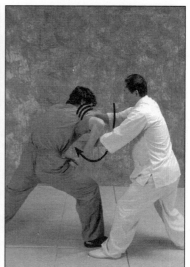

Figure 3–198

Theory:

Dividing the Muscle/Tendon (tendon on the base of the pinkie) and Misplacing the Bone (neck). Your right hand's grabbing is a **Pluck (Cai)**, the final locking position of your right hand and chest is a **Squeeze (Ji)** and your left hand's pushing against his head is a **Rend (Lie)**. Once you have locked your opponent's arm behind him, in order to increase the pain for your control, you should increase the pressure in twisting his pinkie's tendons.

Technique #4: Butterfly Bores Through the Flowers

(Hu Die Chuan Hua) 蝴蝶穿花

This technique is used against your opponent when his hand is approaching you. When your opponent uses his right hand to press or push your chest, again reposition yourself to his right, while also using your left hand to grab his right fingers from the rear side of his palm (Figure 3-197). Next, circle his hand downward while using your right hand to lock his post-arm in to prevent him from stepping and freeing himself (Figure 3-198). Then, step your

| Figure 3–199 | Figure 3–200 | Figure 3–201 |

right leg behind your left leg while circling his right arm behind him (Figure 3-199). Finally, step your left leg behind him, twist his wrist counterclockwise and push his chin to his left with your left hand (Figure 3-200).

Theory:

Dividing the Muscle/Tendon (wrist) and Misplacing the Bone (wrist and shoulder). Your left hand's grabbing is a **Pluck (Cai)**, and the final twisting of his wrist is a **Turning (Zhuan)**. To make this technique most effective, you should twist his wrist strongly toward the rear side of his palm. This can generate great pain.

Technique #5: The Child Worships the Buddha

(Tong Zhi Bai Fo) 童子拜佛

This technique is used against the *An* which has already reached your chest. When your opponent has placed his hand on your upper chest and gets ready to emit his pressing or pushing power, immediately reposition yourself to yield to his pushing while grabbing his right fingers (Figure 3-201). When you do this, you should also place your left hand on his right elbow to immobilize his elbow's movement. Next, turn his wrist 90 degrees clockwise with your right hand and lock it there (Figure 3-202). Finally, bow your body toward him while using your left hand to keep his arm bent, and keep it lower than his wrist (Figure 3-203). This will offer you a great angle for locking.

Theory:

Dividing the Muscle/Tendon (wrist). Your right hand's grabbing is a **Pluck (Cai)**, the twisting of his wrist is a **Turning (Zhuan)**, and the left hand's pushing downward against his elbow is a **Downward Press (An)**. To make this technique most effective, you should keep his elbow lower than his wrist. Naturally, the locking of his wrist from your right hand must be strong.

Figure 3–202

Figure 3–203

Figure 3–204

Figure 3–205

Figure 3–206

Technique #6: Small Wrap Hand

(Xiao Chan Shou) 小纏手

This technique is used against the situation in which your opponent's hands are already on your forearm to seal it downward (Figure 3-204). In this situation, immediately reposition yourself to his right, while at the same time locking his fingers with your left hand and coiling your right hand on the wrist (Figure 3-205). Finally, circle your wrist down to lock his until his body reaches the ground (Figure 3-206).

Theory:

Dividing the Muscle/Tendon (wrist). When you move your right hand to the top of his wrist, it is a **Coil (*Chan*)** and the final downward pressing is a **Downward Press (*An*)**. In order to prevent him from escaping right from the beginning, you should use your fingers to push his index finger toward his wrist and cover all his other fingers tightly onto your forearm. When you press him down, a circular motion can generate a great locking pressure in his wrist.

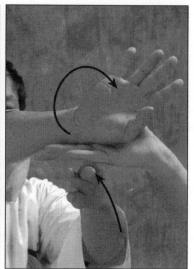

| *Figure 3–207* | *Figure 3–208* | *Figure 3–209* |

Technique #7: Upward Finger Turn

(Shang Fen Zhi) 上分指

When both of your opponent's hands are on your right arm and are pressing it, immediately place your left hand on his right hand (Figure 3-207). Next, reposition yourself to his right to neutralize his pressing or pushing while turning your right arm (Figures 3-208 and 3-209). Finally, use your thumb and index finger to lock his index finger upward (Figure 3-210).

Theory:

Misplacing the Bone (base of index finger). Your left hand's finger locking is a **Pluck (Cai)**. When you control him to the final position, your index finger should be on the base of his index finger with the support of the other three fingers, while the thumb is on the last joint of his index finger. If you can, you should keep his arm straight to have better control (Figure 3-211).

Technique #8: Large Rollback

(Da Lu) 大攦

Again, when both of your opponent's hands are on your right forearm (Figure 3-212), immediately reposition yourself to his right, while using your right hand to hook down and grab his right wrist and using your left forearm to press his elbow upward (Figure 3-213). Then, step your right leg backward. The leverage is generated from both of your hands to lead him down to the ground (Figure 3-214). Your left forearm should press on the rear post-arm tendon located about three inches above his elbow.

Theory:

Pressing the Tendon (post-arm) and Misplacing the Bone (elbow). Your right hand's hooking and grabbing is a **Pluck (Cai)**. In fact, this entire action is **Large Rollback (Da Lu)**.

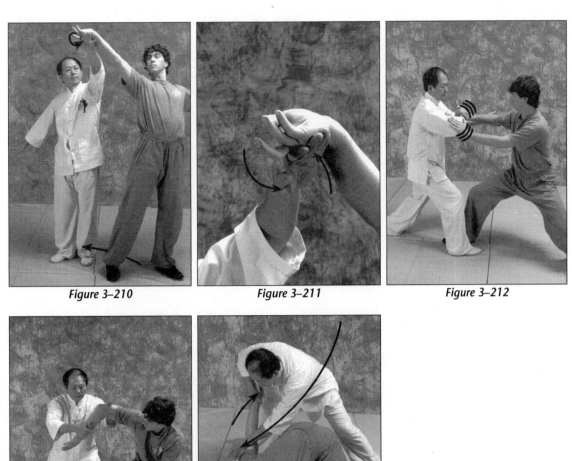

Figure 3–210

Figure 3–211

Figure 3–212

Figure 3–213

Figure 3–214

Press Forward or Press Downward (*An*) is the most common technique in *Taiji* Pushing Hands. Therefore, in order to become a proficient *Taiji* martial artist, you should master those *Qin Na* techniques which can be used against *An* as much as possible. As mentioned earlier, there are many techniques which can be used against open hands, such as *An* in *Taijiquan*. We have only introduced some of the techniques. If you wish to know more about this, you should refer to ***Comprehensive Applications of Shaolin Chin Na***, by YMAA.

▪ Chapter 4 ▪

Qin Na in Cai, Lie, Zhou, and Kao

4-1. Introduction

As mentioned in the second chapter, *Cai*, *Lie*, *Zhou* and *Kao* occupy the four corners in the *Taiji* Eight Trigrams. This implies that, theoretically speaking, these four *Jin* patterns are applied to the corners. However, you should not be strictly limited by these rules. When you apply the techniques, they are all alive and vary according to actual situations. In this chapter, we will introduce those *Qin Na* techniques which can be used from these four *Jin* patterns, and also those which can be used against them.

4-2. Qin Na in Cai

Generally, **Cai** (**pluck**) is done by grabbing or locking part of your opponent's body and then either controlling it immediately, or leading the plucking downward or to the corners for some specific purposes, for example to make him lose balance or to put him into an awkward situation. The part of the body plucked can be the finger, wrist, forearm, elbow, sleeves, clothes, or even the hair. The corners that the *Cai* leads can be to the backward right (Figure 4-1), to the forward right (Figure 4-2), to the backward left (Figure 4-3), or to the forward left (Figure 4-4).

I. QIN NA FOR CAI

You should remember that in *Taijiquan*, *Cai*, like the other seven *Jin* patterns, is only an action which can be used to lock the opponent directly or is followed by pulling the

Figure 4–1

Figure 4–2

Figure 4–3

Figure 4–4

Figure 4–5

Figure 4–6

opponent at an angle which can expose his cavities or vital areas for striking, or make him lose stability. Here, we will introduce some the *Qin Na* techniques which are related to the *Cai* action.

Technique #1: Left Right Cross Elbow

(Zuo You Jiao Zhou) 左右交肘

When both of your opponent's hands are pressing your right forearm (Figure 4-5), immediately turn your body to your right to neutralize his pressing, while at the same time hooking down and grabbing his right wrist and placing your left hand on his right elbow to control his arm (Figure 4-6). From this situation, it is common that your opponent will charge his punch to your face with his left fist. If this happens, immediately raise your left forearm up to intercept his left hand punch (Figure 4-7). Finally, twist both of his arms and use his right arm to lock his left arm (Figure 4-8). If you wish, you may continue your turning until he falls (Figure 4-9).

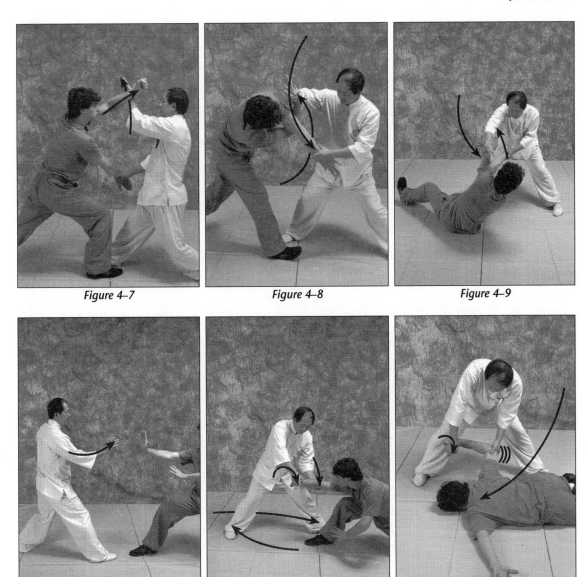

Figure 4–7 | Figure 4–8 | Figure 4–9

Figure 4–10 | Figure 4–11 | Figure 4–12

Theory:

Misplacing the Bone (elbow) or Pressing the Tendon (post-arm). Your two handed grabbing is a **Pluck (*Cai*)**, and the rotation of both arms is **Turning (*Zhuan*)**. In order to make the technique effective, your opponent's left arm must be straight. The pressure generated from his right arm to his left arm should be either directly on the rear side of his elbow or on the tendons located about three inches above his elbow.

Technique #2: White Crane Twists Its Neck

(Bai He Niu Jing) 白鶴扭頸

If your opponent is in front of you with his right hand opened (Figure 4-10), immediately reposition yourself to his right while grabbing his fingers with your right hand, and twist it toward his pinkie to lock his pinkie's base tendons (Figure 4-11). When you do this, you should also place your left hand on his right elbow and press it toward his right pinkie. This will offer you good leverage for locking. Finally, lead him down to the ground (Figure 4-12).

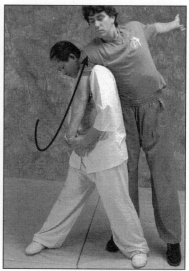

| *Figure 4–13* | *Figure 4–14* | *Figure 4–15* |

Theory:

Dividing the Muscle/Tendon (base of pinkie). Your right hand's grabbing is a **Pluck (Cai)** and your left hand's pressing on his elbow is a **Squeeze (Ji)**. The angle of locking his pinkie's tendon is very important. You should place your mind on this area while you are locking him.

Technique #3: One Post to Support the Heavens

(Yi Zhu Ding Tian) 一柱頂天

When your opponent's right hand is on your right forearm (Figure 4-13), immediately step your left leg to the front of his right leg while leading his arm to your right with your right hand and left elbow (Figure 4-14). Finally, grab his hand with both of your hands, place your left shoulder under his right armpit, straighten out his entire arm, and then lift it upward to lock him (Figure 4-15). Your positioning is very important. The range should be beyond your opponent's left hand strike.

Theory:

Misplacing the Bone (shoulder and elbow). Your two handed grabbing is a **Pluck (Cai)** and your left shoulder's upward supporting is an **Upward Pressing (Kao)**. The trick to using this technique correctly is to keep his entire arm straight and then lift it upward against his shoulder.

Technique #4: Lead the Snake to Enter the Cave

(Yin She Ru Dong) 引蛇入洞

When both of your opponent's hands are pressing your right forearm (Figure 4-16), immediately raise your right arm up to neutralize his pushing or pressing, while using your left hand to grab his left wrist (Figure 4-17). Next, lead his left arm down by locking his left elbow with both of your hands (Figure 4-18). Finally, continue your locking until he is on the ground (Figure 4-19).

Figure 4–16   Figure 4–17   Figure 4–18

Figure 4–19   Figure 4–20   Figure 4–21

Theory:

Misplacing the Bone (elbow). When you raise your right forearm up to neutralize his pressing, it is an **Upward Wardoff (Peng)**. Your left hand's wrist and right hand's elbow grabbing is a **Pluck (Cai)**. To make this technique effective, you must keep his arm straight. The pressure should be directly on the rear side of his elbow.

Technique #5: Hands Grab Double Cavities

(Shou Kou Shuang Xue) 手扣雙穴

This technique is a typical example of using the Pluck (*Cai*) to grab a cavity. When both of your opponent's hands are pressing your right forearm (Figure 4-20), immediately neutralize his pressing to your right, grabbing his right wrist with your right hand while placing your left hand on his elbow (Figure 4-21). Finally, bend his wrist with your right

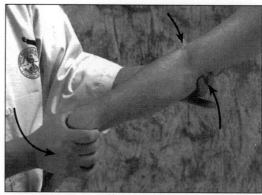

Figure 4–23

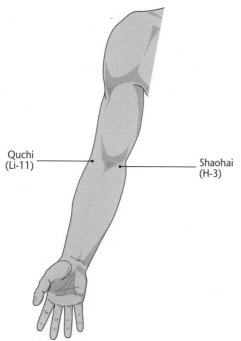

Figure 4–22. Shaohai (H-3) and Quchi (Li-11)

hand while grabbing the two cavities Shaohai (H-3) and Quchi (LI-11) with your left hand (Figures 4-22 and 4-23). You should lock him up so that he cannot either kick you or punch you with his left hand (Figure 4-24).

Theory:
Dividing the Muscle/Tendon (wrist) and Cavity Press (*Shaohai* and *Quchi* cavities). Your right hand's grabbing on his wrist and your left hand's locking on his cavities are **Pluck (*Cai*)**. Occasionally, you will encounter an opponent whose cavities are not as sensitive as others. In this case, this technique will not be effective. If you discover this, immediately use your right leg to kick his groin.

II. QIN NA AGAINST CAI

Since *Cai* is often used in actual *Taiji* combat, there are many *Qin Na* techniques which have been developed against the plucking and grabbing. Here, we will only introduce some of the typical *Qin Nas* useful against *Cai*. If you are interested in knowing more about *Qin Na* techniques against *Cai*, you may refer to the book: ***Comprehensive Applications of Shaolin Chin Na***, by YMAA.

Technique #1: Small Wrap Hand

(*Xiao Chan Shou*) 小纏手

When your opponent's right hand grabs your right wrist and his left hand grabs your elbow (Figure 4-25), immediately reposition yourself to his right hand side, using your left

Figure 4–24   Figure 4–25   Figure 4–26

Figure 4–27

Figure 4–28

hand to pull his index finger toward your wrist while raising your right arm upward to set up a advantageous angle to counter his grabbing (Figure 4-26). Then, wrap your right hand around the top side of his wrist to lock it (Figure 4-27), and finally circle it down to lock him (Finger 4-28).

Theory:

Dividing the Muscle/Tendon (wrist). Your two handed wrapping is **Coil (Chan)** and the final pressing by your right hand is **Press Down (An)**. In order to lock him efficiently, you must use your right fingers to direct your opponent's elbow and keep it slightly lower than his wrist. This will allow you to set up the best controlling angle on his wrist. When you apply this technique, the movement should be round and smooth. Only then are you able to control your opponent naturally, without alerting him to your intention.

Figure 4–29

Figure 4–30

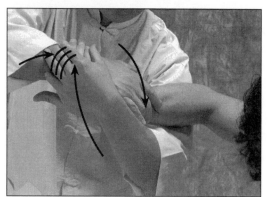

Figure 4–31

Figure 4–32

Technique #2: Large Wrap Hand

(Da Chan Shou) 大纏手

Although this technique is very similar to the previous one, the method of achieving the final control is different. Again, if your opponent's right hand is grabbing your wrist while his left hand is controlling your right elbow (Figure 4-29), reposition yourself to his right hand side, and raise your right arm up while moving your left hand under his forearm until it reaches his right hand (Figure 4-30). Next, use your left hand to push his index finger toward your wrist while wrapping your right hand over his wrist (Figure 4-31). Finally, bend your body toward him and press your right hand toward his wrist to lock him down to the ground (Figure 4-32).

Alternatively, after you have repositioned yourself to his right hand side (Figure 4-33), you may move your left hand over your right palm and pull his index or middle finger

Figure 4-33

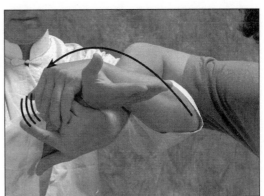

Figure 4-34

Figure 4-35

Figure 4-36

toward your wrist (Figure 4-34) and then wrap your right hand around his wrist (Figure 4-35). Finally, using the leverage of both of your hands, bow toward him and lock him to the ground (Figure 4-36).

Theory:

Dividing the Muscle/Tendon (wrist). Your right hand's grabbing on his wrist and your left hand's locking on his cavities are **Pluck (Cai)**. Your two handed wrapping is **Coil (Chan)** and the final pressing by your right hand is **Press Down (An)**. In order to lock him efficiently, you must use your right fingers to direct your opponent's elbow and keep it slightly lower than his wrist. This will allow you set up the best controlling angle on his wrist.

| Figure 4–37 | Figure 4–38 | Figure 4–39 |

Technique #3: Large Rollback

(Da Lu) 大擺

Again, if your opponent's right hand is grabbing your right wrist while his left hand is controlling your right elbow (Figure 4-37), immediately reposition yourself to his right hand side while raising your right arm up and placing your left forearm on the tendons of the rear of his post-arm (Figure 4-38). Finally, step your right leg backward and use the leverage generated from both of your hands to lead him down to the ground (Figure 4-39).

Theory:

Pressing Tendons (post-arm) and Misplacing the Bone (elbow). Your right hand's grabbing is a **Pluck (*Cai*)** and your left forearm's rolling back motion is a **Rollback (*Lu*)**. In fact, this action is considered **Large Rollback (*Da Lu*)** in *Taijiquan* techniques. In order to make this technique effective, you must press his rear post-arm tendons on the right spot. The accurate position for pressing is about three inches above the elbow on the rear side of his post-arm. Naturally, you may also press his rear elbow to lock his elbow joint.

Technique #4: Reverse Wrist Press and The Crane Spreads Its Wings

(Fan Ya Wan and Bai He Liang Chi) 反壓腕，白鶴亮翅

Again, if your opponent's right hand is grabbing your right wrist while his left hand is controlling your right elbow (Figure 4-40), immediately use your left hand to grab his right hand and try to free your right hand (Figure 4-41). Next, use both of your hands to rotate his right wrist counterclockwise (Figure 4-42). Finally, step your right leg behind his right leg, use your left hand to twist his right wrist continuously, and use your right forearm to push the upper back of his head forward (Figure 4-43).

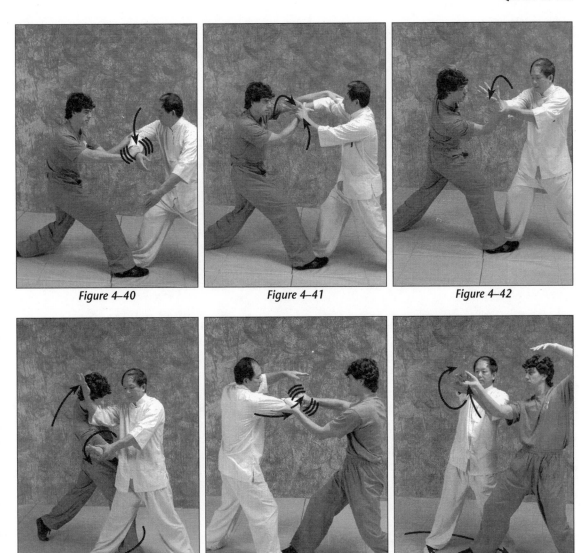

| Figure 4-40 | Figure 4-41 | Figure 4-42 |

| Figure 4-43 | Figure 4-44 | Figure 4-45 |

Theory:

Dividing the Muscle/Tendon (wrist) and Misplacing the Bone (elbow, shoulder, and neck). Your left hand's grabbing is a **Pluck (Cai)**, your right hand's circling to free itself is a **Coil (Chan)** and finally, the forearm's pushing is a **Rend (Lie)**. To make this technique effective, your opponent's right arm should not be bent too much nor kept too straight. A correct set up for the angle between the forearm and post-arm can make a significant difference in this technique.

Technique #5: The Hand Bends the Pine Branch

(Shou Ban Song Zhi) 手扳松枝

When your opponent's right hand is grabbing your right wrist while his left hand is controlling your right elbow (Figure 4-44), immediately reposition yourself to his right hand side, while rotating your right wrist counterclockwise to free yourself from his grabbing and placing your left hand on his index finger area (Figure 4-45). Next, free your right

Figure 4–46

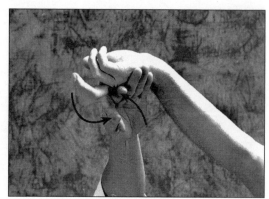

Figure 4–47

wrist while using your left thumb and index finger to lock him up (Figure 4-46). To make this technique most effective, you should place your thumb on the last joint of his index finger and your index finger on the base of his index finger (Figure 4-47).

Theory:

Misplacing the Bone (base of index finger). Your final locking is a **Pluck (*Cai*)**. To make this technique most effective and to prevent your opponent from turning his body, you should keep his arm straight. The trick to keeping his arm straight is to lock his index finger while his arm is in a low position, and then lifting his arm upward. In the final lock, the leverage generated from your thumb and index finger is the key to locking.

Technique #6: Old Man Promoted to General

(Lao Han Bai Jiang) 老漢拜將

When your opponent's right hand is grabbing your right wrist while his left hand is controlling your right elbow (Figure 4-48), immediately step your left leg behind his right leg and cover his right hand with your left hand. Then circle your left elbow over his right arm and place the rear side of his right elbow under your left armpit (Figure 4-49). Next, use the leverage of your hand's grabbing and your left armpit to lock him down to the ground (Figure 4-50). When you lock his arm, you should also use both of your hands to control his right hand (Figure 4-51).

Theory:

Dividing the Muscle/Tendon (wrist) and Misplacing the Bone (elbow). Your two handed grabbing is a **Pluck (*Cai*)** and in the final lock, your shoulder's (armpit's) downward pressing is a **Press Against (*Kao*)**. To make this technique effective, you must keep your opponent's arm straight. If necessary, you may jerk your power and break his elbow easily.

| Figure 4–48 | Figure 4–49 | Figure 4–50 |

| Figure 4–51 | Figure 4–52 | Figure 4–53 |

Technique #7: Wild Chicken Breaks Its Wings

(Ye Ji Ao Chi) 野雞拗翅

When your opponent's right hand is plucking or pressing your right shoulder (Figure 4-52), immediately use your right hand to grab his right hand while circling your left arm to the top of his right elbow (Figure 4-53). Finally, reposition yourself to his right hand side while using the leverage generated from your right hand and left elbow to press him down to the ground (Figure 4-54).

Theory:

Dividing the Muscle/Tendon (wrist) and Misplacing the Bone (elbow). Your two handed grabbing is a **Pluck (Cai)** and in the final lock, your elbow's press is **Elbow (Zhou)**. The shoulder is one of the few common places at which your opponent can pluck you. He can either grab your clothes on the shoulder area and then pull

| Figure 4–54 | Figure 4–55 | Figure 4–56 |

you down to destroy the mobility of your arm, or grab your shoulder tendon to lock your shoulder area. To make this technique effective, you should keep his elbow bent and lower than his wrist. The major pain is generated from his wrist, not from his elbow.

4-3. Qin Na in Lie

As discussed in Chapter 2, *Lie* is the action of using the arm to split or rend in order to put your opponent into a locking position or to make him fall. Very often it is considered a sideways *Peng*. However, strictly speaking, *Peng*'s power is more horizontal, and that of *Lie* is more diagonal. *Lie* action is normally used against the neck (Figure 4-55), shoulder (Figure 4-56), or post-arm (Figure 4-57). Here, we will introduce some typical examples of *Lie* as applied in *Qin Na*.

I. QIN NA FOR LIE

In order to use the arm for *Lie* in *Qin Na*, often you will need to use the other hand to Pluck (*Cai*) or control (*Na*) your opponent's wrist. If the angle of *Lie* is applied accurately, it is very easy to lock your opponent or to make him fall.

Technique #1: Arm Wraps Around the Dragon's Neck

(Bi Chan Long Jing) 臂纏龍頸

When both of your opponent's hands are on your right forearm and are pressing it (Figure 4-58), immediately reposition yourself to his right hand side, and grab his right wrist with your right hand while using your left hand to push his right elbow to bend it (Figure 4-59). Next, pull his right arm against your chest while using your left arm to push his neck backward (Figure 4-60). Finally, circle your left arm around his neck and lock him up until his heels are off the ground (Figure 4-61).

Figure 4–57

Figure 4–58

Figure 4–59

Figure 4–60

Figure 4–61

Figure 4–62

Theory:

Sealing the Breath (neck) and Misplacing the Bone (shoulder and elbow). Your right hand's grabbing is a **Pluck (Cai)**, your left arm's pushing against his neck is a **Rend (Lie)**, and in the final lock the arm's circling is a **Wrap (Chan)**. This technique is derived from one of the *Taiji* postures, Diagonal Flying. This technique can not only to lock his neck to seal his breath, but if necessary, you can also take him down.

Technique #2: Reverse Wrist Press

(Fan Ya Wan) 反壓腕

When your opponent's hands are on your right arm, pressing it or simply sticking with it (Figure 4-62), immediately use your left hand to grab his right wrist and twist it counterclockwise (Figure 4-63). Next, step your right leg behind his right leg while using both

| Figure 4–63 | Figure 4–64 | Figure 4–65 |

hands to twist his right wrist strongly (Figure 4-64). Finally, continue to control his wrist with your left hand and lock his arm on your stomach area, while using your right arm to push the upper back of his head forward to lock his arm (Figure 4-65).

Theory:

Dividing the Muscle/Tendon (wrist) and Misplacing the Bone (shoulder, elbow, and neck). Your left hand's grabbing is a **Pluck (Cai)** and your right arm's pushing against his rear upper neck is a **Rend (Lie)**. The angle of locking is very important. The locking leverage is generated from the left hand's twisting and your right hand's pushing. His arm should not be too straight in the final locking.

Technique #3: White Crane Twists Its Neck

(Bai He Niu Jing) 白鶴扭頸

If your opponent is right in front of you with his right hand opened, or he is trying to use his right hand to grab your chest (Figure 4-66), immediately step your left leg behind his right leg while using your right hand to grab his right fingers, and twist them to the right and then toward him to control the base tendons of his pinkie (Figure 4-67). Next, continue to twist his right fingers with your right hand while using your left hand to push his chin backward (Figure 4-68). Finally, circle him down to the ground as you continue to lock his right arm while using your left hand to push his head to his left (Figure 4-69). This will generate good leverage to lock his fingers, arms, and neck.

Theory:

Dividing the Muscle/Tendon (wrist) and Misplacing the Bone (neck). Your right hand's grabbing is a **Pluck (Cai)** and your left arm's pushing his neck and then circling it down is a **Rend (Lie)**. When you control your opponent's right arm, his arm should be bent 90 degrees for better control. Furthermore, his elbow should be slightly lower than his wrist. This can be done by controlling his pinkie's tendons. Right from the beginning until the end, you should keep his arm locked.

Figure 4–66　　　　Figure 4–67　　　　Figure 4–68

Figure 4–69　　　　Figure 4–70　　　　Figure 4–71

Technique #4: Wild Horses Shear the Mane and Wave Hands in the Clouds

(Ye Ma Fen Zong and Yun Shou) 野馬分鬃，雲手

When both of your opponent's hands are on your right forearm, immediately move your left forearm under his right forearm (Figure 4-70). Next, turn your body to your left to neutralize his pushing, and grab his right wrist with your left hand while placing your right forearm under his post-arm (Figure 4-71). Finally, use the leverage generated from your left hand and right forearm to lock him upward (Figure 4-72). You should stay on his right hand side to keep away from his left hand's possible attack.

Alternatively, you may use your right forearm to lock the tendons on the rear side of his post arm (Figure 4-73).

Theory:

Misplacing the Bone (shoulder) and Pressing the Tendon (post-arm). Your left hand's grabbing is a **Pluck (Cai)** and your right arm's pressing against his post-arm is a **Rend (Lie)**. If you are locking the tendons in his post-arm, the location of your

Figure 4–72

Figure 4–73

Figure 4–74

Figure 4–75

Figure 4–76

Figure 4–77

right forearm's pressing on his post-arm is very important. The correct position should be about three inches above the elbow on the rear side of his post-arm. Often these two *Qin Nas* are only used to uproot or lock your opponent temporarily. After locking, you may then kick his groin with your right knee or even swing him down to the ground.

Technique #5: Grasp Sparrow's Tail

(Lan Que Wei) 攬雀尾

When both of your opponent's hands are on your right forearm (Figure 4-74), immediately reposition yourself to his right hand side and grab his right wrist with your right hand while using your right hand to push his elbow upward to keep it straight (Figure 4-75). Next, pull his right arm toward your right while placing your left shoulder under his armpit (Figure 4-76). Finally, turn your body to your left slightly and pull his right arm down to lock his right arm on your left shoulder (Figure 4-77).

| *Figure 4–78* | *Figure 4–79* | *Figure 4–80* |

Theory:

Misplacing the Bone (elbow and shoulder). Your right hand's grabbing is a **Pluck (Cai)** and your left arm's upward diagonal locking is a **Rend (Lie)**. The other option of locking is to place the tendons on the rear side of his post-arm on your left shoulder and using your left shoulder to press his tendons while pulling his arm down with both of your hands.

II. QIN NA AGAINST LIE

As mentioned earlier, *Lie* is commonly done with two hands. When one hand is grabbing or plucking the opponent's wrist, the other arm is used to generate the rending or splitting force. If your opponent uses *Lie* against you, you have two options in applying *Qin Na*. One is to take care of the hand which is grabbing or plucking your wrist, and the other is to control the arm which is rending you. Since you have already learned how to use *Qin Na* against Pluck (*Cai*) in the last section, we will not repeat it here. Here, we will focus on the *Qin Na* against the rending arm.

Technique #1: Left Right Cross Elbow

(Zuo You Jiao Zhou) 左右交肘

When your opponent's right hand grabs your right wrist while his left arm is on your neck pushing backward (Figure 4-78), immediately use your left hand to intercept his left arm and grab his wrist while raising your right forearm up to loosen his grabbing (Figure 4-79). Next, grab his right wrist with your right hand and cross his arms in front of you (Figure 4-80). Finally, rotate both of his arms counterclockwise and use his right forearm to lock his left arm (Figure 4-81). If you wish, you may sweep your right leg backward to take him down (Figure 4-82).

Figure 4–81

Figure 4–82

Figure 4–83

Theory:

Misplacing the Bone (elbow and shoulder). Your two handed grabbing is a **Pluck (Cai)** and the twisting of both of his arms is a **Turning (Zhuan)**. In order to make the locking effective, you must keep his left arm straight. When you execute this technique, you must be fast. The reason for this is simply that your opponent will have the same opportunity to execute the same technique to lock your arms. The first one executing the technique will be the one who controls.

Technique #2: Carry a Pole on the Shoulder

(Jian Tiao Bian Dan) 肩挑扁擔

Again, when your opponent's right hand grabs your right wrist while his left arm is pressing against your neck, immediately use your left hand to grab his left wrist to prevent him from pressing your neck (Figure 4-83). Next, turn your body to your left while placing the rear tendons of his post-arm or armpit on your right shoulder (Figure 4-84). If his tendons are on your shoulder, you may simply pull his arm down to generate pain in his tendons. However, if his armpit is on your shoulder, then you should pull his arm downward and then push upward toward his shoulder to create pain in his shoulder's tendons and ligaments (Figure 4-85).

Theory:

Misplacing the Bone (elbow and shoulder) and Pressing the Tendon (post-arm). Your left hand's grabbing is a **Pluck (Cai)** and your shoulder's upward pushing is an **Upward Press (Kao)**. If you are locking his tendons, you should raise your stance. This will offer you a better leverage for locking. However, if you are locking his shoulder, then the movement of pulling his arm down to keep it straight first and then pushing it upward against his shoulder is the key to locking.

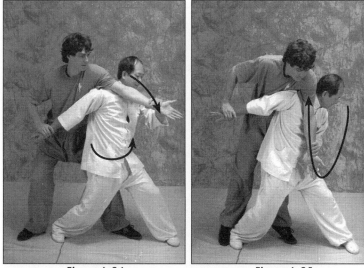

Figure 4–84   Figure 4–85

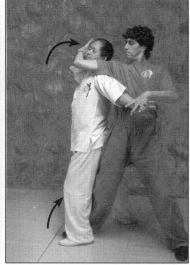
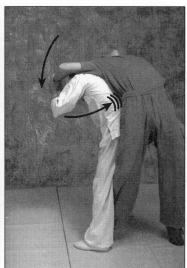

Figure 4–86   Figure 4–87   Figure 4–88

Technique #3: The Old Man Carries the Fish on His Back

(Lao Han Bei Yu) 老漢背魚

When your opponent's left hand grabs your left wrist and his right arm is pushing your neck, immediately use your right hand to grab his right wrist (Figure 4-86). Next, reposition yourself while bending his arm with your right hand and chin (Figure 4-87). Finally, free your left hand and use both hands to pull his arm downward to lock him on your back (Figure 4-88).

Theory:

Misplacing the Bone (elbow and shoulder). Your right hand's grabbing is a **Pluck (Cai)** and the final lock behind you is a **Shoulder Upward Press (Kao)**. Whenever your wrist is grabbed, you should try to free it as soon as possible. The trick to freeing the wrist is to dislodge it through the space between your opponent's thumb and index finger. When you lock your opponent's arm, it should not be either too straight or too bent. The correct angle can make the technique very easy and effective to execute.

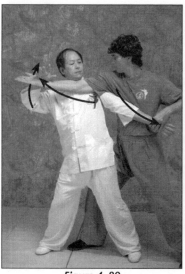

| Figure 4–89 | Figure 4–90 | Figure 4–91 |

Technique #4: Two Children Worship the Buddha

(Shuang Tong Bai Fo) 雙童拜佛

Again, when your opponent's left hand grabs your left wrist while his right arm is pushing your neck, immediately use your right hand to grab his right wrist and push it forward to prevent his locking (Figure 4-89). Then, bow your body downward while pulling his right arm backward and pressing your left shoulder forward (Figure 4-90).

Theory:
Misplacing the Bone (elbow and shoulder). Your right hand's grabbing is a **Pluck (Cai)** and your left shoulder's pressing is a **Downward Press (Kao)**. This technique can only lock your opponent temporarily. If you wish, you may sweep your left leg backward while swinging his body to your right to take him down.

4-4. Qin Na in Zhou

As explained in Chapter 2, the purpose of *Zhou* is to use the elbow to strike the cavity (*Da*), to press the body (*Ji*), to neutralize the opponent's press or push (*Hua*), to wrap or coil the opponent's limbs (*Chan*), or to seal the opponent's attack (*Feng*). In *Taijiquan*, *Zhou* has an important role in *Qin Na* applications. When *Zhou* is used for *Qin Na*, normally it must be coordinated with *Cai* (plucking or grabbing) on the opponent's wrist. Only then can *Zhou Qin Na* be effective and powerful.

I. QIN NA FOR ZHOU

When *Zhou* is used for *Qin Na*, the actions of pressing, neutralizing, wrapping, coiling, and sealing are critical for making the techniques effective. Because of this, the sensitivity of feeling the angles which are pressed, neutralized, wrapping, and sealing are very important. That means the "listening *Jin*" (*Ting Jin*) on the elbow is the key to locking. With a correct angle of locking, the techniques can be executed without too much effort. Here, we will introduce some typical examples.

Figure 4–92

Figure 4–93

Figure 4–94

Figure 4–95

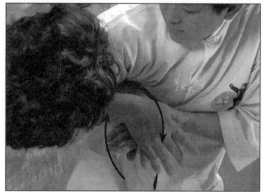

Figure 4–96

Technique #1: Prop Up Elbow

(Shang Jia Zhou) 上架肘

When both of your opponent's hands are on your right arm and are pushing it (Figure 4-91), immediately use your left hand to grab his right hand (Figure 4-92). Next, step your right leg behind his right leg and twist his right wrist with your left hand while circling your right elbow to the outside of his right elbow (Figure 4-93). Finally, use the leverage of your left hand and right elbow to lock his arm (Figure 4-94). If you wish, you can continue to step your left leg behind him while using your right arm and chest area to lock his right arm, while using your left hand to push the upper back of his head forward (Figure 4-95).

Theory:

Misplacing the Bone (elbow and neck) and Dividing the Muscle/Tendon (wrist). Your left hand's grabbing is a **Pluck (Cai)**, your elbow's circling and upward pushing is an **Elbow (Zhou)**, and the final lock using your left hand to push the upper back of his head forward is a **Wardoff (Peng)**. When you circle your elbow to lock his elbow, your left hand's twisting of his right wrist is very important. In fact, in

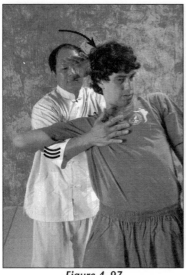

| Figure 4–97 | Figure 4–98 | Figure 4–99 |

order to increase your locking power, you should use both of your hands to handle the job (Figure 4-96). In the final lock, the best way to generate good leverage for the locking is to raise your right arm's locking up while pushing the top of his head forward (Figure 4-97).

Technique #2: Forgive Me for not Going with You

(Shu Bu Tong Xing) 恕不同行

Again, when both of your opponent's hands are on your right forearm and are pushing it (Figure 4-98), immediately use your left hand to grab his left hand (Figure 4-99). Next, circle your right elbow on the top of his left elbow while twisting his left wrist with your left hand (Figure 4-100). Finally, use the leverage of your left hand and right elbow to lock his left arm (Figure 4-101).

Theory:
Misplacing the Bone (elbow) and Dividing the Muscle/Tendon (wrist). Your left hand's grabbing is a **Pluck (Cai)** and your right elbow's circling and pressing is an **Elbow (Zhou)**. When you use your elbow to press him down, his elbow should be bent and slightly lower than his wrist. Naturally, you should position yourself in the right spot, beyond his right hand's attack.

Technique #3: Turn the Body to Seize the Monkey

(Fan Shen Qin Yuan) 翻身擒猿

When your opponent is behind you and his left hand is on your right shoulder (Figure 4-102), immediately use your left hand to grab his left wrist while circling your elbow upward (Figure 4-103). Next, circle your right arm under his left elbow and raise it upward while releasing your left hand's wrist grabbing (Figure 4-104). Finally, extend your right arm and use your right hand to push his chest to generate pain in his entire left arm (Figure 4-105).

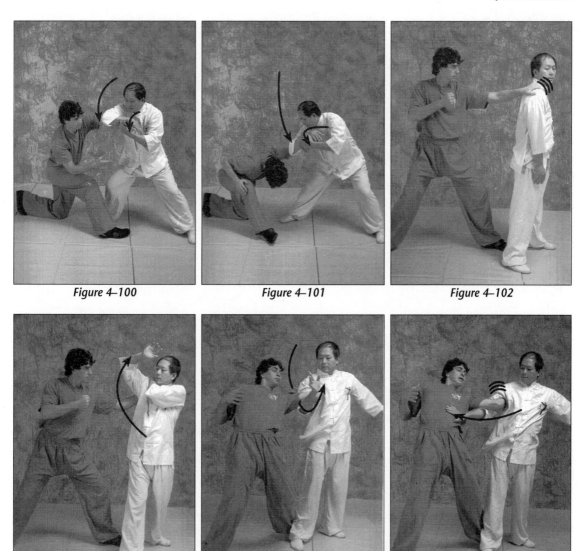

Figure 4–100　　　　　　Figure 4–101　　　　　　Figure 4–102

Figure 4–103　　　　　　Figure 4–104　　　　　　Figure 4–105

Theory:

Misplacing the Bone (elbow and shoulder). Your left hand's grabbing is a **Pluck (Cai)**, your right elbow's circling around his arm is an **Elbow (Zhou)**, and the final position of the hand's pushing is a **Wardoff (Peng)**. When you lock your opponent's arm, prevent him from rotating his arm. If he can do that, he will be able to escape.

Technique #4: The Hero Shows Courtesy

(Ying Xiong You Li) 英雄有禮

When your opponent's right hand is on your left shoulder (Figure 4-106), immediately step your right leg backward, and grab his right hand with your right hand while placing your left elbow on his right elbow (Figure 4-107). Finally, twist his right wrist with your

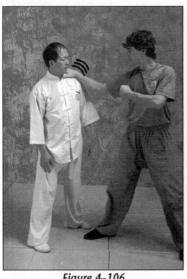
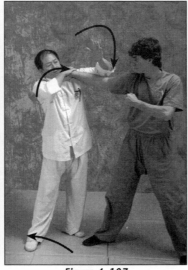

| *Figure 4–106* | *Figure 4–107* | *Figure 4–108* |

right hand, and press his elbow down with your left elbow while bowing your body toward him (Figure 4-108).

Theory:

Dividing the Muscle/Tendon (wrist). Your right hand's grabbing is a **Pluck (*Cai*)** and left elbow's pressing is an **Elbow (*Zhou*)**. The main locking is on his wrist by your right hand. Your elbow's pressing is to maintain a good angle for the wrist's locking. His elbow should be slightly lower than his wrist.

Technique #5: Daoist Greets with Hands

(Dao Zi Zuo Ji) 道子作揖

When your opponent uses his right hand to grab your right wrist, immediately circle your right hand counterclockwise to free the grabbing while placing your left forearm on his right elbow (Figure 4-109). Next, circle your right hand around his right forearm until your right forearm is on his right forearm (Figure 4-110). Finally, press his forearm downward with your right forearm while using your left elbow to push his right elbow upward (Figure 4-111).

Theory:

Misplacing the Bone (elbow and shoulder). In the final locking, your right wrist's downward pressing against his forearm is a **Downward Press (*An*)** and your left elbow's lifting on his elbow is an **Elbow (*Zhou*)**. When you execute this technique, you must be fast. Otherwise, your opponent will have a chance to escape if he feels your locking.

Figure 4–109

Figure 4–110

Figure 4–111

Figure 4–112

Figure 4–113

Figure 4–114

Technique #6: Extending the Neck for Water

(Yin Jing Qiu Shui) 引頸求水

Whenever you have a chance to grab your opponent's right fingers with your right hand, immediately press his elbow to his left (Figure 4-112). Next, coil your left hand around his right arm until it reaches his post-arm near the elbow area and lift his arm upward to lock it (Figure 4-113). Finally, use your right hand to either push his chin upward or push it toward his left (Figure 4-114). This will offer you good leverage to generate pain in his right shoulder.

Theory:

Misplacing the Bone (shoulder). Your right hand's grabbing is a **Pluck (Cai)**, your left hand's circling around his right arm is a **Coil (Chan)**, the left elbow's upward lifting on his forearm is an **Elbow (Zhou)**, and your right hand's lifting on his chin is a **Lift (Ti)**. To make this technique effective, you must keep his right arm bent. If he is able to straighten his arm, it will not be effective. The trick to doing this is to use your left post-arm to prevent him from straightening his arm.

Figure 4–115

Figure 4–116

Figure 4–117

Figure 4–118

Figure 4–119

Technique #7: Forward Upward Turning

(Qian Shang Fan) 前上翻

When your opponent's right hand is on your left forearm (Figure 4-115), immediately neutralize his pushing or grabbing to your left while using your right forearm to pull in his right elbow (Figure 4-116). Next, step your right leg behind his right leg and use both hands to lock his arm backward (Figure 4-117). Finally, let your right hand continue to lock his arm while using your left hand to push the upper back of his head forward to lock him (Figure 4-118). The best method of locking his arm is to make the angle between his forearm and post-arm 90 degrees (Figure 4-119).

Theory:

Misplacing the Bone (elbow, shoulder, and neck). Your two handed locking on his arm is a **Downward Press (*An*)** and the final lock, which uses your elbow to lift up his elbow to lock his arm, is an **Elbow (*Zhou*)**. The leverage generated from your right arm's locking and left hand's pushing on his head is the key to the locking. If you push his head too hard, you will pop his shoulder out of its socket.

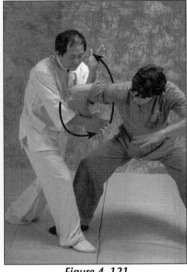

| Figure 4-120 | Figure 4-121 | Figure 4-122 |

II. QIN NA AGAINST ZHOU

For emitting power (*Fa Jin*) in *Taijiquan*, the legs are the root of power, the waist is the steering wheel which controls the direction of the power's manifestation, and the hands are the places from which the power is manifested. The power can also be generated from the arm. For an arm, the shoulder is the root of the movement, the elbow is the steering wheel which controls the direction of the movement, and the hands are the final places where the movement ends. From this, you can see that if you are able to immobilize your opponent's elbow movement, then you have restrained the free movements of his arms. Naturally, you will have governed the entire fighting situation.

Because of this reason, there were many *Qin Na* created in the past which can now be used to control the elbow. This is especially important when your opponent's hands are closed as fists, or when the fighting range is close. When your opponent's hands are closed, it is hard to control the fingers or even the wrist, and when the fighting range is close, the elbows and the shoulders will have become the main weapons for short range fighting. Here, we will introduce some *Qin Na* techniques which were specially designed against the elbow.

Technique #1: Small Wrap Elbow

(Xiao Chan Zhou) 小纏肘

When your opponent uses his elbow to strike your solar plexus area (Figure 4-120), immediately use your right forearm and your left arm to intercept and neutralize the attack (Figure 4-121). Next, reposition yourself, grab his right wrist with your right hand, and use both hands to rotate his arm and force him to bow (Figure 4-122). Finally, step your right leg backward and circle him down to the ground (Figure 4-123).

Theory:

Misplacing the Bone (elbow and shoulder). Your right hand's grabbing is a **Pluck (Cai)** and the entire movement is a **Large Rollback (Da Lu)**. The pressure that makes your opponent follow your circle is generated from the leverage of both hands' controlling instead of pulling. Naturally, if you wish you may also sweep your left leg backward to make him fall.

Figure 4–123

Figure 4–124

Figure 4–125

Figure 4–126

Figure 4–127

Figure 4–128

Technique #2: Pressing Shoulder with a Single Finger or Extending the Neck for Water

(Yi Zhi Ding Jian or Yin Jing Qiu Shui) 一指頂肩，引頸求水

Again, when your opponent uses his elbow to strike your solar plexus, use both arms to intercept and neutralize his attempt (Figure 4-124). Next, reposition yourself, grab his right wrist with your right hand while coiling your left hand around his right arm until it reaches his post-arm near the elbow area, and lock his right arm up (Figure 4-125). Finally, use your right index or middle finger to press his *Jianneiling* (M-UE-48) cavity to create pain (Figure 4-126). Alternatively, you may use your right hand to push his chin upward while lifting his right arm upward (Figure 4-127).

Theory:

Misplacing the Bone (elbow and shoulder). Your right hand's grabbing is a **Pluck (Cai)**, your left hand's circling around his arm is a **Coil (Chan)**, your left arm and elbow's upward lifting to his right arm is **Elbow (Zhou)**, the right index or middle finger's upward pressing to the Jianneiling is a **Point (Dian)**, and finally, your right hand's upward lifting of his chin is a **Lift (Ti)**. Once you have locked his right arm

Figure 4–129

Figure 4–130

Figure 4–131

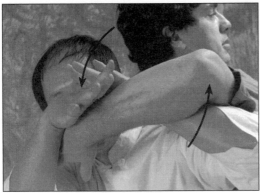

Figure 4–132

behind him, the tendons and ligaments in his shoulder should be very tensed. In this case, if you press his *Jianneiling* (M-UE-48) cavity, significant pain can be produced. This is an example of using **Elbow (Zhou)** against **Elbow (Zhou)**.

Technique #3: Daoist Greets with Hands and The Old Man carries the Fish on His Back

(Dao Zi Zuo Ji and Lao Han Bei Yu)
道子作揖，老漢背魚

Again, when your opponent uses his elbow to attack your solar plexus, immediately use your left forearm to push his elbow downward to neutralize it (Figure 4-128). Next, use your right forearm to lift his right forearm up while pushing his right elbow to his left with your left elbow (Figure 4-129). Finally, rotate his arm until it is locked (Figure 4-130).

Alternatively, you may continue your turning and use your upper back to support the locking of his arm behind your back (Figure 4-131).

Theory:

Misplacing the Bone (elbow and shoulder). Your left forearm's pressing against his elbow strike is a **Downward Press (An)**, and in the final position, your left elbow's upward lifting is an **Elbow (Zhou)**, while your right hand's downward pushing is a **Downward Press (An)**. This is an another example of using the **Elbow (Zhou) against the Elbow (Zhou)**. In the final locking, in order to prevent your opponent from turning around, you may use your left shoulder to push against his shoulder. In this case, your left shoulder's push is a **Press Against (Kao)**. In the optional technique, the support from your back for the locking is a **Press Against (Kao)**. The locking angle of his arm is very important. His arm should be neither too straight nor too bent (Figure 4-132).

| Figure 4–133 | Figure 4–134 | Figure 4–135 |

4-5. Qin Na in Kao

As explained in Chapter 2, the purpose of *Kao* is to use part of your body to bump your opponent's body to make him lose his balance or fall. When your opponent is in the situation of regaining his balance, take this opportunity to execute further action such as kicking or striking. The common *Kaos* are done by the shoulder (*Jian Kao*, shoulder *Kao*), back (*Bei Kao*, Back *Kao*), hip (*Tun Kao*, hip *Kao*), thigh (*Tui Kao*, leg *Kao*), knee (*Xi Kao*, knee *Kao*), and chest (*Xiong Kao*, chest *Kao*). In addition, from the direction of *Kao*, it can be distinguished as: forward *Kao* (*Qian Kao*), downward *Kao* (*Xia Kao*), sideward *Kao* (*Ce Kao*), and upward *Kao* (*Shang Kao*).

I. QIN NA FOR KAO

Though there are many types of *Kao*, there are only a few *Kaos* which can be used for *Qin Na*. Often, *Kao* is used to bump the opponent off his balance instead of locking or controlling. Here, a few examples are introduced from which the *Kao* can be used for *Qin Na*.

Technique #1: Two Children Worship the Buddha

(Shuang Tong Bai Fo) 雙童拜佛

When your opponent locks your right arm with both of his hands (*Rend*)(Figure 4-133), immediately reposition yourself to his right hand side, and spin your right arm counterclockwise to escape from his locking while placing your left arm under his right armpit (Figure 4-134). Next, bow your body forward, pulling his right forearm backward while pushing your left shoulder against his right shoulder, and lock him there (Figure 4-135).

Theory:

Misplacing the Bone (shoulder and elbow). In the final locking, your chest's forward pushing against his arm is a **Chest Press Against (*Xiong Kao*)** while your left shoulder's pressing against his shoulder is a **Shoulder Press Against (*Jian Kao*)**. This technique can be used to control your opponent only temporarily. In fact, it can be used to swing him down to the ground.

Figure 4-136

Figure 4-137

Figure 4-138

Figure 4-139

Technique #2: The Old Man Promoted to General

(Lao Han Bai Jiang) 老漢拜將

When both of your opponent's hands are on your right arm and are pressing (Figure 4-136), immediately use your left hand to grab his left hand while circling your right arm upward (Figure 4-137). Next, turn your body to your left and place your right armpit on his left shoulder (Figure 4-138). Finally, use the leverage generated from both of your hands' grabbing and your right shoulder to press him down to the ground (Figure 4-139).

Theory:

Misplacing the Bone (shoulder and elbow). Your two handed grabbing is a **Pluck (Cai)** and the final lock is a **Shoulder Press Against (Jian Kao)**. To prevent his arm from bending, lock his elbow under your armpit. If necessary, you may use the jerking *Jin* to break his elbow.

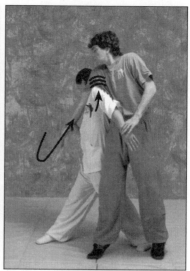

| Figure 4–140 | Figure 4–141 | Figure 4–142 |

Technique #3: Shoulder Carries a Pole

(Jian Tiao Bian Dan) 肩挑扁擔

When your opponent uses his right arm to rend your neck while grabbing your left wrist with his left hand, immediately grab his right wrist with your right hand (Figure 4-140). Next, turn your body to your right and place his post-arm on your left shoulder (Figure 4-141). Finally, pull his arm first downward, and then lift it upward against his shoulder to generate strain in his shoulder's tendons and ligaments (Figure 4-142). Naturally, you may use your left shoulder to press upward against his tendons on his post-arm.

Theory:

Misplacing the Bone (shoulder and elbow) and Pressing the Tendon (post-arm). Your right hand's grabbing is a **Pluck (Cai)** and your shoulder's upward pressing is an **Upward Press Against (Kao)**. If you are locking his shoulder, to make the technique effective, first you pull his arm downward to straighten it out, and then push straight upward against his shoulder. This motion can generate great pain in his shoulder.

Technique #4: The Old Man Carries the Fish on His Back

(Lao Han Bei Yu) 老漢背魚

Again, when your opponent uses his left hand to grab your left wrist while using his right arm to rend your neck, immediately use your right hand to grab his right wrist to prevent his rending (Figure 4-143). Next, turn your body to your right and bend his arm while trying to free your left hand (Figure 4-144). Finally, bow forward and use both of your hands to pull his arm down to lock him behind your back (Figure 4-145).

Theory:

Misplacing the Bone (shoulder and elbow). Your right hand's grabbing is a **Pluck (Cai)** and in the final position, your back's upward press is a **Press Against (Kao)**. When you control his arm, to make this technique effective, his arm should be neither too bent nor too straight.

Figure 4-143

Figure 4-144

Figure 4-145

Figure 4-146

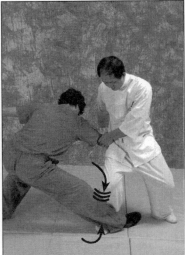

Figure 4-147

Figure 4-148

Technique #5: The Knee Presses the Enemy's Leg

(Xi Ding Di Tui) 膝頂敵腿

This technique uses the knee to press against the opponent's leg or knee. When the distance between you and your opponent is short, immediately hook your right leg behind his right leg (Figure 4-146). Next, use the leg near the knee to press against internal side of his calf to lock his right leg (Figure 4-147). The angle of pressing is the key to the locking (Figure 4-148). With correct locking, you may lock his leg or even force him down easily.

Theory:

Misplacing the Bone (knee). This action is a **Knee Press Against (*Xi Kao*)**. In a battle, this technique can be used very quickly, which allows you to put your opponent in a locked position temporarily or to make him fall. This technique is not designed to lock his leg permanently.

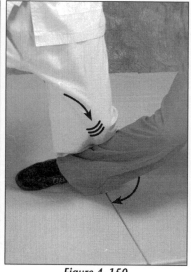

| Figure 4–149 | Figure 4–150 | Figure 4–151 |

Technique #6: The Leg Twists the Enemy's Leg

(Tui Ban Di Tui) 腿絆敵腿

This technique is very similar to the previous one. The only difference is that you are locking from the external side of his leg. Again, when the distance between you and your opponent is short, you may immediately use your left foot to hook his right leg near the ankle area (Figure 4-149). Then, use the upper part of your calf or knee to press him down (Figure 4-150).

Theory:

Misplacing the Bone (knee). This action is a **Knee Press Against (*Xi Kao*)**. In a battle, this technique can be used very quickly, which allows you to put your opponent in a locked position temporarily or make him fall. This technique is not designed to lock his leg permanently.

II. QIN NA AGAINST KAO

Most *Qin Na* techniques against *Kao* focus on the shoulder *Kao*. The reason for this is that, when your opponent uses his shoulder to Press Against (*Kao*), then you may have a chance to control his arms. If he uses another portion of the body, such as his chest, back, thigh or knee, then it is very hard to execute any *Qin Na* technique against him. In this section, we will introduce some of the techniques useful against shoulder *Kao*.

Technique #1: Large Rollback

(Da Lu) 大擺

When your opponent uses his right shoulder or upper arm to stroke you (Figure 4-151), immediately use your right hand to control his right forearm while placing your left forearm on the rear tendon of his right post-arm (Figure 4-152). Your left palm should face downward. Next, step your right leg backward and use the leverage of your right hand

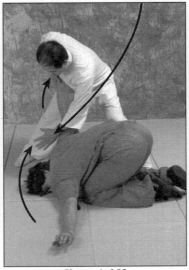

| Figure 4–152 | Figure 4–153 | Figure 4–154 |

and left forearm to press him down to the ground (Figure 4-153). When you press him down, you should press your left forearm hard on his rear post-arm tendon while rotating your left forearm counterclockwise until your left palm is facing you. This left forearm rotation action will generate great pain in your opponent's post arm and therefore follow your leading to the ground.

Theory:

Misplacing the Bone (shoulder and elbow) and Pressing the Tendon (rear post-arm). This technique uses **Large Rollback (Da Lu)** against the *Kao*. Your right hand's controlling of his forearm is a **Pluck (Cai)**. If your opponent uses his shoulder or upper arm to stroke you, the way to prevent his attacking power from reaching you is to control his post-arm. Therefore, this technique can be effectively used against this stroke. Naturally, you should use the circular motion to destroy his balance while both of your arms are leading him down to the ground.

Technique #2: Two Children Worship the Buddha

(Shuang Tong Bai Fo) 雙童拜佛

Again, when your opponent is pressing against your chest with his shoulder (Figure 4-154), immediately use your right hand to control his right forearm while inserting your left arm under his right arm and pressing against his stomach area (Figure 4-155). Then, bow your body forward while using the leverage generated from your right hand's pulling and left shoulder's downward pressing to lock his right arm (Figure 4-156).

Theory:

Misplacing the Bone (shoulder and elbow) and Pressing the Tendon (rear post-arm). This technique uses **Shoulder Press Against (Kao)** to counterattack the **Shoulder Press Against (Kao)**. Naturally, your right hand's controlling is a **Pluck (Cai)**. This technique can only be used to lock your opponent temporarily for further attack, such as using your right hand to strike his face, or even to circle him down.

Figure 4–155

Figure 4–156

Figure 4–157

Figure 4–158

Figure 4–159

Technique #3: Daoist Greets with Hands and The Old Man carries the Fish on His Back

(Dao Zi Zuo Ji and Lao Han Bei Yu) 道子作揖，老漢背魚

When your opponent uses his right shoulder to press against your chest (Figure 4-157), immediately use your right hand to control his right forearm while using your left forearm to press his elbow down (Figure 4-158). Next use the leverage generated from both of your hands and left elbow to lock his arm up (Figures 4-159 and 4-160).

Alternatively, you may continue your turning and use your upper back to support the locking of his arm behind your back (Figures 4-161 and 4-162).

Theory:

Misplacing the Bone (elbow and shoulder). Your left forearm's pressing against his elbow strike is a **Downward Press (An)**, and in the final position, your left elbow's upward lifting is an **Elbow (Zhou)** while your right hand's downward pushing is a

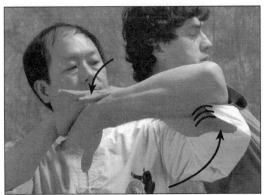

Figure 4-160

Figure 4-161

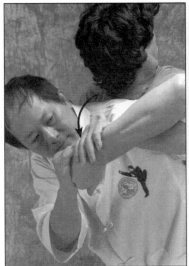

Figure 4-162

Figure 4-163

Figure 4-164

Downward Press (An). In the final locking, in order to prevent your opponent from turning around, you may use your left shoulder to push against his shoulder. In this case, your left shoulder's push is a **Press Against (Kao)**. In the optional technique, the support from your back for the locking is a **Press Against (Kao)**. The locking angle of his arm is very important. His arm should be neither too straight nor too bent.

Technique #4: Arm Wraps Around the Dragon's Neck

(Bi Chan Long Jing) 臂纏龍頸

When your opponent is pressing against your chest with his right shoulder, immediately control his right forearm with your right hand and press his elbow down with your left forearm (Figure 4-163). Next, reposition yourself, and pull his right arm backward against your chest while circling your left arm toward his neck (Figure 4-164). Finally, lock his arm on your chest while wrapping his neck with your left arm (Figure 4-165).

Figure 4–165

Theory:

Misplacing the Bone (shoulder and elbow) and Seal the Breath (neck). This technique uses **Rend (Lie)** to counterattack the **Shoulder Press Against (Kao)**. Your right hand's controlling is a **Pluck (Cai)**, and your left arm's wrapping is a **Rend (Lie)** and **Coil (Chan)**.

From the techniques discussed in Chapter 3 and Chapter 4, you should have realized and comprehended two important points. First, the same technique can be applied in different situations, even though the set up and execution of the technique can be different. Second, among the eight basic *Taiji* technical movements, it is easy to use one against the other in *Qin Na*. This is not surprising, given that these eight basic patterns were created to mutually support and conquer each other. Third, almost all *Qin Na* techniques introduced here can be applied in *Taiji* Pushing Hands. This is again not surprising. This is simply because all the *Taiji* Pushing Hands techniques are built upon the common foundation of these eight basic moving technical patterns.

▪ Chapter 5 ▪

QIN NA APPLICATIONS IN TAIJIQUAN POSTURES

5-1. Introduction

In the last two chapters we have discussed the possible *Qin Na* applications in the eight basic *Taiji* moving patterns: *Peng, Lu, Ji, An, Cai, Lie, Zhou,* and *Kao.* In addition, *Qin Na* which may be used against these eight basic moving actions have also been introduced. However, if you analyze the 37 postures of *Taiji* movement (*Yang* Style), you will realize that, although most of the postures are derived from the same eight basic movements, many others do not carry the same patterns and theory.

In this chapter, we will try to find the possible and reasonable *Qin Na* applications for these other *Taiji* postures. There are, however, a very few of these postures from which I cannot find reasonable *Qin Na* techniques, and thus they will not be discussed. Furthermore, because I am only familiar with *Yang* Style *Taijiquan,* I can only offer you the possible *Qin Na* in *Yang* Style. However, since the basic theories of *Qin Na* remain the same in every style, after you have reached a good level of understanding, you may apply these same theories in other styles. If you would like to know more about striking and wrestling (taking down) techniques in *Taijiquan,* you may refer to **Advanced Yang Style Tai Chi Chuan, Vol. 2 — Martial Applications**.

Other than introducing those *Qin Na* categorized as "Dividing the Muscle/Tendon" and "Misplacing the Bone," we would also like to offer you some information about "Cavity Pressing" or "Cavity Striking" in this chapter.

The technique of Cavity Grabbing, Pressing, or Striking is known as one of the highest martial techniques in China. You should know that, strictly speaking, **when a cavity is attacked by grabbing and/or pressing it is classified as *Qin Na*. However, if the cavity**

is attacked by striking or kicking, then it will be classified in the fighting categories of striking and kicking.

In ancient times, almost every Chinese martial style trained "Cavity Pressing or Striking" techniques. However, usually the highest level of these techniques was only taught to the trusted students who had stayed with the master for more than ten years. There are two main reasons for this. First, the theory is very deep, and the training is much harder than other martial training. Therefore, it is very difficult for a beginner to learn and reach a high level. Second, when many of the cavities are struck, it can cause death easily. Due to this reason, unless a student's morality is very high, normally a master would prefer to keep these secrets to himself, instead of passing them down to immoral students.

It is the same in *Taijiquan*. Although it is well known in China that *Taijiquan* specializes in cavity press techniques, not too many *Taiji* practitioners today know about it or train it. The main reason for this is that training cavity press takes a great deal of time and patience. It is especially hard to train in today's lifestyle, when most people are busy earning money for surviving or spending most of their leisure time in entertainment. In addition to this, there are not too many *Taiji* masters today who still have the knowledge and capability for teaching this art. Furthermore, even after you have trained this art today, you will never have a chance to use it, since it can cause death so easily. This situation is not the same as in ancient times, when every martial technique was critical for survival. It was more frequent that you had the opportunity to verify the effectiveness of your techniques. Today, most *Taiji* masters emphasize Pushing Hands and teach students how to destroy the opponent's root, center, and balance. Actual combat in *Taijiquan* has lost its meaning.

In this chapter, though you will see some introduction to Cavity Grabbing or Striking, it is not intended to teach you and make you become a proficient *Taiji* Cavity Press expert. In the second section of this chapter, some common hand forms for Cavity Press in *Taijiquan* will also be summarized. Finally, in the third section, those *Qin Na* applications and cavity attacks for the *Taijiquan* postures will be discussed.

5-2. Hand Forms for Cavity Press

In this section, we will summarize some of the hand forms which are commonly used in *Taiji* Cavity Press. Since we do not intend to discuss this subject at an in-depth and profound level, we will not include how to condition the hand forms, the herbs required for training, and the most important part of the cavity press - the detailed skills and timing of striking. The reason for this is simply that it would take another entire book to discuss these subjects.

A. Hand Forms of Cavity Grabbing

1. Crane Claw (Figure 5-1)
2. Eagle Claw (Figure 5-2)
3. Double Finger Grabbing

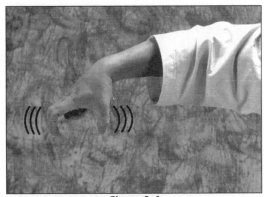

Figure 5–1

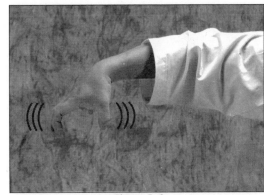

Figure 5–2

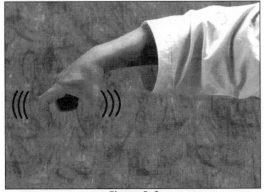

Figure 5–3

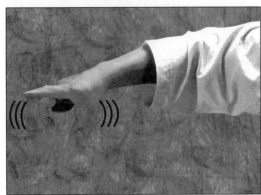

Figure 5–4

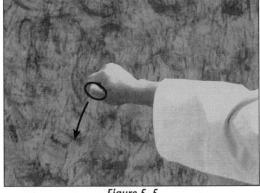

Figure 5–5

Figure 5–6

    a. Thumb and Index Finger (Figure 5-3)
    b. Thumb and Middle Finger (Figure 5-4)

B. Hand Forms for Cavity Striking

1. Thumb
    a. Knuckle of Thumb (Figure 5-5)
    b. Tip of Thumb (Figure 5-6)

2. Finger Tips
    a. Crane Beak (Figure 5-7)
    b. Eagle Beak (Figure 5-8)

Figure 5–7

Figure 5–8

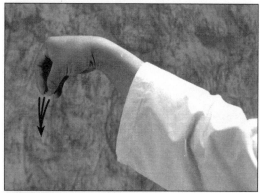

Figure 5–9

Figure 5–10

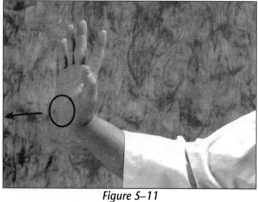

Figure 5–11

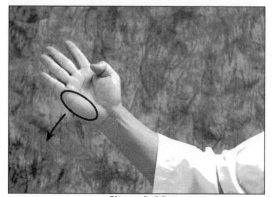

Figure 5–12

    c. Finger Tip Hand (Figure 5-9)

    d. Sword Secret Hand (Figure 5-10)

3. Palm

    a. Base of Palm (Figure 5-11)

    b. Edge of Palm (Figure 5-12)

4. Fist

    a. Horizontal Fist (Figure 5-13)

    b. Vertical Fist (Figure 5-14)

    c. Back of Fist (Figure 5-15)

    d. Phoenix Eye Fist (Figures 5-16 and 5-17)

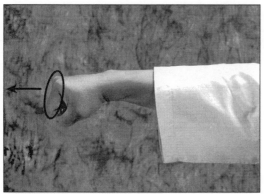

Figure 5–13

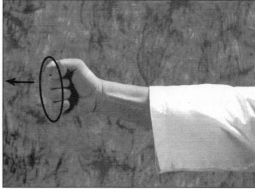

Figure 5–14

Figure 5–15

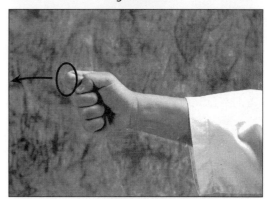

Figure 5–16

Figure 5–17

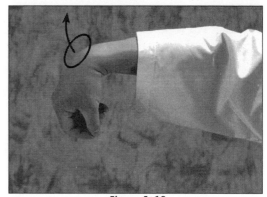

Figure 5–18

5. Wrist

    a. Top Side of Wrist (Figure 5-18)

6. Elbow

    a. External Side of Elbow (Figure 5-19)

7. Foot

    a. Top of Foot (Figure 5-20)

    b. Heel (Figure 5-21)

    c. Side of Foot (Figure 5-22)

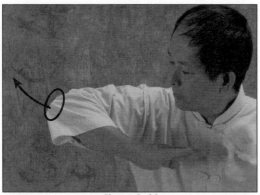

Figure 5–19

Figure 5–20

Figure 5–21

Figure 5–22

5-3. Qin Na and Cavity Press in Taiji Postures

The first movement, **Taiji Beginning** (*Taiji Qi Shi*) does not have actual combat applications. This movement is to coordinate the mind, leading the *Qi* to the Lower *Dan Tian*. Therefore, often this form is also called "**Sink *Qi* to *Dan Tian***" (*Qi Chen Dan Tian*). It is a preparatory movement which can bring the mind to your center and sink the *Qi* firmly to the Lower *Dan Tian*.

In addition, there are no combat applications for the last movement of *Taijiquan*. This movement is commonly named "**Returning the *Taiji* to Its Origin**" (*Taiji Huan Yuan*) or "**Lead the *Qi* to Return to Its Origin**" (*Yin Qi Gui Yuan*). From the name, you can see that after practicing the entire *Taiji* form, this movement is again used to return the *Qi* to its origin—the Lower *Dan Tian*.

1. GRASP SPARROW'S TAIL (*Lan Qiu Wei, You*) 攬雀尾

A. RIGHT (*You*) 右

Movements:

Turn your body to your right, move your right hand up with your left hand slightly touching the middle portion of your right forearm (Figure 5-23).

Analysis:

This is an action of *Peng*. The right arm is used as *Peng* to neutralize the oncoming attack upward, and the left hand is used to support the right arm to enhance its neutralizing strength.

| Figure 5-23 | Figure 5-24 | Figure 5-25 |

| Figure 5-26 | Figure 5-27 | Figure 5-28 |

Qin Na:

Technique #1: Wardoff Upward the Opponent's Elbow

(Shang Peng Di Zhou) 上掤敵肘

In this technique, your left hand is used to Pluck (*Cai*) your opponent's wrist while your right arm is wardingoff upward to lock his elbow (Figures 5-24 and 5-25).

Technique #2: Backward Upward Turning

(Hou Shang Fan) 後上翻

This posture is used to neutralize the opponent's attack first, then follow with *Qin Na*. First, use your right forearm to wardoff the opponent's attack upward and to your right (Figure 5-26). Immediately step your right leg to his right, and use your left hand to grab his right hand while circling your right elbow until it reaches his elbow (Figure 5-27). Finally, twist his wrist with your left hand while lifting his elbow upward with your right elbow (Figure 5-28). Alternatively, you may step your left leg behind him, and lock his

143

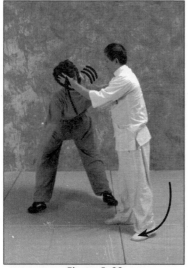

Figure 5–29

Figure 5–30

Figure 5–31

Figure 5–32

Figure 5–33

right arm with your right hand and chest area while using your left arm to push the upper part of his head forward (Figures 5-29 and 5-30).

Technique #3: Small Elbow Wrap

(Xiao Chan Zhou) 小 纏 肘

Again, first use your right forearm to upward wardoff your opponent's right hand attack (Figure 5-31). Next, step your left leg to the front of his right leg, and hook and grab his right wrist with your right hand while placing your left forearm upward against his elbow (Figure 5-32). Then, bow forward, using the leverage of your left forearm and right hand to bend his arm and circle forward (Figure 5-33). Finally, pull his body to your front while sweeping your left leg backward to make him fall (Figure 5-34).

| Figure 5–34 | Figure 5–35 | Figure 5–36 |

Figure 5–37

Technique #4: Arm Wraps Around the Dragon's Neck

(Bi Chan Long Jing) 臂纏龍頸

Again, first use your right forearm to upward wardoff your opponent's right hand attack (Figure 5-35). Next, immediately hook your right hand down and grab his right wrist, and step your left leg behind his right leg while using your left forearm to push his neck backward (Figure 5-36). Finally, lock his right arm with your chest and right hand while circling your left arm around his neck to lock him up (Figure 5-37).

From the above four examples, you can see that there are limited techniques which can be used directly from this posture. However, you will not be surprised to learn that this posture was originally designed to neutralize the opponent's attack or to set up and create an opportunity for the following technique.

Cavity Press or Strike:

When you use your right arm to wardoff the oncoming attack, you have exposed many of your opponent's cavities under his right arm (Figure 5-38). This will offer you a great opportunity for the following attacks (Figures 5-39 and 5-40).

Figure 5–38 *Figure 5–39* *Figure 5–40*

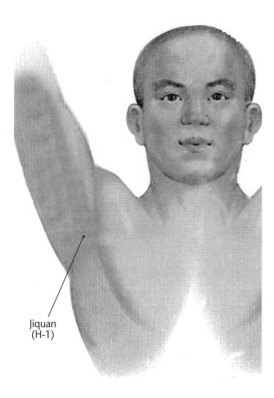

Figure 5–41

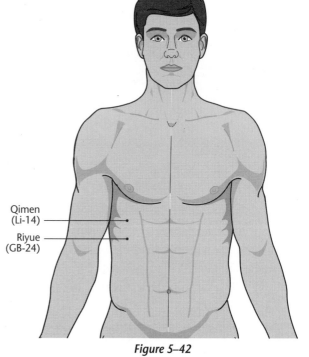

Figure 5–42

Cavity Name	Hand Form(s)	Possible Results
Jiquan (H-1)(Figure 5-41)	Sword Secret	Cause Heart Attack
Qimen (Li-14)(Figure 5-42)	Phoenix Eye Fist	Seal the Breath and Shock the Liver
Riyue (GB-24)(Figure 5-42)	Phoenix Eye Fist	Seal the Breath and Shock the Liver

Figure 5–43

Figure 5–44

B. Left *(Zuo)* 左

Movements:

From last posture, move both of your hands toward the center of your body and center yourself (Figure 5-43). Then, move your right hand downward while **Rending (*Lie*)** your left forearm upward and diagonally to your left (Figure 5-44).

Analysis:

This action is a movement of *Lie*. This posture is commonly used right after Grasp Sparrow's Tail (Right). The power of *Lie* on your left arm is generated from the balancing force of your right leg and right arm. One of the main forces is from the expanding of the chest, which is one of the two major bows in the body able to generate great power. The other bow is the torso.

Qin Na:

Technique #1: Carry a Pole on the Shoulder

(Jian Tiao Bian Dan) 肩挑扁擔

After your right arm has wardedoff your opponent's right hand attack, immediately hook his arm down and grab his wrist while using your left arm to push his right post-arm (Figure 5-45). Next, turn his right arm until his palm is facing upward while using your left shoulder to lift his post-arm upward from the tendons (Figure 5-46).

Cavity Press or Strike:

Once you step your left leg behind his right leg, you have changed the distance, allowing you to use your elbow to strike the cavities. Generally, striking power generated from the elbow is much stronger than that of the fist (Figure 5-47). When you attack, if possible, you should pull his right arm backward. This will enhance the striking power.

Figure 5–45

Figure 5–46

Figure 5–47

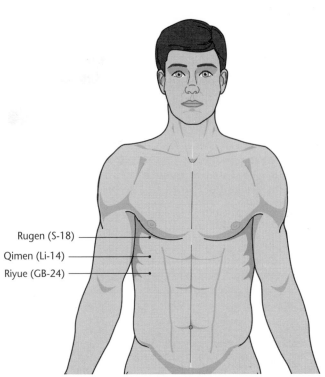

Rugen (S-18)
Qimen (Li-14)
Riyue (GB-24)

Figure 5–48

Figure 5–49

Other than striking cavities, you may also use your left fist to strike upward to his nose or downward to his groin.

Cavity Name	Hand Form(s)	Possible Results
Rugen (S-18)(Figure 5-48)	Elbow	Seal the Breath
Qimen (Li-14)(Figure 5-48)	Elbow	Seal the Breath and Shock the Liver
Riyue (GB-24)(Figure 5-48)	Elbow	Seal the Breath and Shock the Liver

| *Figure 5–50* | *Figure 5–51* | *Figure 5–52* |

2. WARDOFF *(Peng)* 掤

Movements:

First you move your left arm upward with the fingers upward and the palm facing your face. Then rotate your left hand clockwise while turning your body to your left (Figure 5-49). While you are doing so, also draw your right leg back to your left leg while moving your right arm down and toward your body. Next, step your right leg forward while pressing your left hand down and lifting your right forearm upward and forward (Figure 5-50).

Analysis:

When *Peng* is used for striking, the entire forearm is used to uproot the opponent or bounce him off his balance. Since the forearm cannot generate sharp pointing pressure or penetrating power, it cannot be used for cavity striking. Normally, after you have used your left forearm to neutralize the oncoming attack (Figure 5-51), use your right forearm to push his chest forward or upward (Figure 5-52). In fact, as explained in Chapter 2, *Peng* is also commonly used as a defensive action for neutralization.

Qin Na:

Please refer to Chapter 3.

Cavity Press or Strike:

None.

Figure 5–53

Figure 5–54

3. ROLLBACK *(Lu)* 擺

Movements:

The movement is normally from the posture from which one of your arms has already extended forward (Figure 5-53). Then, you sit backward and change your stance from Bow-Arrow Stance into Four-Six Stance, while moving both of your hands backward and to the side (Figure 5-54).

Analysis:

Lu is commonly used to yield, lead, and neutralize the opponent's power. Although it is commonly considered a defensive action, you should understand that when the situation allows, *Lu* can be used for offense.

Qin Na:

Please refer to Chapter 3.

Cavity Press or Strike:

When you rollback, in order to immobilize your opponent's arm, your left hand and right hand can grab and press three cavities (Figure 5-55).

Cavity Name	**Hand Form(s)**	**Possible Results**
Shaohai (H-3)(Figure 5-56)	Fingers	Cause Numbness
Quchi (LI-11)(Figure 5-56)	Fingers	Cause Numbness
Neiguan (P-6)(Figure 5-56)	Fingers	Cause Numbness or Fainting

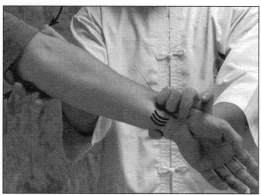

Figure 5-55

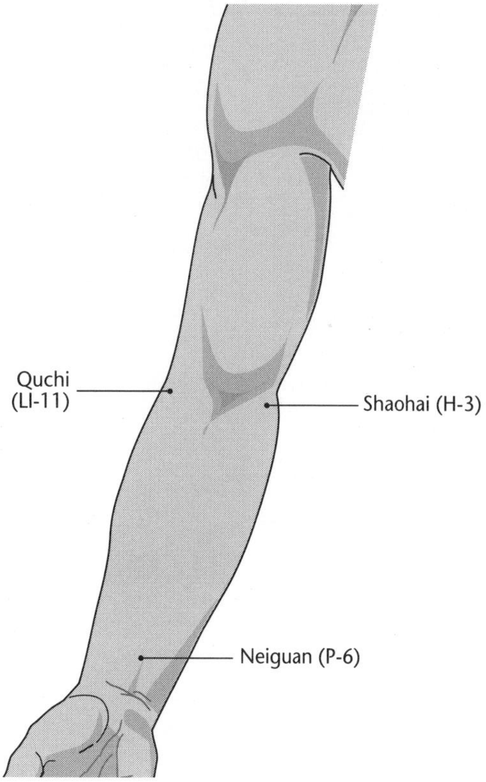

Quchi
(LI-11)

Shaohai (H-3)

Neiguan (P-6)

Figure 5-56

Figure 5-57

4. PRESS OR SQUEEZE *(Ji)* 擠

Movements:

In *Taijiquan* posture, when *Ji* is executed, the left hand is on the wrist area of the right hand and is pressing forward (Figure 5-57).

Analysis:

Ji can be used for both defense and offense. When *Ji* is used for defense, it is commonly executed with both hands squeezing toward each other. However, when *Ji* is used for attacking, it can be done by either squeezing both hands toward each other or pressing forward. In the *Taijiquan* sequence, it is commonly executed as forward pressing.

Qin Na:

Please refer to Chapter 3.

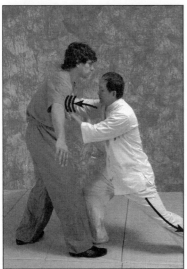

Figure 5–58

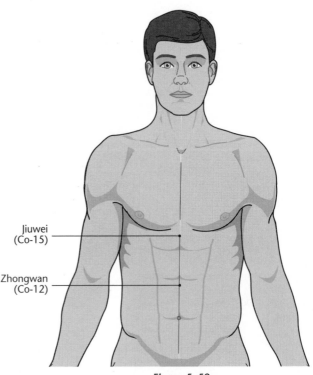

Jiuwei
(Co-15)

Zhongwan
(Co-12)

Figure 5–59

Cavity Press or Strike:

When you have a chance, use your left hand to press against your right wrist. You may then either press your opponent's chest or even use Jerking Jin to strike him (Figure 5-58).

Cavity Name	Hand Form(s)	Possible Results
Jiuwei (Co-15)(Figure 5-59)	Wrist	Seal the Breath or Heart Attack
Zhongwan (Co-12)(Figure 5-59)	Wrist	Seal the Breath and Vomiting

5. SETTLE DOWN THE WRIST *(An)* 按

Movements:

First, you sit backward into a Four-Six Stance while raising both of your arms up (Figure 5-60). Then, start to shift your weight to your front leg, and change into Bow-Arrow Stance while pointing your fingers forward. Finally, right before both of your hands reach to their maximum extension, settle your wrists down and press forward (Figure 5-61).

Analysis:

An can be used to seal the movement of your opponent's arm (Figure 5-62). It can also be used to neutralize the opponent's oncoming attack upward (Figure 5-63), and then to strike his chest area either with a single palm or double palms (Figure 5-64).

Figure 5–60

Figure 5–61

Figure 5–62

Figure 5–63

Figure 5–64

Qin Na:

Please refer to Chapter 3.

Cavity Press or Strike:

When *An* is used to attack, you can either use single or double hands to strike the cavity. In fact, the palm strike is one of the most common attacking techniques in *Taijiquan*. There are many cavities which can be used for palm striking. We will only introduce some of the typical ones.

Cavity Name	Hand Form(s)	Possible Results
Ruzhong (S-17)(Figure 5-65)	Palm	Seal the Breath
Rugen (S-18)(Figure 5-65)	Palm	Seal the Breath
Jiuwei (Co-15)(Figure 5-65)	Palm	Seal the Breath or Heart Attack
Zhongwan (Co-12)(Figure 5-65)	Palm	Seal the Breath and Vomiting

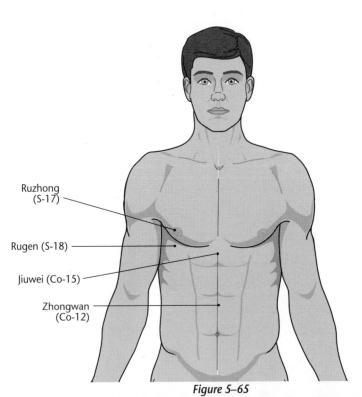

Ruzhong
(S-17)

Rugen (S-18)

Jiuwei (Co-15)

Zhongwan
(Co-12)

Figure 5–66

Figure 5–65

Figure 5–67

Figure 5–68

Figure 5–69

6. SINGLE WHIP *(Dan Bian)* 單鞭

Movement:

This posture includes three movements. In the first movement, both of your hands are in front of your waist area and you use your body's turning momentum to move the hands to your left (Figure 5-66). The second movement is moving your left hand down to face the right palm (Figure 5-67) and then coiling your right arm upward and backward (Figure 5-68). Thirdly, turn your body to your left, deflect your left arm to the left (Figure 5-69), and then step your left leg forward while pushing *(An)* your left hand forward (Figure 5-70).

Figure 5–70

Figure 5–71

Figure 5–72

Figure 5–73

Analysis:

The first movement is the body's rotational movement. From the body's rotational momentum, the swinging power of the arms is generated. The second movement is from the coiling action of the right arm; the opponent's power is led upward and neutralized. Finally, the last movement is the action of *An* which is applied to your opponent's chest.

Qin Na:

Technique #1: Use Both Hands to Lead the Cow

(Shuang Shou Qian Niu) 雙手牽牛

In this *Qin Na*, the first movement of Single Whip, the rotation, is adopted. When you have a chance to use your left hand to grab your opponent's left wrist, immediately use your right hand to lock and press his elbow (Figure 5-71). You can then lead him down to the ground or break his elbow.

Technique #2: Diagonal Flying

(Xie Fei Shi) 斜飛式

This *Qin Na* uses the second movement of Single Whip, coiling, to execute the technique. When your opponent uses his right hand to punch you, coil your right hand around his right wrist (Figure 5-72). Next, grab his right wrist with your right hand, step your left leg behind his right leg, and use your left arm to push against his neck while locking his right arm in front of your chest (Figure 5-73).

| Figure 5–74 | Figure 5–75 | Figure 5–76 |

Technique #3: Roast Peking Duck

(Bei Ping Kao Ya) 北平烤鴨

From the same situation, when your opponent punches you with his right fist, immediately intercept with your left forearm and circle around his wrist and grab it (Figure 5-74). While you are doing so, also move your left hand upward to keep his right arm bent. Then, rotate his right palm until his palm faces upward and use your left and right hands to lock his arm upward (Figure 5-75).

Cavity Press or Strike:

In the first movement, you are grabbing and leading his arm. In this grabbing, three cavities are usually used. In the final movement, it is an action of *An*. The common places for executing this *An* are on the chest area (Figure 5-76).

Cavity Name	Hand Form(s)	Possible Results
Shaohai (H-3)(Figure 5-77)	Fingers	Cause Numbness
Quchi (LI-11)(Figure 5-77)	Fingers	Cause Numbness
Neiguan (P-6)(Figure 5-77)	Fingers	Cause Numbness or Fainting
Ruzhong (S-17)(Figure 5-78)	Palm	Seal the Breath
Rugen (S-18)(Figure 5-78)	Palm	Seal the Breath

7. LIFT HANDS AND LEAN FORWARD *(Ti Shou Shang Shi)* 提手上勢

Movements:

First, move both of your hands toward your center (Figure 5-79), then extend your right arm up and out while stepping your right leg forward and touch the ground with your heel (Figure 5-80).

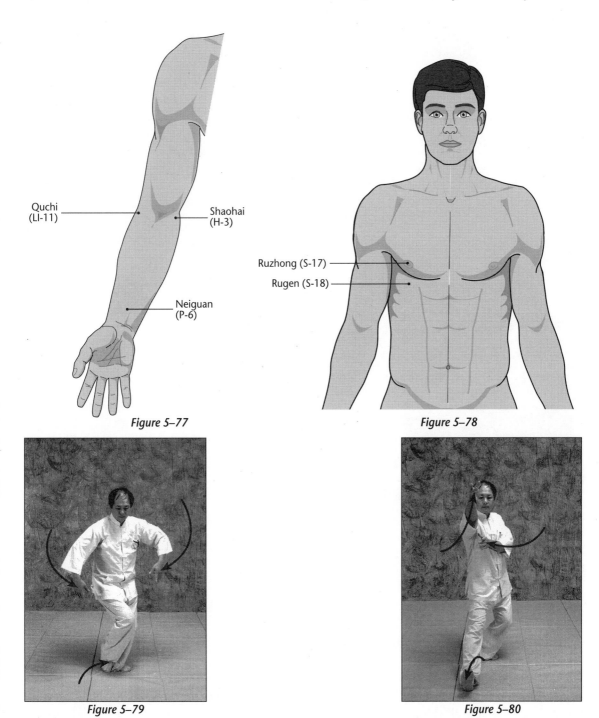

Quchi
(LI-11)

Shaohai
(H-3)

Neiguan
(P-6)

Figure 5–77

Ruzhong (S-17)

Rugen (S-18)

Figure 5–78

Figure 5–79

Figure 5–80

Analysis:

In this posture, the right arm's upward and forward lifting is used to intercept the attack, and the right leg is used to kick the opponent's knee or groin. In addition, the left hand on the front of the chest is ready for an attack.

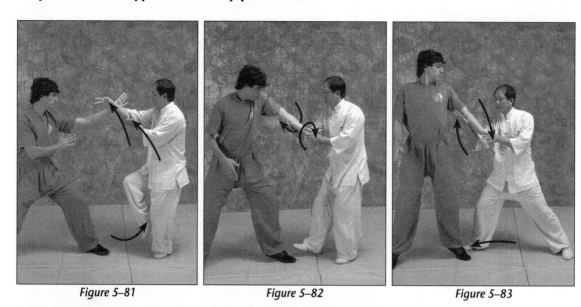

Figure 5–81   Figure 5–82   Figure 5–83

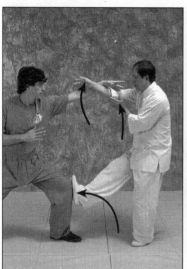   

Figure 5–84   Figure 5–85

Qin Na:

Technique #1: Heaven King Supports the Pagoda

(Tian Wang Tuo Ta) 天王托塔

When your opponent punches you with his left fist, immediately raise your right arm up to intercept his attack (Figure 5-81). Next, coil your left arm up to his elbow while using your left hand to grab his left wrist (Figure 5-82). Finally, step your right leg beside his left leg, and use the leverage generated from both of your hands to lock him up (Figure 5-83).

Cavity Press or Strike:

The right arm's upward and forward movement is an interception. The right leg's movement was designed to either kick the knee or groin (Figure 5-84). The left hand hidden underneath the right elbow is for a follow-up attack (Figure 5-85).

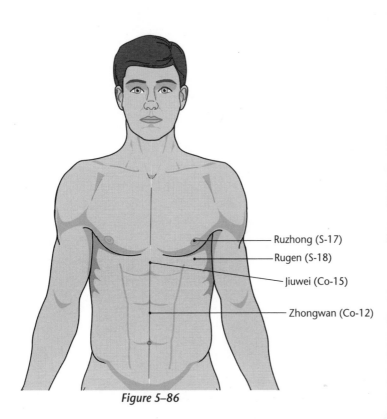

Figure 5-86

Figure 5-87

Figure 5-88

In Figure 5-86:
- Ruzhong (S-17)
- Rugen (S-18)
- Jiuwei (Co-15)
- Zhongwan (Co-12)

Cavity Name	Hand Form(s)	Possible Results
Ruzhong (S-17)(Figure 5-86)	Palm or Fist	Seal the Breath
Rugen (S-18)(Figure 5-86)	Palm or Fist	Seal the Breath
Jiuwei (Co-15)(Figure 5-86)	Palm or Fist	Seal the Breath or Heart Attack
Zhongwan (Co-12)(Figure 5-86)	Palm or Fist	Seal the Breath and Vomiting

8. THE CRANE SPREADS ITS WINGS *(Bai He Liang Chi)* 白鶴亮翅

Movements:

First, move both of your hands toward your center (Figure 5-87), then open them outward while touching the ground with your left toes (Figure 5-88).

Analysis:

This posture includes two movements; one is closing and the other is opening. The movement is generated from the chest instead just the arms. Therefore, the upward spreading has a feeling of **Wardoff (Peng)**. The stance on your left leg is called False Stance, because it can be used for easy and sudden kicks.

Figure 5–89

Figure 5–90

Figure 5–91

Figure 5–92

Figure 5–93

Figure 5–94

Qin Na:

Technique #1: Left Right Cross Elbow

(Zuo You Jiao Zhou) 左右交肘

When your opponent punches you with his right fist, first intercept it with your right hand (Figure 5-89) and then pluck it down (Figure 5-90). In this situation, it is very easy for your opponent to attack you with his left hand (Figure 5-91). When this happens, immediately use your left forearm to intercept his left hand punch and pluck it down, then rotate both of his arms to lock him up (Figure 5-92).

Technique #2: The Crane Spreads Its Wings

(Bai He Liang Chi) 白鶴亮翅

When your opponent punches you with his right fist, first use your left hand to cover his punch (Figure 5-93). Next, grab his right wrist with your left hand and immediately use

Figure 5–95

Figure 5–96

Figure 5–97

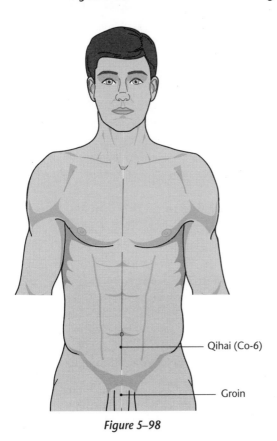

Qihai (Co-6)

Groin

Figure 5–98

both hands to twist his wrist counter-clockwise (Figure 5-94). Finally, continue your left hand's twisting while using your right forearm to push his neck to your right (Figure 5-95). This will offer you good leverage for locking.

Cavity Press or Strike:

The arms' closing and opening is used to seal or to lock. There is no striking purpose. However, from the arms' closing and opening, you may have set up a chance for your kicking (Figure 5-96). Your left leg is then used to kick the lower part of his body (Figure 5-97).

Cavity Name	Hand Form(s)	Possible Results
Qihai (Co-6)(Figure 5-98)	Heel	Death
Groin (Organ)(Figure 5-98)	Toes or Heel	Death

| Figure 5–99 | Figure 5–100 | Figure 5–101 |

9. BRUSH KNEE AND STEP FORWARD (Lou Xi Yao Bu) 摟膝拗步

Movements:

First you turn your body to your right while rotating your right hand clockwise and also pushing your left forearm to your right (Figure 5-99). Next, step your left leg forward and coil your left hand downward (Figure 5-100). Finally, use your right hand to Press Forward (*An*) (Figure 5-101).

Analysis:

This posture includes two major parts. The first part is the neutralization and then coiling down the left arm, and the second part is the right hand's *An*.

Qin Na:

Technique #1: Reverse Elbow Wrap

(Fan Chan Zhou) 反纏肘

This technique uses the first part of the postural movement. When your opponent punches you with his right fist, first intercept with your right forearm while using your left forearm to seal his right elbow (Figure 5-102). Next, step your left leg behind his right leg while coiling your left hand around his right arm until it reaches his post-arm near the elbow (Figure 5-103). Finally, use the leverage generated from your left elbow and hand to press and circle him down to the ground (Figure 5-104).

Technique #2: Small Elbow Wrap

(Xiao Chan Zhou) 小纏肘

In the same situation as the last one, again use your right forearm to intercept the attack while using your left forearm to seal his elbow (Figure 5-105). Next, step your left leg to the front of his right leg, grabbing his right wrist with your right hand and pressing

Figure 5–102

Figure 5–103

Figure 5–104

Figure 5–105

Figure 5–106

Figure 5–107

his elbow down with your left hand (Figure 5-106). Finally, sweep your left leg backward while using the leverage generated from your right hand and left forearm to swing him down to the ground (Figure 5-107).

Technique #3: Both Hands Twist the Neck

(Shuang Shou Niu Jing) 雙手扭頸

In the same situation, right after you have neutralized his right hand's attack (Figure 5-108), step your left leg behind his right leg while moving your right hand to his chin and left hand behind his head (Figure 5-109). Then, use the leverage generated from both of your hands to break his neck (Figure 5-110).

Figure 5–108

Figure 5–109

Figure 5–110

Figure 5–111

Figure 5–112

Cavity Press or Strike:

Right after you have neutralized the oncoming attack (Figure 5-111), step your left leg behind his right leg to keep away from his left hand, while using your left hand to push the center of his back forward and using your right palm to strike his chest area (Figure 5-112). To obtain a better angle for the attack, you should focus on the front upper body area.

Cavity Name	Hand Form(s)	Possible Results
Tiantu (Co-22)(Figure 5-113)	Thumb	Seal the Breath
Yingchuang (S-16)(Figure 5-113)	Palm or Phoenix Eye Fist	Seal the Breath
Ruzhong (S-17)(Figure 5-113)	Palm or Phoenix Eye Fist	Seal the Breath
Rugen (S-18)(Figure 5-113)	Palm or Phoenix Eye Fist	Seal the Breath
Jiuwei (Co-15)(Figure 5-113)	Palm	Seal the Breath or Heart Attack
Zhongwan (Co-12)(Figure 5-113)	Palm	Seal the Breath and Vomiting

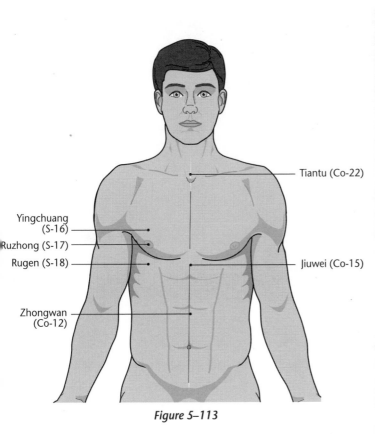

Tiantu (Co-22)

Yingchuang (S-16)

Ruzhong (S-17)

Rugen (S-18)

Jiuwei (Co-15)

Zhongwan (Co-12)

Figure 5–113

Figure 5–114

Figure 5–115

10. PLAY THE GUITAR *(Shou Hui Pi Pa)* 手揮琵琶

Movements:

First move your right leg next to your left leg while lifting your right arm upward (Figure 5-114). Next, step your left leg forward and enter a False Stance while moving your left hand under your right elbow, extending forward and moving your right hand to your left armpit area (Figure 5-115).

Analysis:

Your right arm's upward movement is used to neutralize the oncoming attack upward. Your left hand's following movement is to repel your opponent's arm to the side and your left leg's stepping is used for kicking. After your neutralization and repelling, your right hand is ready for further attack.

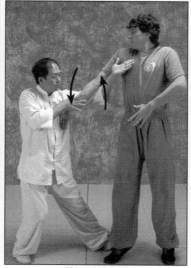

| Figure 5–116 | Figure 5–117 | Figure 5–118 |

Qin Na:

Technique #1: Heaven King Supports the Pagoda

(Tian Wang Tuo Ta) 天王托塔

When your opponent attacks you with his right hand, immediately use your right forearm to intercept his right forearm while placing your left forearm under his right elbow (Figure 5-116). Next, grab his right wrist with your right hand and use the leverage generated from your right hand and left forearm to lock his right elbow (Figure 5-117).

Alternatively, right after you have intercepted his right arm (Figure 5-118), you may also use your left hand to push his elbow upward to lock it (Figure 5-119).

Technique #2: Forward Upward Turning

(Qian Shang Fan) 前上翻

When your opponent punches you with his left hand, immediately step your right leg backward and lift your right arm upward to intercept his attack (Figure 5-120). Next, step your left leg behind his left leg, and use your left forearm to pull his left elbow toward you while pushing his wrist toward him with your right hand (Figure 5-121). Finally, lock his left arm with your left arm while pushing the upper back of his head forward to lock his arm firmly (Figure 5-122).

Cavity Press or Strike:

Right after you have neutralized the oncoming attack with your right arm (Figure 5-123), you can grab his right wrist with your right hand while locking his elbow with your left hand. From this situation, you may then kick the lower part of his body (Figure 5-124). Alternatively, you may step your left leg behind his right leg to avoid his left hand's attack while using your left hand to seal his elbow and using your right fist to attack him (Figure 5-125).

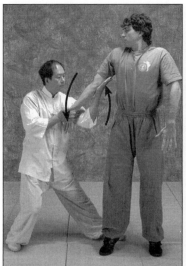

Figure 5-119

Figure 5-120

Figure 5-121

Figure 5-122

Figure 5-123

Figure 5-124

Figure 5-125

Figure 5–127

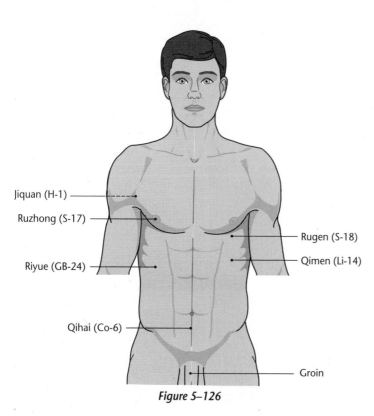

Jiquan (H-1)
Ruzhong (S-17)
Rugen (S-18)
Qimen (Li-14)
Riyue (GB-24)
Qihai (Co-6)
Groin

Figure 5–126

Cavity Name	Hand Form(s)	Possible Results
Qihai (Co-6)(Figure 5-126)	Heel	Death
Groin (Organ)(Figure 5-126)	Toes or Heel	Death
Jiquan (H-1)(Figure 5-126)	Sword Secret	Cause a Heart Attack
Ruzhong (S-17)(Figure 5-126)	Palm or Phoenix Eye Fist	Seal the Breath
Rugen (S-18)(Figure 5-126)	Palm or Phoenix Eye Fist	Seal the Breath
Qimen (Li-14)(Figure 5-126)	Phoenix Eye Fist	Seal the Breath and Shock the Liver
Riyue (GB-24)(Figure 5-126)	Phoenix Eye Fist	Seal the Breath and Shock the Liver

11. TWIST BODY AND CIRCLE FIST *(Pei Shen Chui)* 撇身捶

Movements:

First turn your body to your left while lowering your right arm and moving it toward your left (Figure 5-127). Next, turn your body to your right, circling your right arm upward and then downward (Figure 5-128). Finally, move your right hand to the side of your right waist while covering your left forearm downward (Figure 5-129).

Analysis:

Your right arm's downward movement is used to neutralize the lower attack to your left and the right arm's upward and forward circling is used to strike the opponent.

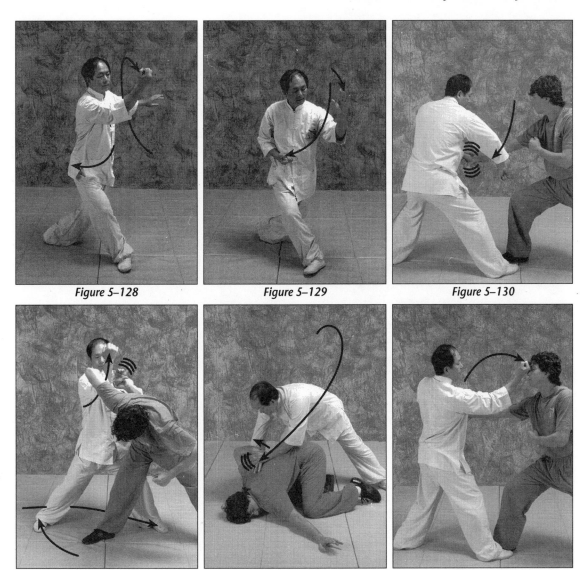

| Figure 5–128 | Figure 5–129 | Figure 5–130 |

| Figure 5–131 | Figure 5–132 | Figure 5–133 |

Qin Na:

Technique #1: Large Elbow Wrap

(Da Chan Zhou) 大纏肘

When your opponent attacks your lower body with his right hand, immediately use your right forearm to neutralize his attack to your left while also using your left hand to grab his right wrist (Figure 5-130). Next, reposition yourself while circling your right arm upward to bend his right arm (Figure 5-131). Finally, place your right hand on his post-arm near the elbow and use the leverage generated from both of your hands to lock him down to the ground (Figure 5-132).

Cavity Press or Strike:

After your right arm's neutralization, you can easily circle your right hand upward and then forward to strike him (Figure 5-133).

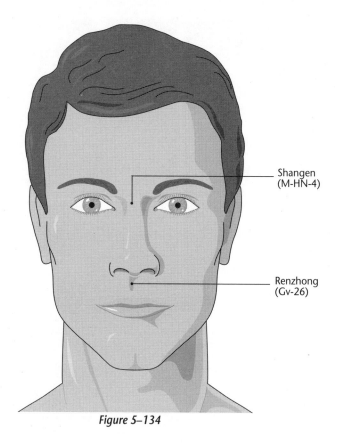

Shangen
(M-HN-4)

Renzhong
(Gv-26)

Figure 5–134

Figure 5–135

Figure 5–136

Cavity Name	**Hand Form(s)**	**Possible Results**
Shangen (M-HN-4)(Figure 5-134)	Back of Fist	Fainting, Nose Bleed
Renzhong (Gv-26)(Figure 5-134)	Back of Fist	Fainting

12. STEP FORWARD, DEFLECT DOWNWARD, PARRY AND PUNCH

(Shang Bu Ban Lan Chui) 上步扳攔捶

Movements:

First turn your body to your right while covering your left arm downward (Figure 5-135), then step your left leg forward while punching your right hand forward (Figure 5-136).

Analysis:

Your left arm's covering is used to neutralize the attack downward. Right after the neutralization, immediately punch your right fist forward for an attack.

Figure 5–137

Figure 5–138

Figure 5–139

Figure 5–140

Qin Na:

Technique #1: Step Forward and Deflect Downward

(Shang Bu Ban Zhou) 上步扳肘

When your opponent attacks you with his right fist, immediately intercept it with your right forearm and then grab his wrist while covering your left forearm on his elbow (Figure 5-137). Next, step your left leg behind his right leg, bow forward and use the leverage of both of your hands to lock his arm down to the ground (Figure 5-138).

Cavity Press or Strike:

Right after you cover his attack, you may continue to lead his right arm to your left while stepping your left leg behind his right leg to avoid his left hand's attack and using your right fist to attack his abdominal area (Figure 5-139) or the groin (Figure 5-140).

Figure 5–142

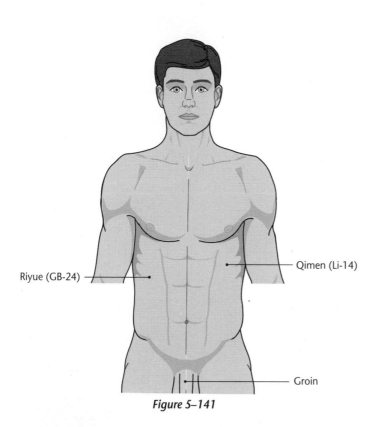

Riyue (GB-24)

Qimen (Li-14)

Groin

Figure 5–141

Cavity Name	Hand Form(s)	Possible Results
Qimen (Li-14)(Figure 5-141)	Fist	Seal the Breath and Shock the Liver
Riyue (GB-24)(Figure 5-141)	Fist	Seal the Breath and Shock the Liver
Groin (Organ)(Figure 5-141)	Palm	Death

13. SEAL TIGHTLY *(Ru Feng Si Bi)* 如封似閉

Movements:

First, slide your left hand inward along your right arm until you reach the right elbow (Figure 5-142), next coil to the bottom of the elbow and then outward (Figure 5-143). Keep extending your left hand forward while withdrawing your right hand and sitting back into Four-Six Stance (Figure 5-144). Finally, strike your right palm forward and change the stance into Bow-Arrow Stance (Figure 5-145).

Analysis:

This posture is designed for use against grabbing. While you try to free your right arm, you are also coiling your left hand around your right arm until you reach your opponent's body either to grab him or to lock him. This will provide you with an opportunity to attack.

Figure 5–143

Figure 5–144

Figure 5–145

Figure 5–146

Figure 5–147

Figure 5–148

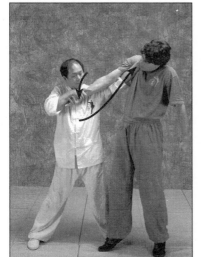

Figure 5–149

Qin Na:

Technique #1: Roast Peking Duck

(Bei Ping Kao Ya) 北平烤鴨

When your opponent uses his right hand to grab your right wrist (Figure 5-146), immediately circle your right hand counterclockwise to reverse the grabbing while extending your left hand under his right arm (Figure 5-147). Next, step your left leg behind his right leg, grab his right wrist and continue extending your left arm until it reaches his neck (Figure 5-148). Finally, rotate his arm until his palm is facing upward and press it downward while straightening out your left arm to lock him up (Figure 5-149).

Figure 5–150	Figure 5–151	Figure 5–152
Figure 5–153	Figure 5–154	Figure 5–155

Technique #2: Low Outward Wrist Press

(Xia Wai Ya Wan) 下外壓腕

Once you have an opportunity to grab your opponent's right wrist with your right hand, immediately move your left arm under his right arm (Figure 5-150). Next, step your left leg behind his right leg while coiling your left hand until it reaches his elbow (Figure 5-151). Finally, bend his wrist while continuing to lock his right elbow until his body is on the ground (Figure 5-152).

Cavity Press or Strike:

Your left hand's coiling is trying to reach your opponent to catch his arm while you try to free your right hand (Figure 5-153). Naturally, if you are able to lock his right arm, you may use your left hand to press the cavities beside his neck to seal his breath (Figure 5-154). Alternatively, right after you have grabbed his right arm with your left hand, you may immediately use your right hand to attack his chest area (Figure 5-155).

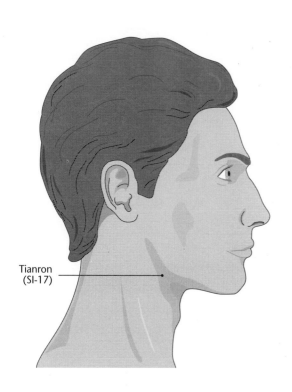

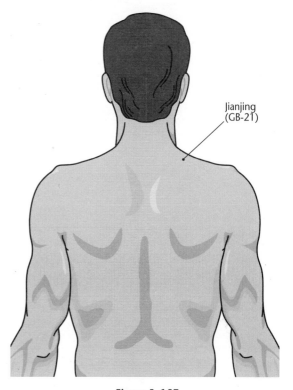

Tianron
(SI-17)

Jianjing
(GB-21)

Figure 5–156

Figure 5–157

Cavity Name	Hand Form(s)	Possible Results
Tianrong (SI-17)(Figure 5-156)	Thumb	Seal the Artery
Jianjing (GB-21)(Figure 5-157)	Grabbing	Fainting or Numbness
Ruzhong (S-17)(Figure 5-158)	Palm	Seal the Breath
Rugen (S-18)(Figure 5-158)	Palm	Seal the Breath
Qimen (Li-14)(Figure 5-158)	Fist	Seal the Breath and Shock the Liver
Riyue (GB-24)(Figure 5-158)	Fist	Seal the Breath and Shock the Liver

14. EMBRACE TIGER AND RETURN TO THE MOUNTAIN

(Bao Hu Gui Shan) 抱虎歸山

Movements:

Cross both of your arms in front of you until they are as high as your head (Figure 5-159). Next, squat your right leg downward and continue to circle both of your arms down (Figure 5-160). Finally, keep both of your arms in front of your chest and stand upward in a Horse Stance (Figure 5-161).

Analysis:

This is an opening and closing action in *Taijiquan*. These kinds of actions are commonly used to seal or to immobilize the arm movement of your opponent.

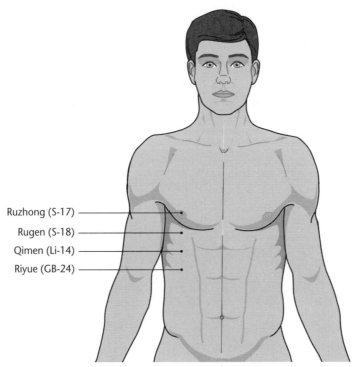

Ruzhong (S-17) ———
Rugen (S-18) ———
Qimen (Li-14) ———
Riyue (GB-24) ———

Figure 5–158

Figure 5–159

Figure 5–160

Figure 5–161

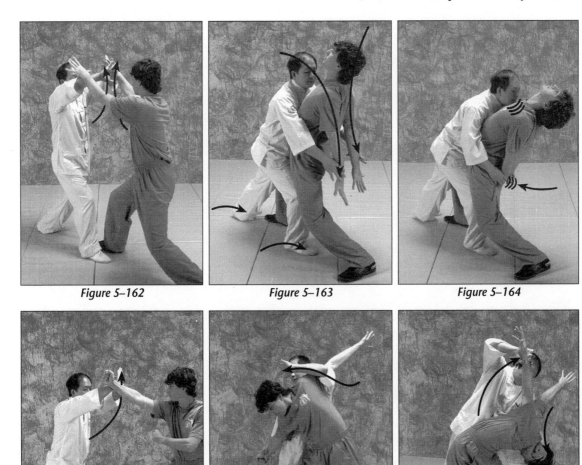

Figure 5–162

Figure 5–163

Figure 5–164

Figure 5–165

Figure 5–166

Figure 5–167

Qin Na:

Technique #1: Embrace Tiger and Return to the Mountain

(Bao Hu Gui Shan) 抱虎歸山

When your opponent tries to use both of his hands to grab you, immediately intercept his two arms upward (Figure 5-162). Next, step both of your legs in and get closer to him while circling both of his arms to his back (Figure 5-163). Finally, use your chin to press his right upper chest while holding both of his arms behind him (Figure 5-164).

Technique #2: Large Python Coils the Neck

(Da Mang Chan Jing) 大蟒纏頸

When your opponent punches you with his right arm, immediately use your right hand to seal the punch upward (Figure 5-165). Next, step your left leg behind him while inserting your left hand under his armpit and try to reach his neck (Figure 5-166). Finally, use your left hand to lock his neck while lifting his right arm upward (Figure 5-167).

Figure 5–168 Figure 5–169 Figure 5–170

Figure 5–171 Figure 5–172 Figure 5–173

Technique #3: Large Ape Bends the Branch *(Da Yuan Pan Zhi)* 大猿攀枝

Again, if your opponent uses his right fist to punch you, immediately intercept it with your right forearm and then pluck it down (Figure 5-168). In this case, it is very possible that your opponent will execute his second punch from his left hand. Once you notice this, immediately use your left forearm to intercept it upward and grab it (Figure 5-169). Next, step your left leg behind him and circle both of his arms behind him (Figure 5-170). Finally, use your right leg to push his sacrum forward to lock him in place (Figure 5-171).

Cavity Press or Strike:

The major part of this posture is the seal. Only at the end point of the action can it be used for grabbing or striking. For example, once you have sealed his right arm's attack (Figure 5-172), immediately step your left leg beside his right leg while using both of your hands to attack his groin area (Figure 5-173).

Cavity Name	**Hand Form(s)**	**Possible Results**
Groin (organ)	Grabbing	Death

Figure 5-174

Figure 5-175

Figure 5-176

Figure 5-177

Figure 5-178

15. FIST UNDER THE ELBOW (*Zhou Di Kan Chui*) 肘底看捶

Movements:

From Single Whip posture (Figure 5-174), move your right leg next to the left leg while moving your right hand above your head (Figure 5-175). Next, step your right leg to your right (Figure 5-176) and then shift your weight to your right leg, and at the same time cover your right arm downward (Figure 5-177). Finally, extend your left arm above your right hand while stepping your left leg forward into a False Stance (Figure 5-178).

Analysis:

This posture is a training for stepping into the opponent's left empty door. When stepping your right leg to your right and then turning to the left, you have occupied the space on your opponent's left hand side which allows you to attack. Your right hand's movement is to coordinate the stepping in protecting yourself, and your left hand's extending movement is for attacking. If you pay attention to the name of this posture, you can see that the meaning is "beware of the fist under the elbow." That means the right fist under your left elbow is used to attack.

| *Figure 5–179* | *Figure 5–180* | *Figure 5–181* |

Qin Na:

Technique #1: Left Right Cross Elbow

(Zuo You Jiao Zhou) 左右交肘

When your opponent attacks you with his right hand, first step your right leg to your right to dodge the attack while covering his forearm with your right arm (Figure 5-179). Next, grab his right wrist with your right hand and pull it down. This will offer your opponent an opportunity to execute his second punch with his left hand. In this case, raise your left arm up to block his punch while moving your left leg to your front (Figure 5-180). Finally, rotate both of his arms and use his right arm to lock his left arm in place (Figure 5-181). His left arm should be kept straight.

Technique #2: Twist the Wrist under the Elbow

(Zhou Di Zhi Wang) 肘底制腕

When you discover your opponent is extending his left hand to grab you, immediately cover his left fingers with your right hand and twist it counterclockwise (Figure 5-182). Then, step your left leg behind his left leg, continue to twist his left fingers and push them toward his armpit while using your left elbow to press his neck (Figure 5-183). This will cause great pain in his pinkie's tendon.

Technique #3: Daoist Greets with Hands

(Dao Zhi Zuo Ji) 道子作揖

This *Qin Na* uses the right hand's cover and left arm's lifting motion in the posture. When your opponent attacks you with his right hand, use your right forearm to intercept his right forearm while using your left forearm to intercept his right elbow (Figure 5-184). Then, step your left leg behind his right leg, press his forearm downward while using your left elbow to lift his elbow up to lock him (Figure 5-185).

Figure 5–182	*Figure 5–183*	*Figure 5–184*

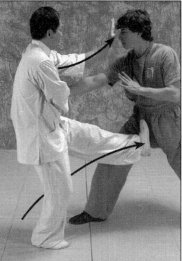

Figure 5–185	*Figure 5–186*	*Figure 5–187*

Cavity Press or Strike:

There are three attacking opportunities in this posture. The first one is the left leg's kicking. The second is normally the left hand's attack to his face (Figure 5-186). Normally, this face strike is a fake attack which is used to distract your opponent's attention or to tempt him to block upward. This will create an opportunity for the third attack, which is the hidden fist under the left elbow (Figure 5-187).

Cavity Name	**Hand Form(s)**	**Possible Results**
Qihai (Co-6)(Figure 5-188)	Heel	Death
Groin (Organ)(Figure 5-188)	Toes or Heel	Death
Tiantu (Co-22)(Figure 5-188)	Sword Secret	Seal the Breath
Jiuwei (Co-15)(Figure 5-188)	Palm or Fist	Seal the Breath or Heart Attack
Zhongwan (Co-12)(Figure 5-188)	Palm or Fist	Seal the Breath and Vomiting
Ruzhong (S-17)(Figure 5-188)	Palm or Phoenix Eye Fist	Seal the Breath
Rugen (S-18)(Figure 5-188)	Palm or Phoenix Eye Fist	Seal the Breath
Qimen (Li-14)(Figure 5-188)	Phoenix Eye Fist or Fist	Seal the Breath and Shock the Liver
Riyue (GB-24)(Figure 5-188)	Phoenix Eye Fist or Fist	Seal the Breath and Shock the Liver

Figure 5–189

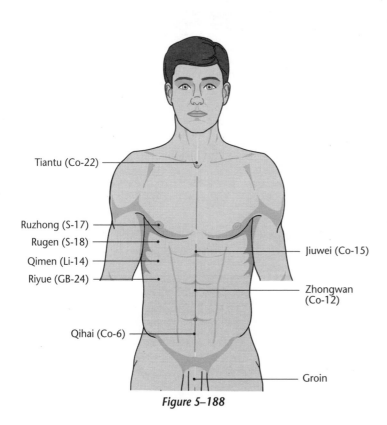

Tiantu (Co-22)

Ruzhong (S-17)
Rugen (S-18)
Qimen (Li-14)
Riyue (GB-24)

Jiuwei (Co-15)

Zhongwan
(Co-12)

Qihai (Co-6)

Groin

Figure 5–188

16. STEP BACK AND REPULSE MONKEY *(Dao Nian Hou)* 倒攆猴

Movements:

In the beginning posture your left hand extends forward, your right hand is on your right waist, and you are standing in a Four-Six Stance (Figure 5-189). Next, stand up with your right leg, and rotate your left hand until the palm is facing upward while circling your right hand to the right ear area (Figure 5-190). Then, turn your right foot until the toes are facing forward (Figure 5-191). Finally, step your left leg backward, pushing your right hand forward while pulling your left hand backward (Figure 5-192).

Analysis:

Your left hand's turning is against a grabbing. From this rotational action, you will be able to free your hand. Your stepping backward is used as a yield or withdrawal. Often, this stepping can also be used as a strategic movement. Naturally, your right hand's forward Pushing (*An*) is used for striking.

Qin Na:

Technique #1: Twist the Wrist and Push the Neck

(Niu Wan Tui Jing) 扭腕推頸

When your opponent punches you with his right fist, immediately step your right leg backward while using your left forearm to cover the punch (Figure 5-193). Next, move your left leg backward and move your right leg behind his right leg while using both hands to twist

Figure 5–190

Figure 5–191

Figure 5–192

Figure 5–193

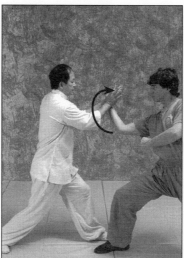

Figure 5–194

Figure 5–195

his right wrist (Figure 5-194). Finally, continue his wrist's twisting with your left hand while pushing your right hand against his neck (Figure 5-195). This will lock his arm in position.

Cavity Press or Strike:

Your left hand's twisting can either be used to escape from your opponent's grabbing or to control his wrist. Once you have controlled your opponent's wrist, then you will be able to use the other hand to attack the front of his body (Figure 5-196).

Cavity Name	Hand Form(s)	Possible Results
Tiantu (Co-22)(Figure 5-197)	Sword Secret	Seal the Breath
Jiuwei (Co-15)(Figure 5-197)	Palm or Fist	Seal the Breath or Heart Attack
Zhongwan (Co-12)(Figure 5-197)	Palm or Fist	Seal the Breath and Vomiting
Ruzhong (S-17)(Figure 5-197)	Palm or Phoenix Eye Fist	Seal the Breath
Rugen (S-18)(Figure 5-197)	Palm or Phoenix Eye Fist	Seal the Breath
Qimen (Li-14)(Figure 5-197)	Phoenix Eye Fist or Fist	Seal the Breath and Shock the Liver
Riyue (GB-24)(Figure 5-197)	Phoenix Eye Fist or Fist	Seal the Breath and Shock the Liver

Figure 5–196

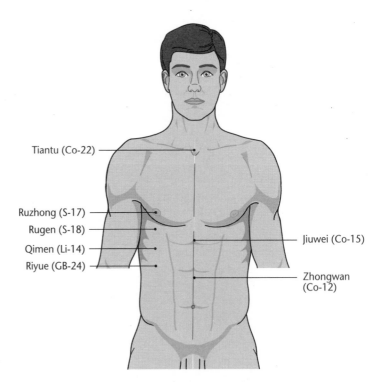

Tiantu (Co-22)

Ruzhong (S-17)

Rugen (S-18)

Qimen (Li-14)

Riyue (GB-24)

Jiuwei (Co-15)

Zhongwan (Co-12)

Figure 5–197

Figure 5–198

Figure 5–199

Figure 5–200

17. DIAGONAL FLYING (Xie Fei Shi) 斜飛勢

Movements:

Move your left leg back next to your right leg while circling your left hand down and your right hand up (Figure 5-198). Then step your left leg forward while splitting both of your arms diagonally (Figure 5-199).

| *Figure 5–201* | *Figure 5–202* | *Figure 5–203* |

Analysis:

This is a combination of **Wardoff (*Peng*)** and **Rend (*Lie*)**. The downward and upward diagonal movements are able to generate good leverage for the Rend power.

Qin Na:

Technique #1: Diagonal Flying to Support the Arm

(Xie Fei Cheng Bi) 斜飛撐臂

When your opponent punches you with his right hand, use your right hand to intercept and then coil to the right (Figure 5-200). Next, step your left leg behind his right leg, grab his right wrist and pull it down while using your left shoulder to lock his right postarm (Figure 5-201).

Cavity Press or Strike:

Your right hand's grabbing and pulling his right arm downward is to expose his head area to your attack (Figure 5-202). For example, when the throat is chopped, the breath can be sealed (Figure 5-203) and when the side of the neck is chopped, the artery can be sealed.

Cavity Name	Hand Form(s)	Possible Results
Throat	Edge of Palm	Seal the Breath
Futu (LI-18)(Figure 5-204)	Edge of Palm	Seal the Artery
Taiyang (M-HN-9)(Figure 5-204)	Phoenix Eye Fist	Death (Rupture the Artery)
Jiache (S-6)(Figure 5-204)	Back of Fist	Fainting

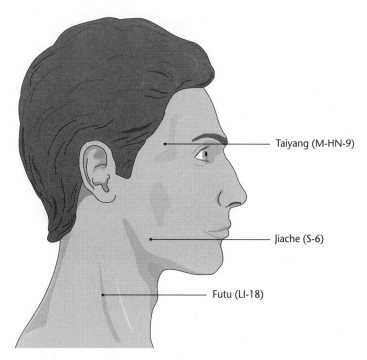

Figure 5–204

| Figure 5–205 | Figure 5–206 | Figure 5–207 |

18. PICK UP NEEDLE FROM SEA BOTTOM *(Hai Di Lao Zhen)* 海底撈針

Movements:

From the movement in which your right arm is pushing forward and your left hand is beside your left waist (Figure 5-205), move your left leg backward and enter a False Stance while lifting your right arm upward and your left hand in front of your chest (Figure 5-206). Finally, sink your right arm downward and at the same time squat into a low posture (Figure 5-207).

| *Figure 5–208* | *Figure 5–209* | *Figure 5–210* |

Analysis:

When your opponent is attacking your chest, use your right arm to intercept the attack upward to expose his lower body for your strike. Your left hand pushes his elbow to immobilize his arm's movement, which offers you an opportunity for your right hand attack. Often, after the right arm's upward intercepting, it is used to **Pluck (Cai)** the opponent's wrist and pull it down to expose his head or to make him lose balance.

Qin Na:

Technique #1: Upward Pushing Enemy's Elbow

(Shang Tui Di Zhou) 上推敵肘

When your opponent attacks you with his right hand, immediately withdraw your left leg while using your right arm to intercept the attack upward and your left hand to seal his elbow (Figure 5-208). Then, step your left leg forward and pull his right wrist down while pushing his elbow upward with your left hand (Figure 5-209). In this case, you have locked his right arm. Naturally, if you use power, you may break his elbow.

Technique #2: Step Forward and Deflect Downward

(Shang Bu Ban Zhou) 上步扳肘

When your opponent attacks you with his right fist, immediately intercept it with your right forearm and then grab his wrist while pushing your left hand upward on his elbow (Figure 5-210). Next, reposition yourself, bow forward and use the leverage of both of your hands to lock his arm down to the ground (Figure 5-211).

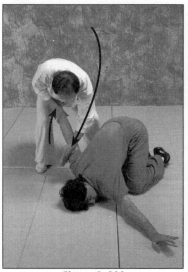
Figure 5–211

Figure 5–212

Figure 5–213

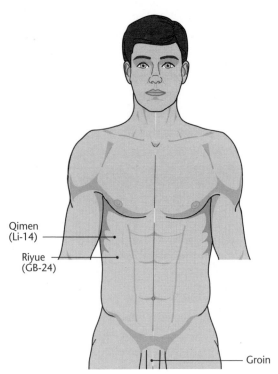

Qimen
(Li-14)

Riyue
(GB-24)

Groin

Figure 5–214

Cavity Press or Strike:

Right after you have intercepted your opponent's attack upward, you will have opened up many cavities on the forward right hand side of his body for your attack. This will naturally include the left leg's kicking to his knee (Figure 5-212). You may use your left hand to seal his right arm while using your right hand to attack the side of his body (Figure 5-213).

Cavity Name	Hand Form(s)	Possible Results
Qimen (Li-14)(Figure 5-214)	Fist	Seal the Breath and Shock the Liver
Riyue (GB-24)(Figure 5-214)	Fist	Seal the Breath and Shock the Liver
Groin (Organ)(Figure 5-214)	Palm	Death

| *Figure 5–215* | *Figure 5–216* | *Figure 5–217* |

19. FAN BACK *(San Tong Bei)* 扇通背

Movements:

First, move your left leg back and stand in False Stance while placing your left hand in front of you and your right hand above and in front of your head (Figure 5-215). Next, step your left leg forward and push both of your hands forward with your body (Figure 5-216).

Analysis:

The first movement is used for yielding and the second movement can be used either for sealing or for pushing.

Technique #1: Forward Upward Turning

(Qian Shang Fan) 前上翻

When your opponent punches you with his right hand, immediately step your left leg backward and lift your right arm upward to intercept his attack while using your left hand to seal his elbow (Figure 5-217). Next, step your left leg behind his right leg, and use your left forearm to pull his right elbow toward you while pushing his wrist toward him with your right hand (Figure 5-218). Finally, lock his right arm with your left arm while pushing the upper back of his head forward to lock his arm firmly (Figure 5-219).

Technique #2: Daoist Greets with Hands

(Dao Zhi Zuo Ji) 道子作揖

Again, when your opponent punches you with his right hand, withdraw your left leg while using your right forearm to intercept his attack upward and your left hand to seal his elbow (Figure 5-220). Then, use the leverage of your left and right hands to lock his right arm up (Figure 5-221).

Figure 5–218

Figure 5–219

Figure 5–220

Figure 5–221

Figure 5–222

Figure 5–223

Cavity Press or Strike:

When your opponent's arm is blocked upward, his armpit and the right hand side of his body will be exposed for your attack (Figure 5-222). Naturally, you may also use your left hand to grab the tendons under his armpit to numb his arm's movement (Figure 5-223).

Cavity Name	Hand Form(s)	Possible Results
Jiquan (H-1)(Figure 5-224)	Sword Secret	Cause a Heart Attack
Yuanye (GB-22)(Figure 5-224)	Phoenix Eye Fist	Seal the Breath
Dabao (Sp-21)(Figure 5-224)	Phoenix Eye Fist	Seal the Breath

20. WAVE HANDS IN THE CLOUDS (Yun Shou) 雲手

Movements:

First, turn your body to your right while pressing your left hand downward (Figure 5-

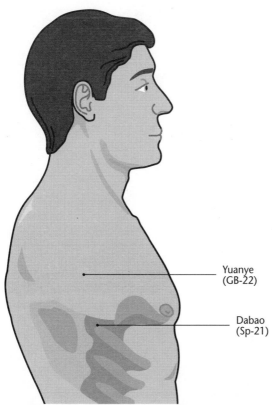

Yuanye
(GB-22)

Dabao
(Sp-21)

Figure 5–224

| *Figure 5–225* | *Figure 5–226* | *Figure 5–227* |

225). Next, raise your right forearm (Figure 5-226) and then turn your body to your right (Figure 5-227).

Analysis:

Both of your hands' actions are used to seal or to lock your opponent's arm. Your body's turning is to throw your opponent off balance or to break his elbow.

Figure 5–228

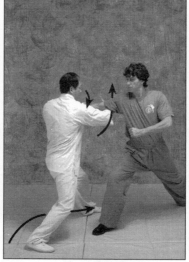

Figure 5–229

Figure 5–230

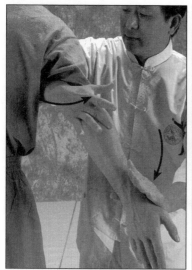

Figure 5–231

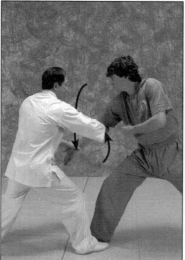

Figure 5–232

Figure 5–233

Qin Na:

Technique #1: Cloud Hands to Lock the Elbow

(Yun Shou Jia Zhou) 雲 手 架 肘

When your opponent attacks you with his right hand, immediately use your left forearm to intercept (Figure 5-228). Next, step your left leg to his right hand side while pressing his wrist down with your left hand and propping up his right post-arm or elbow with your right forearm (Figure 5-229). Finally, push his wrist forward, and pull his post-arm or elbow inward while pressing your right elbow to the side of his chest to lock him up (Figures 5-230 and 5-231).

| *Figure 5-234* | *Figure 5-235* | *Figure 5-236* |

Technique #2: Large Elbow Wrap

(Da Chan Zhou) 大纏肘

Again, if your opponent attacks you with his right hand, use your left forearm to intercept his punch and then press his arm downward while using your right hand to lock his elbow (Figure 5-232). Next, step your left leg behind his right leg and raise up your right arm to bend his right arm (Figure 5-233). Finally, step your right leg backward while using the leverage generated from both of your hands to lock him down to the ground (Figure 5-234).

Cavity Press or Strike:

Once you have locked your opponent's arm with both of your hands, you may also use your right elbow to strike the sides of his upper body (Figure 5-235). In addition, the lower section of his body will also be exposed for your knee attack (Figure 5-236).

Cavity Name	Hand Form(s)	Possible Results
Qihai (Co-6)(Figure 5-237)	Knee	Death
Groin (Organ)	Knee	Death
Yuanye (GB-22)(Figure 5-237)	Elbow	Seal the Breath
Dabao (Sp-21)(Figure 5-237)	Elbow	Seal the Breath

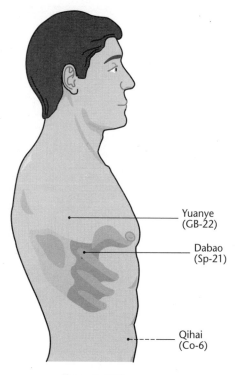

Yuanye
(GB-22)

Dabao
(Sp-21)

Qihai
(Co-6)

Figure 5–237

Figure 5–238

Figure 5–239

Figure 5–240

Figure 5–241

21. STAND HIGH TO SEARCH OUT THE HORSE *(Gao Tan Ma)* 高探馬

Movements:

Begin with your right hand pressing forward (Figure 5-238). Withdraw your left leg and stand in False stance, while moving your right hand to the front and slightly above your head, and your left hand in front of your chest (Figure 5-239).

Analysis:

This movement is just like the first movement of the Fan Back in Posture #19, which is used to neutralize the upper body attack (Figure 5-240). The left leg is set up for a kicking (Figure 5-241).

Figure 5–242

Figure 5–243

Qin Na:

Please refer to #19, Fan Back.

Cavity Press or Strike:

Please refer to #19, Fan Back.

22. TOE KICK *(Ti Tui)* 踢腿

Movements:

First, turn your body to your left while crossing your arms in front of your chest (Figure 5-242). Next, open both of your arms and kick your right toes out to your right (Figure 5-243).

Analysis:

The arms' closing and opening are used to intercept the opponent's attack upward, which will expose the opponent's middle and lower body to your kicking.

Qin Na:

No *Qin Na* applications.

Cavity Press or Strike:

Although the name is called Toe Kick in *Taijiquan*, if you use the toes to kick, the only place which you can attack is the groin. However, if you also use the side of your foot or your heel to kick, then you may kick the side of the ribs to rupture the liver.

Figure 5–245

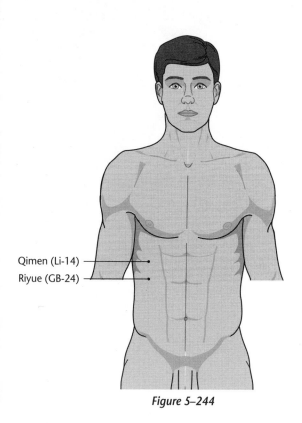

Qimen (Li-14)
Riyue (GB-24)

Figure 5–244

Figure 5–246

Cavity Name	Hand Form(s)	Possible Results
Qimen (Li-14)(Figure 5-244)	Side of Foot or heel	Seal the Breath and Rupture the Liver
Riyue (GB-24)(Figure 5-244)	Side of Foot or heel	Seal the Breath and Rupture the Liver
Groin (Organ)	Toes	Death

23. HEEL KICK *(Deng Tui)* 蹬腿

Movements:

First, cross both of your arms in front of your chest (Figure 5-245). Next, open both of your arms and kick your heel out in front of you (Figure 5-246).

Analysis:

Both of your hands are used to grab your opponent's arm or even clothes, and then the heel is used to kick the center of his body. Naturally, if the distance is too short, you may also use your knee to kick.

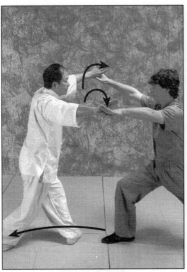

| *Figure 5–247* | *Figure 5–248* | *Figure 5–249* |

Qin Na:

Technique #1: Fair Lady Picks the Peach

(Xian Niu Zhai Tao) 仙女摘桃

When your opponent intends to use both of his hands to grab you or both palms to strike your chest, immediately step your right leg backward while using both of your hands to grab his fingers on both hands (Figure 5-247). Next, turn his left fingers clockwise and his right fingers counterclockwise, and bend them down (Figure 5-248). Naturally, under this locking situation, you may be able to use your right leg to kick him (Figure 5-249).

Cavity Press or Strike:

Once you have used both of your arms to intercept both of your opponent's hands, his lower body will be exposed for your kicking.

Cavity Name	Hand Form(s)	Possible Results
Zhongwan (Co-12)(Figure 5-250)	Heel	Seal the Breath and Vomiting
Qihai (Co-6)(Figure 5-250)	Heel	Death
Groin (Organ)	Heel	Death

Figure 5–251

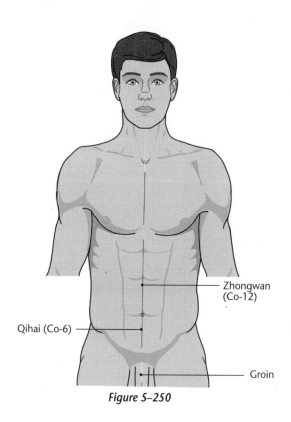

Zhongwan
(Co-12)

Qihai (Co-6)

Groin

Figure 5–250

Figure 5–252

24. STEP FORWARD AND STRIKE DOWN WITH THE FIST

(Jin Bu Zai Chui) 進步栽捶

Movements:

First, turn your body to your right while covering your left arm to your right (Figure 5-251). Next, step your left leg forward, repel your left arm to your left and down, while punching your right fist down (Figure 5-252).

Analysis:

Both of your hands are used to intercept the lower punch or kick. Naturally, your right fist is for attack.

Figure 5–253

Figure 5–254

Figure 5–255

Figure 5–256

Figure 5–257

Qin Na:

Technique #1: Two Children Worship the Buddha

(Shuang Tong Bai Fo) 雙童拜佛

When your opponent punches your lower body with his left fist, immediately use your left arm to neutralize his attack to your left (Figure 5-253). Next, step your right leg behind his right leg, and hook his left arm upward while inserting your right arm under his left armpit and reaching his abdomen area (Figure 5-254). Then you pull his left arm backward while pressing your right shoulder against his left shoulder, and push his left thigh with your left hand (Figure 5-255). Finally, use this leverage to circle him down to the ground (Figure 5-256).

Cavity Press or Strike:

Once you have used your left arm to clear his attack, you may use your right fist to attack the lower section of his body (Figure 5-257).

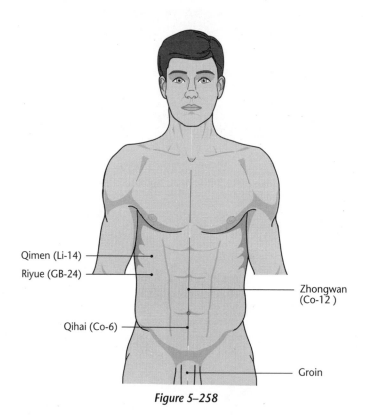

Figure 5–258

Cavity Name	Hand Form(s)	Possible Results
Qimen (Li-14)(Figure 5-258)	Fist	Seal the Breath and Rupture the Liver
Riyue (GB-24)(Figure 5-258)	Fist	Seal the Breath and Rupture the Liver
Zhongwan (Co-12)(Figure 5-258)	Fist	Seal the Breath and Vomiting
Qihai (Co-6)(Figure 5-258)	Fist	Death
Groin (Organ)	Fist	Death

25. STRIKE THE TIGER POSTURE *(Da Hu Shi)* 打虎勢

Movements:

First, move your right arm upward and to your right while shifting your body forward into Bow-Arrow Stance (Figure 5-259). Next, move your left arm under your right arm and extend it forward while withdrawing your right hand back to your right waist (Figure 5-260). Finally, squat down into the Taming the Tiger Stance while pulling your left arm back to your left, and strike with your right hand in a circular motion (Figure 5-261).

Analysis:

Your right arm's upward movement is for interception. Then, take this opportunity to grab his wrist with your left hand. Finally, pull him down with your left hand while using your right hand to strike.

Figure 5–259

Figure 5–260

Figure 5–261

Figure 5–262

Figure 5–263

Figure 5–264

Figure 5–265

Qin Na:

Technique #1: The Arm Locks the Python's Neck

(Bi Suo Mang Jing) 臂鎖蟒頸

When your opponent punches you with his left fist, first use your right arm to intercept the punch (Figure 5-262). Next, use your left hand to grab his left wrist (Figure 5-263). Then, reposition yourself behind him while circling your right arm around his neck (Figure 5-264). Finally, pull his left arm back while locking his neck with your right arm (Figure 5-265).

Figure 5–266

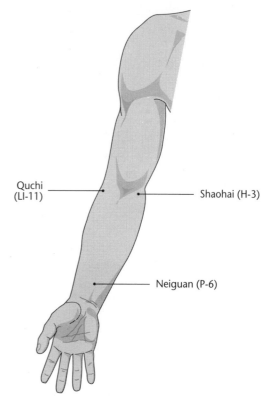

Figure 5–267

Cavity Press or Strike:

This technique aims at an attack on the side or the back of his body (Figure 5-266).

Cavity Name	Hand Form(s)	Possible Results
Shaohai (H-3)(Figure 5-267)	Fingers (Left)	Cause Numbness
Quchi (LI-11)(Figure 5-267)	Fingers (Left)	Cause Numbness
Neiguan (P-6)(Figure 5-267)	Fingers (Left)	Cause Numbness or Fainting
Naohu (Gv-17)(Figure 5-268)	Fist	Fainting, Shock the Brain
Tianzong (SI-11)(Figure 5-268)	Phoenix Eye Fist	Numbness
Lingtai (Gv-10)(Figure 5-268)	Fist	Death

26. TWO WINDS PASS THROUGH THE EARS

(Shuang Feng Guan Er) 雙風貫耳

Movements:

First, move your right leg back and stand in False Stance while lowering both of your arms in front of your chest (Figure 5-269). Then, circle both of your arms upward toward the center (Figure 5-270).

Analysis:

You move your right leg backward so you can yield your body backward easily. Both of your arms' downward motion is to protect or to seal the attack to your chest. Your right leg's False Stance can be used to kick anytime, since there is no weight on it. Finally, the arms' circling is to strike the opponent.

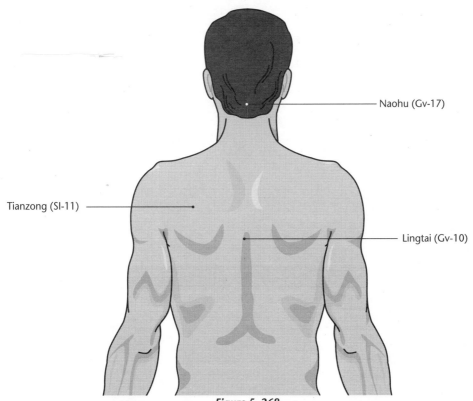

Figure 5–268

| *Figure 5–269* | *Figure 5–270* | *Figure 5–271* |

Qin Na:

Technique #1: Force the Bow

(Qiang Po Ju Gong) 強迫鞠躬

When your opponent attacks you with his right fist, immediately use your right hand to intercept the punch while stepping backward to yield (Figure 5-271). Next, step your left leg behind him, and circle your right hand around his right arm while inserting your

Figure 5–272

Figure 5–273

Figure 5–274

Figure 5–275

Taiyang (M-HN-9)

Ermen (TB-21)

Yifeng (TB-17)

Jiache (S-6)

Futu
(LI-18)

Figure 5–276

left arm under his left arm (Figure 5-272). Finally, use both of your hands to press the upper back of his head downward to lock his neck (Figure 5-273).

Cavity Press or Strike:

Once you have neutralized the opponent's attack, either by pressing it downward or by repelling to the side (Figure 5-274), immediately attack the cavities on his head and neck (Figure 5-275).

Cavity Name	Hand Form(s)	Possible Results
Yifeng (TB-17)(Figure 5-276)	Thumb Tip	Seal the Artery
Futu (LI-18)(Figure 5-276)	Thumb Tip	Seal the Artery
Taiyang (M-HN-9)(Figure 5-276)	Phoenix Eye Fist	Death (Rupture the Artery)
Ermen (TB-21)(Figure 5-276)	Knuckle of Thumb	Fainting
Jiache (S-6)(Figure 5-276)	Back of Fist	Fainting

Figure 5–277

Figure 5–278

27. WILD HORSES SHEAR THE MANE *(Ye Ma Fen Zong)* 野馬分鬃

Movements:

First, turn your body to your left, withdraw your right leg so that it is next to your left leg, move your left arm upward and then sideways while lowering your right arm down (Figure 5-277). Next, step your right leg forward while spreading both of your arms diagonally (Figure 5-278).

Analysis:

This is the movement of **Rend (Lie)**. Your right leg withdrawing is yielding to the opponent's attack. Your left hand's upward and sideways movement is for intercepting and neutralizing. Naturally, the spreading action is for an attack.

Qin Na:

Technique #1: Wild Horses Shear the Mane

(Ye Ma Fen Zong) 野馬分鬃

When your opponent punches you with his right fist, immediately withdraw your right leg back while using your left forearm to intercept and neutralize the attack (Figure 5-279). Then, step your right leg in while using your right forearm to lock the tendons of his post-arm (Figures 5-280 and 5-281).

Cavity Press or Strike:

Once you have used your left arm to clear his attack, you have exposed the right hand side of his body to your attack. You can then use your fist or even elbow to attack (Figure 5-282).

Figure 5–279

Figure 5–280

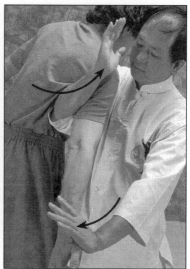

Figure 5–281

Figure 5–282

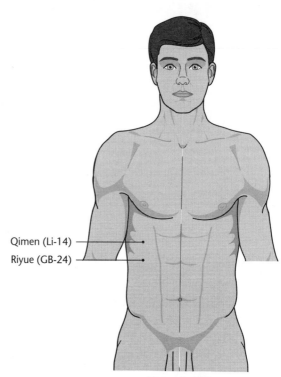

Qimen (Li-14)
Riyue (GB-24)

Figure 5–283

Cavity Name	Hand Form(s)	Possible Results
Qimen (Li-14)(Figure 5-283)	Phoenix Eye Fist or Elbow	Seal the Breath and Rupture the Liver
Riyue (GB-24)(Figure 5-283)	Phoenix Eye Fist or Elbow	Seal the Breath and Rupture the Liver

| *Figure 5–284* | *Figure 5–285* | *Figure 5–286* |

28. FAIR LADY WEAVES WITH SHUTTLE *(Yu Niu Chuan Suo)* 王女穿梭

Movements:

First, lower your left arm down while circling your left hand to your left waist (Figure 5-284), then shift your weight to your right and enter a Bow-Arrow Stance while raising your right arm up and starting to push your left hand forward (Figure 5-285). Finally, turn your body to your right, while rotating your right arm to your right and pushing your left palm forward (Figure 5-286).

Analysis:

Your right arm is used to neutralize the opponent's power upward and to the side. Therefore, it is a **Wardoff (Peng)**. Your left hand's palm attack is a **Press Forward (An)**.

Qin Na:

Technique #1: Forward Upward Turning

(Qian Shang Fan) 前上翻

When your opponent is punching you with his right fist, immediately use your right forearm to intercept and neutralize his attack upward and to your right, while using your left hand to seal his right elbow (Figure 5-287). Next, step your right leg behind his right leg while pressing his elbow inward and pushing his wrist forward to make it bend and lock it (Figure 5-288). Finally, let your left hand take over the control of his wrist and arm while using your right hand to push the upper back of his head forward (Figure 5-289).

Figure 5–287

Figure 5–288

Figure 5–289

Figure 5–290

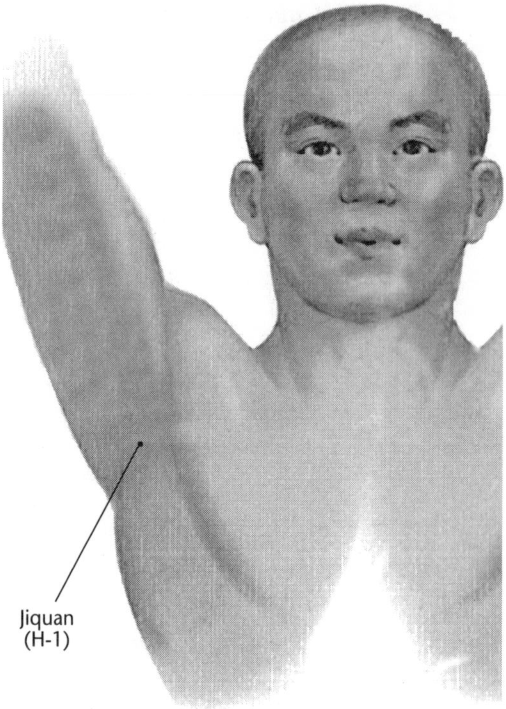

Jiquan
(H-1)

Figure 5–291

Cavity Press or Strike:

Once you have used your right arm to intercept and neutralize your opponent's power upward and to the side, you have exposed the area under his armpit to your attack. In this case, you may either use the palm to strike his lower ribs, phoenix eye fist to attack the nerves between his ribs, or fingers to attack his cavity (Figure 5-290).

Cavity Name	Hand Form(s)	Possible Results
Jiquan (H-1)(Figure 5-291)	Sword Secret	Cause a Heart Attack

| *Figure 5–292* | *Figure 5–293* | *Figure 5–294* |

29. LOWER THE SNAKE BODY *(She Shen Xia Shi)* 蛇身下勢

Movements:

From the Single Whip Posture (Figure 5-292), first move your left hand toward you with the palm facing you while squatting down on your right leg. Then you extend your left arm out along the inner side of your left leg (Figure 5-293).

Analysis:

Although in the practice you squat down very low to train your knees' strength, in actual application you only squat down enough to yield to the oncoming attack. The key application of his posture is the left arm's **Coiling (Chan)**.

Qin Na:

Technique #1: Reverse Elbow Wrap

(Fan Chan Zhou) 反纏肘

When your opponent attacks you with his right fist, immediately squat down and sit backward while using your left forearm to intercept and neutralize the attack to your right (Figure 5-294). Next, coil your left hand around his right arm until it reaches his post-arm (Figure 5-295). Finally, use the leverage generated from your left hand and elbow to press him down to the ground (Figure 5-296).

Cavity Press or Strike:

Your left hand's coiling movement can lead and neutralize your opponent's attack to his right (Figure 5-297). Naturally, you should use this opportunity and immediately attack his right body with your right hand.

Figure 5–295

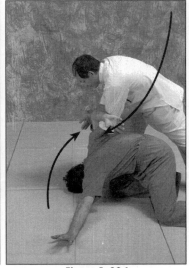

Figure 5–296

Figure 5–297

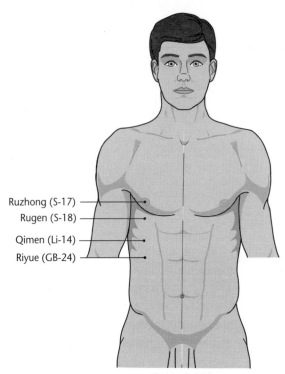

Ruzhong (S-17)
Rugen (S-18)
Qimen (Li-14)
Riyue (GB-24)

Figure 5–298

Cavity Name	Hand Form(s)	Possible Results
Ruzhong (S-17)(Figure 5-298)	Palm	Seal the Breath
Rugen (S-18)(Figure 5-298)	Palm	Seal the Breath
Qimen (Li-14)(Figure 5-298)	Fist or Phoenix Eye Fist	Seal the Breath and Rupture the Liver
Riyue (GB-24)(Figure 5-298)	Fist or Phoenix Eye Fist	Seal the Breath and Rupture the Liver

Figure 5–299

Figure 5–300

30. GOLDEN ROOSTER STANDS ON ONE LEG *(Jin Ji Du Li)* 金雞獨立

Movements:

First, turn your body to the left while starting to raise your right arm (Figure 5-299). Then, raise your right knee up while lifting your right arm until the palm is as high as your face (Figure 5-300).

Analysis:

Your left arm can be used to repel the oncoming attack, and the right hand and the knee are used to attack.

Qin Na:

Technique #1: Golden Rooster Locks the Arm

(Jin Ji Suo Bi) 金雞鎖臂

In fact, this *Qin Na* is only used to lock your opponent's arm, which can therefore create an opportunity for your leg's attack. When you have a chance to grab your opponent's left wrist with your left hand, immediately insert your right forearm behind his post-arm (Figure 5-301). Then, using the leverage of your left hand and right arm, you may lock your opponent's right arm (Figure 5-302). This technique can only lock your opponent for a short time. It is not practical to lock it for a long time, since his left hand is able to reach you easily. Therefore, right after your locking, you should immediately kick his groin with your right knee.

Cavity Press or Strike:

Right after your left hand's neutralization, you may use your right hand to attack his upper body while using your right knee to attack his lower body (Figure 5-303).

Figure 5–301

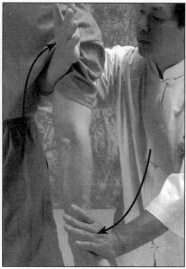

Figure 5–302

Figure 5–303

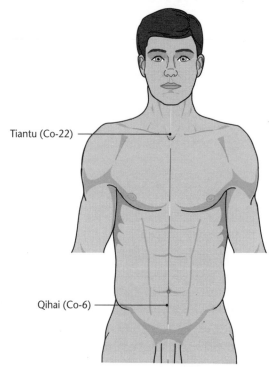

Tiantu (Co-22)

Qihai (Co-6)

Figure 5–304

Cavity Name	Hand Form(s)	Possible Results
Throat	Fingers' Grabbing	Seal the Breath
Tiantu (Co-22)(Figure 5-304)	Thumb	Seal the Breath
Qihai (Co-6)(Figure 5-304)	Knee	Death
Groin (Organ)	knee	Death

| Figure 5–305 | Figure 5–306 | Figure 5–307 |

31. WHITE SNAKE TURNS BODY AND SPITS POISON *(Bai She Tu Xin)* 白蛇吐信

Movements:

From the Fan Back Posture (Figure 5-305), turn your body to your right while lowering your right arm (Figure 5-306). Then, shift your weight to your right leg and enter a Bow-Arrow Stance while repelling your right arm to your right and striking your left palm forward (Figure 5-307).

Analysis:

Normally, this posture is used against the opponent's attack from behind. Your right arm is used to repel the attack while the left hand is used to attack his face with great speed, just like a snake spitting poison from its mouth.

Qin Na:

Technique #1: Lock the Arm and Push the Neck

(Suo Bi Tui Jing) 鎖臂推頸

When your opponent punches your lower body, use your right forearm to repel his attack to your right (Figure 5-308). Next, step your left leg behind his right leg while hooking his right arm up with your right arm, and extending your left arm to lock his neck (Figure 5-309). If you wish to take him down, simply sweep your left leg forward while pressing his neck backward.

Cavity Press or Strike:

Your right arm is used to repel the attack to the side, while your left hand catches the opportunity to attack (Figure 5-310).

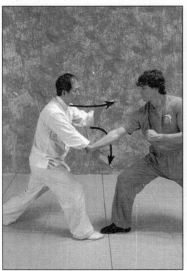

Figure 5–308

Figure 5–309

Figure 5–310

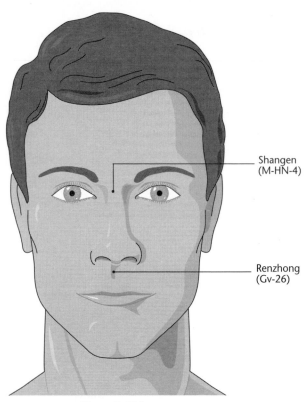

Shangen
(M-HN-4)

Renzhong
(Gv-26)

Figure 5–311

Figure 5–312

Cavity Name	Hand Form(s)	Possible Results
Eyes	Fingers	Blinding
Shangen (M-HN-4)(Figure 5-311)	Fist	Fainting, Nose Bleeding
Renzhong (Gv-26)(Figure 5-311)	Fist	Fainting

Figure 5–313

Figure 5–314

Figure 5–315

32. CROSS HANDS *(Shi Zi Shou)* 十字手

Movements:

From the Stand High to Search Out the Horse posture (Figure 5-312), step your left leg forward and enter a Bow-Arrow Stance while covering your right arm down and extending your left arm upward and forward (Figure 5-313).

Analysis:

Your right arm's covering is used to neutralize the attack downward, which can therefore expose the opponent's face to your attack.

Qin Na:

Technique #1: Daoist Greets with Hands

(Dao Zhi Zuo Ji) 道子作揖

This technique uses the arm's crossing action to lock the opponent's arm. When your opponent attacks you with his right hand, immediately use your right hand to intercept his right forearm, while using your left hand to push his right elbow to your right (Figure 5-314). Then, step your left leg behind his right leg and use both of your hands to rotate his right arm and lock it in place (Figures 5-315 and 5-316).

Cavity Press or Strike:

Your left hand is used to neutralize the attack to your left and then downward (Figure 5-317). After your neutralization, you may immediately attack his face with your left hand (Figure 5-318). Naturally, you may use your right fist to attack his right lower rib area immediately following your left hand's face attack.

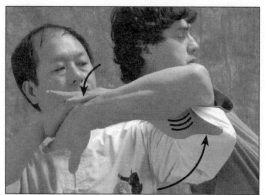

Figure 5–316

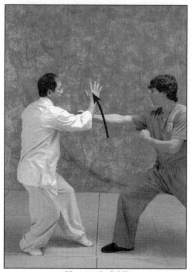

Figure 5–317

Figure 5–318

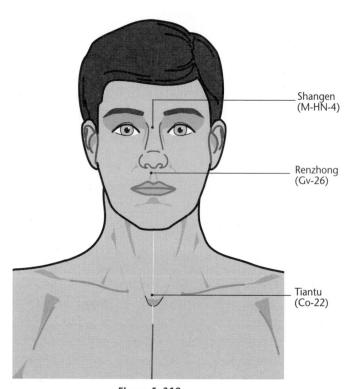

Figure 5–319

Cavity Name	Hand Form(s)	Possible Results
Eyes	Fingers	Blinding
Shangen (M-HN-4)(Figure 5-319)	Fist	Fainting, Nose Bleeding
Renzhong (Gv-26)(Figure 5-319)	Fist	Fainting
Throat	Fingers' Grabbing	Seal the Breath
Tiantu (Co-22)(Figure 5-319)	Thumb	Seal the Breath

| *Figure 5-320* | *Figure 5-321* | *Figure 5-322* |

33. THE WORD "TEN" LEG *(Shi Zi Tui)* 十字腿

Movements:

First, cross both of your arms in front of your chest while moving your right leg back (Figure 5-320). Next, open both of your arms and use your right leg to kick (Figure 5-321).

Analysis:

The meaning of this posture's name is "The Ten Word Leg Posture." It is because the posture is shaped like the Chinese word "Ten." Both of your arms are used to intercept the chest's attack or grab, and the leg is used to kick.

Qin Na:

Technique #1: The Word "Ten" Pressing Leg

(Shi Zi Ding Tui) 十字頂腿

When your opponent punches your chest with his right fist, immediately use your right forearm to intercept the attack and grab his wrist (Figure 5-322). Next, pull his right wrist down; this will offer your opponent a chance to attack you with his left hand. In this situation, immediately use your left hand to intercept the punch and grab his left wrist (Figure 5-323). Then, reposition yourself to his back while pulling both of his arms down behind him (Figure 5-324). Finally, use your right leg to press his sacrum forward to lock him in place (Figure 5-325).

Cavity Press or Strike:

Once you have used both of your hands to grab both of his wrists, you may kick the lower section of his body with your right leg (Figure 5-326). This technique can also be used against your opponent's grabbing or attacking from your back (Figure 5-327). In this case, first turn your body and use your right hand to grab his wrist (Figure 5-328). Then, immediately kick his right lower rib area with your right leg (Figure 5-329).

Figure 5-323

Figure 5-324

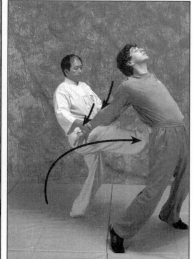

Figure 5-325

Figure 5-326

Figure 5-327

Figure 5-328

Cavity Name	Hand Form(s)	Possible Results
Riyue (GB-24)(Figure 5-330)	Heel	Seal the Breath and Rupture the Liver
Zhongwan (Co-12)(Figure 5-330)	Heel	Seal the Breath and Vomiting
Qihai (Co-6)(Figure 5-330)	Heel	Death
Groin (Organ)	Heel or Toes	Death

34. STEP FORWARD TO SEVEN STARS *(Shang Bu Qi Xing)* 上步七星

Movements:

From the posture, Lower the Snake Body (Figure 5-331), shift your weight to your left leg while raising your left arm (Figure 5-332). Then step your right leg forward into False Stance while punching your right fist forward (Figure 5-333).

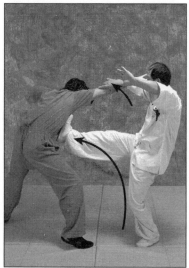

Figure 5–329

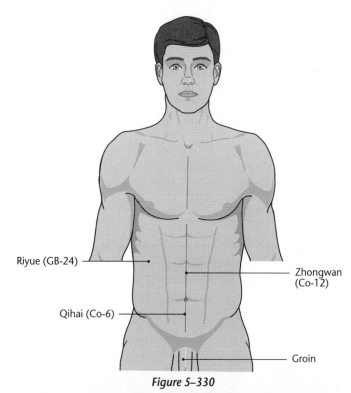

Riyue (GB-24)

Zhongwan (Co-12)

Qihai (Co-6)

Groin

Figure 5–330

Figure 5–331

Figure 5–332

Figure 5–333

Analysis:

Your right arm is used to deflect the opponent's power upward; it can be extended forward either for punching or locking his elbow. Naturally, your right leg can be used for kicking.

Figure 5–334

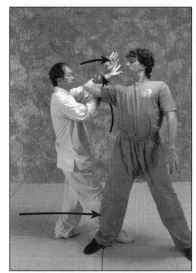

Figure 5–335

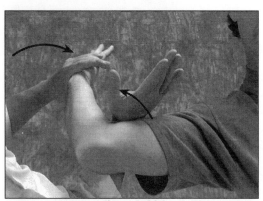

Figure 5–336

Figure 5–337

Figure 5–338

Qin Na:

Technique #1: Seven Star to Lock the Throat (Qi Shen Shuo Hou) 七星鎖喉

When your opponent attacks you with this right fist, first use your left forearm to repel his punch (Figure 5-334). Next, step your right leg forward, pushing his right forearm forward while using your right forearm to pull in his elbow (Figures 5-335 and 5-336). Finally, grab his throat with your right hand while still locking his right arm (Figures 5-337 and 5-338).

Figure 5–339

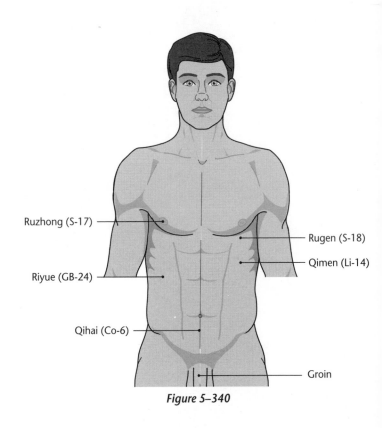

Figure 5–340

Cavity Press or Strike:

Once you have used your left arm to clear his attack, you may use your right fist to attack the right hand side of his body (Figure 5-339).

Cavity Name	Hand Form(s)	Possible Results
Ruzhong (S-17)(Figure 5-340)	Fist	Seal the Breath
Rugen (S-18)(Figure 5-340)	Fist	Seal the Breath
Qimen (Li-14)(Figure 5-340)	Fist	Seal the Breath and Rupture the Liver
Riyue (GB-24)(Figure 5-340)	Fist	Seal the Breath and Rupture the Liver
Qihai (Co-6)(Figure 5-340)	Heel	Death
Groin (Organ)	Toes	Death

35. STEP BACK TO RIDE THE TIGER *(Tui Bu Kua Hu)* 退步跨虎

Movements:

From the posture, Step Forward to Seven Stars (Figure 5-341), step your right leg backward while spreading both of your arms apart diagonally (Figure 5-342).

Analysis:

Both of your arms are used to spread out the oncoming attack while your left leg is ready for kicking.

Qin Na:

No *Qin Na* available.

Figure 5–341

Figure 5–342

Figure 5–343

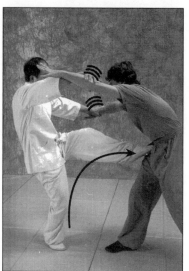

Figure 5–344

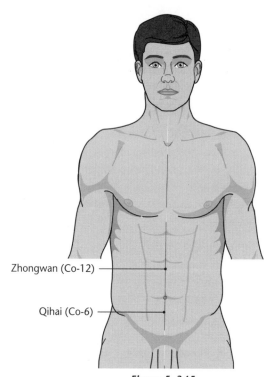

Zhongwan (Co-12)

Qihai (Co-6)

Figure 5–345

Cavity Press or Strike:

Once you have used both of your arms to repel your opponent's attack outward (Figure 5-343), you will have exposed the center area of his body for your kicking (Figure 5-344).

Cavity Name	Hand Form(s)	Possible Results
Zhongwan (Co-12)(Figure 5-345)	Heel	Seal the Breath and Vomiting
Qihai (Co-6)(Figure 5-345)	Heel	Death
Groin (Organ)	Heel or Toes	Death

Figure 5–346

Figure 5–347

36. STEP FORWARD TO SWEEP LOTUS *(Shang Bu Bai Lian)* 上步擺蓮

Movements:

First, turn your body to your left while crossing both of your arms in front of your chest (Figure 5-346). Then, spread both of your arms outward while lifting your knee upward (Figure 5-347).

Analysis:

If your chest has been grabbed by both of your opponent's hands, you can use both of your arms to repel his grabbing outward and then grab his arms or shoulder area. In this situation, he will not be able to escape, and this will allow you to kick him with your right knee.

Qin Na:

Technique #1: Two Hands Push the Chest

(Shuang Shou Tui Xiong) 雙手推胸

When both of your opponent's hands are grabbing your upper chest, immediately use both of your arms to repel his grabbing outward (Figure 5-348). Next, coil both of your arms to the outside of both of his arms, and then push both of your hands toward his chest to lock his arms (Figures 5-349 and 5-350).

Cavity Press or Strike:

Once you have locked both of his arms, you may use your right knee to kick the lower section of his body (Figure 5-351).

Figure 5–348

Figure 5–349

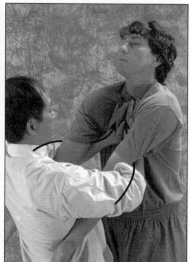

Figure 5–350

Figure 5–351

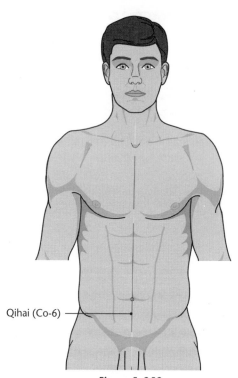

Qihai (Co-6)

Figure 5–352

Cavity Name	**Hand Form(s)**	**Possible Results**
Qihai (Co-6)(Figure 5-352)	Knee	Death
Groin (Organ)	Knee	Death

Figure 5–353

Figure 5–354

Figure 5–355

Figure 5–356

37. DRAW THE BOW AND SHOOT THE TIGER

(Wan Gong She Hu) 彎弓射虎

Movements:

First, step your left leg backward while scooping your right arm upward (Figure 5-353). Then, raise your right arm up to your right while punching your left fist forward (Figure 5-354).

Analysis:

Your backward stepping is to yield to the oncoming power, and your right arm's upward movement is for intercepting and neutralizing. Naturally, your left fist's forward action is for an attack.

Qin Na:

Technique #1: Roast Peking Duck

(Bei Ping Kao Ya) 北平烤鴨

When your opponent uses his right hand to grab or punch your upper chest, immediately use your right forearm to intercept the oncoming attack and then grab it while inserting your left arm under his right arm until it reaches his neck (Figure 3-355). Next, twist his arm counterclockwise until his right palm faces upward, then pull his arm down while lifting your left elbow to lock his right arm (Figure 3-356).

Figure 5–357

Figure 5–358

Technique #2: Lock the Arm and Push the Neck

(Suo Bi Tui Jing) 鎖臂推頸

When your opponent punches your chest with his right fist, immediately use your right forearm to intercept and then grab his right wrist, while using your left forearm to push his right elbow to keep his arm bent (Figure 3-357). Then, step your left leg behind his right leg, and pull his right arm against your chest while extending your left arm to his neck and lock him there (Figure 3-358).

Technique #3: The Old Man Carries the Fish on His Back

(Lao Han Bei Yu) 老漢背魚

In the last technique, right after you have neutralized his right arm's attack (Figure 3-357), immediately step your left leg behind his right leg, turn your body to your right and then pull his arm downward to lock his right arm (Figure 3-359).

Cavity Press or Strike:

Once you have used your right arm to neutralize the oncoming attack, you will have exposed the area under his armpit to your attack (Figure 3-360).

Cavity Name	Hand Form(s)	Possible Results
Jiquan (H-1)(Figure 5-361)	Sword Secret	Cause a Heart Attack
Yuanye (GB-22)(Figure 5-361)	Phoenix Eye Fist	Seal the Breath
Dabao (Sp-21)(Figure 5-361)	Phoenix Eye Fist	Seal the Breath

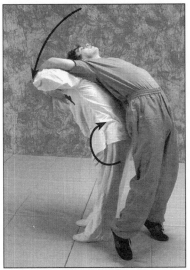

Figure 5–359

Figure 5–360

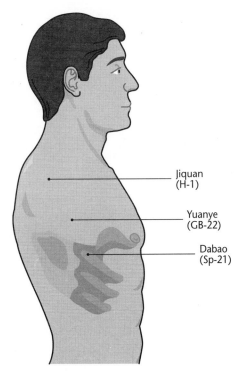

Jiquan
(H-1)

Yuanye
(GB-22)

Dabao
(Sp-21)

Figure 5–361

■ Chapter 6 ■

QIN NA IN TAIJI
PUSHING HANDS

6-1. Introduction

We know that *Taijiquan* is a martial art which was created and designed for combat. *Qin Na* is only one of the four categories of fighting techniques. Furthermore, we also know that in order to reach the final goal of fighting capability in *Taijiquan*, a *Taiji* practitioner must follow the designed training steps to build up the required fighting skills.

Traditionally, when you start *Taijiquan* practice, you will first be taught some simple *Taiji Qigong* and breathing techniques. These are the first few steps which can lead you to the entrance of understanding and feeling the *Qi* circulation in your body. Next, you will learn how to use your mind to lead the *Qi* (*Yi Yi Yin Qi*, 以意引氣). Only when you understand and are able to feel the *Qi*, and further know how to use your mind to lead the *Qi*, will you have built up a firm foundation of the internal side of *Taijiquan* practice. *Taiji Qigong* should be practiced at all times in *Taijiquan* practice. It is not merely trained only at the beginner stage. The more advanced levels of *Taijiquan* reach the deeper *Qigong* practice which should also be trained.

Often, when you start your *Taiji Qigong*, you will also be taught some basic relaxation movements and fundamental stances. After you have become familiar with the basic relaxation movements, the *Taijiquan* sequence will be taught. Although there are only 37 postures in the traditional *Yang* Style *Taijiquan* 105 movement routine, there are more than 250 martial applications, including **striking**, **kicking**, **wrestling**, and **Qin Na**, which can be derived from the 37 postures. Traditionally, the secrets of these martial techniques must be revealed by a master. Only when you have learned the martial applications can every

Taijiquan movement exhibit its essence, root, and meaning. Otherwise, the movements will only be some relaxation exercises. If *Taijiquan* becomes merely a type of relaxation exercise, then anybody will be able to create his own style, and the movements of the style can be classified only as relaxation health *Qigong* instead of *Taijiquan*.

In order to help you understand the martial applications of *Taijiquan*, normally *Taiji* Pushing Hands practice is introduced first. From Pushing Hands practice, you will learn how to feel the opponent's *Jin* (martial power) and *Qi*. From this feeling (i.e., listening *Jin*, 聽勁), you will learn how to stick and adhere your body to your opponent's body. Sticking and adhering allows you to direct and neutralize your opponent's attacking power into emptiness. Naturally, in order to reach this goal, your body must be soft, especially your spine and waist. Not only that, your *Qi* must be strong, and must circulate smoothly and freely. All of these are basic requirements for health. Therefore, *Taiji* Pushing Hands practice is one of the most effective ways of maintaining and improving your health. In addition, through practice, both *Qi* and ideas can exchanged between you and your partner. This can also establish good *Qi* feelings and friendship. Normally, it will take many years of Pushing Hands training to reach a high level of skill. Only after you are able to reach a high level of Pushing Hands, will your striking by hands and kicking by legs be effective, since your opponent will always be under your control.

From the above, you can see that Pushing Hands practice is actually a required and necessary step to reaching the final goal of *Taiji* fighting practice. Since, in *Taijiquan* Pushing Hands, you must stick and adhere your hands or even body to your opponents, the range is close and mutual contact is constantly maintained. *Qin Na* is the most efficient and effective technique for placing your opponent into a controlled situation.

This chapter will summarize and review some of the *Qin Na* techniques which can be used in Pushing Hands situations. Naturally, **since most *Taiji* Pushing Hands techniques are derived from the eight basic technical moving patterns, *Peng, Lu, Ji, An, Cai, Lie, Zhou*, and *Kao*, it is not surprising to see that many of the *Qin Na* techniques in this chapter are refinements of those techniques which have already been introduced in Chapters 3 and 4.** You should focus on learning how to apply all the *Qin Na* introduced in Chapters 3 and 4 into *Taiji* Pushing Hands by yourself. In this chapter, we will review some of them. Hopefully through this effort, you will obtain a guideline and understanding of how *Qin Na* can be adopted in *Taiji* Pushing Hands. Naturally, since there are so many *Qin Na* techniques available, you will discover that some of the techniques introduced in this chapter were not discussed earlier. If you are interested in learning more about the internal aspects of *Taiji Qigong* practice, you may refer to the book **The Essence of Tai Chi Chi Kung** by YMAA. In addition, if you are interested in learning more about *Qin Na* techniques, you may refer to the books: **Analysis of Shaolin Chin Na** and **Comprehensive Applications of Shaolin Chin Na**, by YMAA.

6-2. Qin Na in Taiji Pushing Hands

In *Taiji* Pushing Hands, it is desirable to control your opponent's joints as much as possible. The reason for this is simply because when the joints are controlled, the mobility of his arms will be restricted. Therefore, in this section, we will divide the sample *Qin*

Figure 6–1

Figure 6–2

Figure 6–3

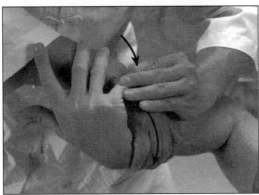

Figure 6–4

Na techniques which can be used in Pushing Hands into three categories: *Qin Na* Against Hands on Your Wrist or Forearm, *Qin Na* Against Hands on Your Elbow Joints, and *Qin Na* Against Hands on Your Shoulder Joints.

I. AGAINST HANDS ON YOUR WRIST JOINTS OR FOREARMS

Technique #1: Small Wrap Finger

(Xiao Chan Zhi) 小纏指

When your opponent's right hand is on your right wrist (Figure 6-1), immediately reposition yourself to his right hand side while neutralizing his pressing to your right. As you do this, also use your left hand to pull his pinkie toward your right wrist while wrapping your right hand around his wrist (Figure 6-2). Finally, press his wrist down with your right hand while pulling his pinkie strongly toward your right wrist (Figure 6-3). When you control him, his elbow should be lower than his wrist (Figure 6-4). Otherwise, he will be able to turn his body counterclockwise to release the control, and the technique will not be effective.

Figure 6–5

Figure 6–6

Figure 6–7

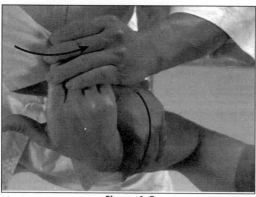

Figure 6–8

Technique #2: Small Wrap Hand

(Xiao Chan Shou) 小纏手

This technique is very similar to the last one, the only difference is that instead of controlling the pinkie, you pull his index finger toward your wrist.

Again, if your opponent's right hand is on your right wrist (Figure 6-5), immediately turn your body to your right to neutralize the press, while using your left hand to pull his index finger toward your right wrist and wrapping your right hand around his right wrist (Figure 6-6). Then, reposition yourself to his right hand side while pressing your right hand down against his right wrist (Figure 6-7). Again, to make the control effective, his elbow should be lower than his wrist (Figure 6-8).

| Figure 6–9 | Figure 6–10 | Figure 6–11 |

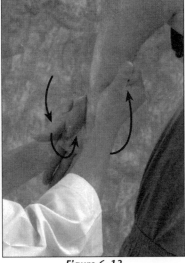

| Figure 6–12 | Figure 6–13 |

Technique #3: Back Wrap Hand

(Fan Chan Shou) 反纏手

When your opponent's right hand is on your right wrist, again turn your body to your right to neutralize his pressing (Figure 6-9). Next, use your left hand to grab his right fingers (Figure 6-10). Then, use both hands to circle his arm downward (Figure 6-11) and follow with an upward circle to lock his wrist (Figure 6-12). To make the technique most effective, you should use your left hand to twist his wrist as much as possible, while using your right hand to lock his forearm and generate good leverage for your left hand's twisting (Figure 6-13).

Figure 6–14

Figure 6–15

Figure 6–16

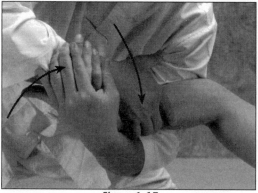
Figure 6–17

Technique #4: Large Wrap Hand

(Da Chan Shou) 大纏手

When your opponent presses your right wrist with his right hand, immediately turn your body to your right to neutralize the pressing (Figure 6-14). Next, reposition yourself to his right hand side while circling your left hand under his right arm until it reaches his right index finger, and wrap your right hand around his right wrist (Figure 6-15). Finally, press his wrist down while pushing his index finger toward your right wrist (Figures 6-16 and 6-17).

Technique #5: Upward Elbow Wrap

(Shang Chan Zhou) 上纏肘

Again, when your opponent's right hand is on your right wrist, immediately turn your body to your right to neutralize the pressing or grabbing, while using your left hand to grab his right hand (Figure 6-18). Next, circle his arm upward with both of your hands (Figure 6-19). Then, reposition yourself to his right hand side while twisting his wrist with

Figure 6–18   Figure 6–19   Figure 6–20

Figure 6–21   Figure 6–22   Figure 6–23

your left hand and lifting his elbow with your right hand to lock him up (Figures 6-20 and 6-21). You may also lock his right arm with your right hand and stomach area, while using your left forearm to push his neck away to generate pain (Figure 6-22).

Technique #6: Small Elbow Wrap

(Xiao Chan Zhou) 小纏肘

In order to neutralize your opponent's right hand pressing on your right wrist, turn your body to your right (Figure 6-23). Next, step your left leg to the front of his right leg, and grab his right wrist with your right hand while pressing his elbow downward with your left forearm (Figure 6-24). Finally, sweep your left leg backward while using the leverage generated from both of your hands to circle him down to the ground (Figure 6-25).

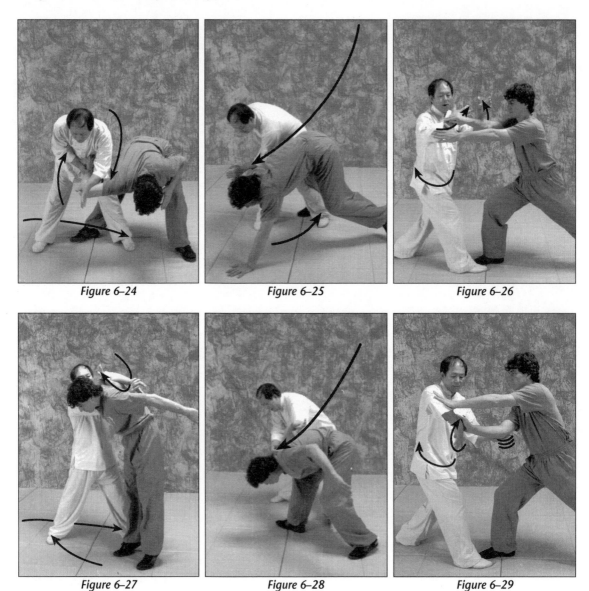

Figure 6–24   Figure 6–25   Figure 6–26

Figure 6–27   Figure 6–28   Figure 6–29

Technique #7: Reverse Elbow Wrap

(Fan Chan Zhou) 反纏肘

Again, you turn your body to your right to neutralize your opponent's right hand pressing on your right wrist (Figure 6-26). Next, reposition yourself to his right hand side, and grab his right wrist with your right hand while coiling your left hand around his arm until it reaches his post-arm near the elbow (Figure 6-27). Finally, use the leverage generated from your left hand and elbow to circle him down to the ground (Figure 6-28).

Technique #8: Upward Elbow Press

(Shang Ya Zhou) 上壓肘

When your opponent's right hand is on your right wrist, immediately turn your body to your right while placing your left hand on his right elbow (Figure 6-29). Then, reposi-

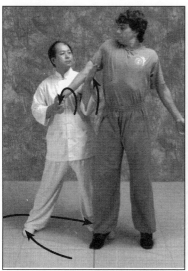

Figure 6–30 *Figure 6–31* *Figure 6–32*

tion yourself to his right, circle your right hand and grab his right wrist, and press his right wrist down while using your left hand to push his right elbow upward (Figure 6-30).

Technique #9: Daoist Greets with Hands

(Dao Zhi Zuo Ji) 道子作揖

This technique is very similar to the last one. The only difference is that this technique can be used if your opponent keeps his arm straight, which can prevent you from locking his elbow as executed in the last technique.

Again, turn your body to your right to neutralize his right hand pressing or grabbing on your right wrist, while placing your left forearm on his elbow (Figure 6-31). Then, reposition yourself to his right hand side, circle your right hand to grab his right wrist and pull it down while pushing his elbow upward to keep it bent (Figure 6-32). This will allow you to lock his right arm. To prevent him from turning his body, simply use your left shoulder to push his right shoulder. This will stop him from turning.

Technique #10: The Old Man Carries the Fish on his Back

(Lao Han Bei Yu) 老漢背魚

In the last technique, right after you have neutralized the opponent's pressing to your right (Figure 6-33), step your right leg behind him, and pull his right arm down while using your back to lock his arm in place (Figure 6-34). To make this control effective, your opponent's arm should be neither too straight nor too bent.

Figure 6–33

Figure 6–34

Figure 6–35

Figure 6–36

Figure 6–37

Figure 6–38

Technique #11: Send the Devil to Heaven

(Song Mo Shang Tian) 送魔上天

When your opponent's right hand is on your right wrist, pulling your right arm to his right (Figure 6-35), immediately step your right leg to his right, moving your right arm up and to his right while using your left hand to grab his right hand (Figure 6-36). Then, step your left leg behind him and use your body's left turning momentum to lock him up (Figure 6-37). The most effective way to lock his arm is to use your left hand to twist his right wrist while using your right hand to grab his fingers and bend them downward (Figure 6-38).

Figure 6–39

Figure 6–40

Figure 6–41

Figure 6–42

II. AGAINST HANDS ON ELBOW JOINTS:

Technique #1: Feudal Lord Lifts the Tripod

(Ba Wang Tai Ding) 霸王抬鼎

When your opponent's left hand is adhering on your right elbow (Figure 6–39), immediately scoop your right arm upward while using your left hand to grab his left hand (Figure 6–40). Next, twist his left wrist with your left hand while using your right hand to push his left elbow to keep it bent (Figure 6–41). Finally, raise your body up while locking his left arm in front of you (Figure 6-42).

Figure 6–43   Figure 6–44   Figure 6–45

Figure 6–46   Figure 6–47   Figure 6–48

Technique #2: Arm Wraps Around the Dragon's Neck

(Bi Chan Long Jing) 臂纏龍頸

From the same situation, when your opponent's left hand is on your right elbow (Figure 6-43), immediately scoop your right arm upward while using your left hand to grab his left hand (Figure 6-44). Next, lock his left arm on your stomach area while extending your right arm to his neck (Figure 6-45). Finally, circle your right arm around his neck while continuing to lock his left arm (Figure 6-46).

Technique #3: The Crane Spreads Its Wings

(Bai He Liang Chi) 白鶴亮翅

This technique is very similar to the last technique. Again, when your opponent's left hand is on your right elbow, scoop your right arm upward while using your left hand to grab his left hand (Figure 6-47). Next, twist his left wrist with your left hand while using

Figure 6–49

Figure 6–50

Figure 6–51

Figure 6–52

your right hand to push his forearm (Figure 6-48). Finally, expand your right arm on his neck while continuing to twist his wrist (Figure 6-49). This will provide you with good leverage for his arm's locking.

III. AGAINST HANDS ON SHOULDER JOINTS:

Technique #1: The Hero Shows Courtesy

(Ying Xiong You Li) 英雄有禮

When your opponent's right hand is on your left shoulder, immediately use your right hand to grab his right hand (Figure 6-50). Next, circle your left arm over his forearm (Figure 6-51), reposition yourself and use the leverage generated from your left arm and right hand to lock his right wrist (Figure 6-52).

Figure 6–53   *Figure 6–54*   *Figure 6–55*

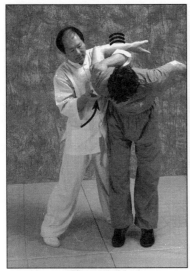

Figure 6–56   *Figure 6–57*

Technique #2: Press Shoulder with Single Finger and Extending the Neck for Water

(Yi Zhi Ding Jian or Yin Jing Qiu Shui) 一指頂肩 ， 引頸求水

Again, when your opponent's right hand is on your left shoulder, immediately use your right hand to grab his right hand (Figure 6-53). Next, free your left hand and place it on your opponent's right elbow (Figure 6-54). Then, reposition yourself to his right hand side while coiling your left hand around his right arm until it reaches his post-arm, and raise it upward to lock his arm (Figure 6-55). Finally, use your right index finger to press his Jianneiling cavity to increase the pain (Figure 6-56). Alternatively, you may use your hand to press his chin upward to generate good leverage for locking (Figure 6-57).

Figure 6–58

Figure 6–59

Figure 6–60

Figure 6–61

Technique #3: Old Man Promoted to General

(Lao Han Bai Jiang) 老漢拜將

When your opponent's right hand is on your left shoulder (Figure 6-58), again use your right hand to grab his right hand while circling your left arm over his right arm (Figure 6-59). Next, place his right elbow under your left armpit while lifting his wrist upward (Figure 6-60). Finally, use the leverage generated from both of your hands and left shoulder to press him down to the ground (Figure 6-61).

Remember, this chapter only offers you some of the *Qin Na* applications. You should study Chapters 3 and 4 carefully and apply them into your Pushing Hands. The best method of learning is practicing with a partner.

▪ Chapter 7 ▪

CONCLUSION

Although this book only offers you some of my personal knowledge about the possible *Qin Na* applications in *Yang* Style *Taijiquan*, it can provide you with an idea and correct concept of how *Qin Na* can be applied in *Taijiquan*. I hope that from this book you are inspired and encouraged to get involved in more study and research into the martial applications of *Taijiquan*. Naturally, if you are already an expert in any style of *Taijiquan*, and have also mastered the martial applications of the style, you should not hesitate to write them down, offer seminars, and introduce them to *Taijiquan* society. Only then can this art remain alive and develop continuously.

To help you achieve an in-depth understanding of *Taijiquan*, both in theory and application, you may refer to the books: ***Advanced Yang Style Tai Chi Chuan, Vol. 1. and Vol. 2.*** However if you would like to know more about the internal cultivation of *Qi*, and how *Qi* is applied in *Taijiquan*, then you should read ***The Essence of Tai Chi Chi Kung.***

If this book has inspired you to become interested in knowing more about Qin Na, then you may refer to ***Analysis of Shaolin Chin Na*** and ***Comprehensive Applications of Shaolin Chin Na***. All of these books are available from YMAA.

■ Appendix A ■

NAMES OF QIN NA
TECHNIQUES

▪ Appendix B ▪

TRANSLATION OF THIRTY-SEVEN POSTURES

1. **Grasp Sparrow's Tail** (*Lan Qiu Wei, You*) 攬雀尾
2. **Wardoff** (*Peng*) 掤
3. **Rollback** (*Lu*) 擺
4. **Press or Squeeze** (*Ji*) 擠
5. **Settle Down the Wrist** (*An*) 按
6. **Single Whip** (*Dan Bian*) 單鞭
7. **Lift Hands and Lean Forward** (*Ti Shou Shang Shi*) 提手上勢
8. **The Crane Spreads Its Wings** (*Bai He Liang Chi*) 白鶴亮翅
9. **Brush Knee and Step Forward** (*Lou Xi Yao Bu*) 摟膝拗步
10. **Play the Guitar** (*Shou Hui Pi Pa*) 手揮琵琶
11. **Twist Body and Circle Fist** (*Pei Shen Chui*) 撇身捶
12. **Step Forward, Deflect Downward, Parry and Punch** (*Shang Bu Ban Lan Chui*) 上步扳攔捶
13. **Seal Tightly** (*Ru Feng Si Bi*) 如封似閉
14. **Embrace Tiger and Return to the Mountain** (*Bao Hu Gui Shan*) 抱虎歸山
15. **Fist Under the Elbow** (*Zhou Di Kan Chui*) 肘底看捶
16. **Step Back and Repulse Monkey** (*Dao Nian Hou*) 倒撺猴
17. **Diagonal Flying** (*Xie Fei Shi*) 斜飛勢
18. **Pick up Needle from Sea Bottom** (*Hai Di Lao Zhen*) 海底撈針
19. **Fan Back** (*San Tong Bei*) 扇通背
20. **Wave Hands in the Clouds** (*Yun Shou*) 雲手
21. **Stand High to Search Out the Horse** (*Gao Tan Ma*) 高探馬
22. **Toe Kick** (*Ti Tui*) 踢腿
23. **Heel Kick** (*Deng Tui*) 蹬腿

24. **Step Forward and Strike Down with the Fist**
(*Jin Bu Zai Chui*) 進步栽捶

25. **Strike the Tiger Posture** (*Da Hu Shi*) 打虎勢

26. **Two Winds Pass Through the Ears** (*Shuang Feng Guan Er*) 雙風貫耳

27. **Wild Horses Shear the Mane** (*Ye Ma Feng Zong*) 野馬分鬃

28. **Fair Lady Weaves with Shuttle** (*Yu Niu Chuan Suo*) 王女穿梭

29. **Lower the Snake Body** (*She Shen Xia Shi*) 蛇身下勢

30. **Golden Rooster Stands on One Leg** (*Jin Ji Du Li*) 金雞獨立

31. **White Snake Turns Body and Spits Poison** (*Bai She Tu Xin*) 白蛇吐信

32. **Cross Hands** (*Shi Zi Shou*) 十字手

33. **The Word "Ten" Leg** (*Shi Zi Tui*) 十字腿

34. **Step Forward to Seven Stars** (*Shang Bu Qi Xing*) 上步七星

35. **Step Back to Ride the Tiger** (*Tui Bu Kua Hu*) 退步跨虎

36. **Step Forward to Sweep Lotus** (*Shang Bu Bai Lian*) 上步襬蓮

37. **Draw the Bow and Shoot the Tiger** (*Wan Gong She Hu*) 彎弓射虎

▪ Appendix C ▪

TRANSLATION AND GLOSSARY OF CHINESE TERMS

Aikido 合氣道
A style of Japanese martial arts which uses the same theory of Chinese Taijiquan and Qin Na.

An 按
Means "pressing or stamping." One of the eight basic Taiji Jin patterns.

Ba Kua Chang (Baquazhang) 八卦掌
Means "Eight Trigram Palms." The name of one of the Chinese internal martial styles.

Baguazhang (Ba Kua Zhang) 八卦掌
Means "Eight Trigram Palms." The name of one of the Chinese internal martial styles.

Bai He 白鶴
Means "White Crane." One of the Chinese southern martial styles.

Bei Kao 背靠
To use the back to lean or press against someone or something. One of the basic Taiji Jin patterns.

Bi 閉
Means "close" or "seal."

Bi Qi 閉氣
Qi here means "air." It means oxygen we inhale. Therefore Bi Qi means to "seal the oxygen supply" or "seal the breath."

Cai 採
Plucking.

Ce Kao 側靠
To lean or to press sideways.

Chai (Sai) 釵
A kind of hairpin for ancient Chinese women. Later, it was derived into a kind of southern Chinese weapon.

Chan 纏
To wrap or to coil. A common Chinese martial arts technique.

Chan Jin 纏勁

The martial power of wrapping or coiling.

Chang Chuan (Changquan) 長拳

Means "Long Range Fist." Chang Chuan includes all northern Chinese long range martial styles.

Chang San-Feng 張三丰

Chang San-Feng is credited as the creator of Taijiquan during the Song dynasty in China (960-1127 A.D.)

Chang Xiang-San 張詳三

A well known Chinese martial artist in Taiwan.

Changquan (Chang Chuan) 長拳

Means "Long Range Fist." Changquan includes all northern Chinese long range martial styles.

Chen Style 陳氏

The family of Chen.

Chen Yan-Lin 陳炎林

A well known Taijiquan master in China during the 1940's.

Cheng Gin-Gsao 曾金灶

Dr. Yang Jwing-Ming's White Crane master.

Chi (Qi) 氣

The energy pervading the universe, including the energy circulating in the human body.

Chi Kung (Qigong) 氣功

The Gongfu of Qi, which means the study of Qi.

Chin (Qin) 擒

Means 'to catch" or "to seize."

Chin Na (Qin Na) 擒拿

Literally means "grab control." A component of Chinese martial arts which emphasizes grabbing techniques, to control your opponent's joints, in conjunction with attacking certain acupuncture cavities.

Cuo 錯

To misplace or to disorder.

Cuo Gu 錯骨

Cuo means "to misplace" or "to disorder" and Gu is "bone." Therefore, Cuo Gu means "to misplace the bone or joint."

Da 打

To strike. Normally, to attack with the palms, fists, or arms.

Da Lu 大攦

Large Rollback. One of the common Taiji techniques.

Da Mo 達摩

The Indian Buddhist monk who is credited with creating the Yi Jin Jing and Xi Sui Jing while at the Shaolin monastery. His last name was Sardili, and he was also known as Bodhidarma. He was once the prince of a small tribe in southern India.

Da Quan 大圈

Large circle. One of the common fighting distances.

Da Xue 打穴

A striking cavity.

Dabao (Sp-21) 大包

An acupuncture cavity belonging to the Spleen channel.

Dan Tian 丹田

"Elixir field." Located in the lower abdomen. It is considered the place which can store Qi energy.

Dao 道

The "way," by implication the "natural way."

Dian 點

"To point" or "to press."

Dian Mai (Dim Mak) 點脈

Mai means "the blood vessel" (Xue Mai) or "the Qi channel" (Qi Mai). Dian Mai means "to press the blood vessel or Qi channel."

Dian Xue 點穴

Dian means "to point and exert pressure" and Xue means "the cavities." Dian Xue refers to those Qin Na techniques which specialize in attacking acupuncture cavities to immobilize or kill an opponent.

Diao 刁

Hooking.

Dim Mak (Dian Mai) 點脈

Cantonese of "Dian Mai."

Ding 定

"To stabilize" or "to firm."

Dong Jin 懂勁

"Understanding Jin." One of the Jins which uses the feeling of the skin to sense the opponent's energy.

Du Mai 督脈

Usually translated Governing Vessel. One of the eight extraordinary vessels.

Duan 斷

"To break" or "to seal."

Duan Mai 斷脈

Duan means "to break" and Mai means "the blood vessel." Duan Mai means "to seal or to break the blood vessel."

Dui 兌

One of the Eight Trigrams.

Emei 峨嵋

Name of a mountain in Sichuan province, China.

Ermen (TB-21) 耳門

An acupuncture cavity belonging to the Triple Burner channel.

Fa Jin 發勁

"Emitting Jin." Jin is martial power, in which muscular power is manifested to its maximum from mental concentration and Qi circulation.

Fen 分

"To divide."

Fen Jin 分筋

Fen means "to divide" and Jin means "muscles/tendons." Fen Jin means "to divide the muscles/tendons."

Feng 封

"To seal" or "to cover."

Fo 火

"Fire." One of the five elements.

Futu (LI-18) 伏兔

An acupuncture cavity belonging to the Large Intestine channel.

Gen 艮

One of the Eight Trigrams.

Gongfu (Kung Fu) 功夫

Means "energy-time." Anything which will take time and energy to learn or to accomplish is called Gongfu.

Gu 骨

Means "bone."

Gung Li Chuan 功力拳

The name of a barehand sequence in Chinese Long Fist martial arts.

Guoshu 國術

Abbreviation of "Zhongguo Wushu," which means "Chinese Martial Techniques."

Han 漢

A dynasty in Chinese history (206 B.C.-221 A.D.)

Han Ching-Tang 韓慶堂

A well known Chinese martial artist, especially in Taiwan in the last forty years. Master Han is also Dr. Yang Jwing-Ming's Long Fist grandmaster.

He 合

Means "to close."

Hou Tian Fa 後天法

Means "Post-Heaven Techniques." An internal Qigong style known from 550 A.D.

Hsing Yi Chuan (Xingyiquan) 形意拳

A style of internal Chinese martial arts.

Hua 化

Means "to neutralize."

Hua Jin 化勁

The Jin (martial power) used to neutralize the opponent's attacking.

Ji 擠

Means "to squeeze" or "to press."

Jiache (S-6) 頰車

Name of an acupuncture cavity. It belongs to the Stomach channel.

Jian Kao 肩靠

To use the shoulder to lean or to press against something or someone.

Jianjing (GB-21) 肩井

An acupuncture cavity belonging to the Gall Bladder channel.

Jianneiling (M-UE-48) 肩內陵

Name of an acupuncture cavity. A special point.

Jin 筋

Means "tendons."

Jin (Jing) 勁

Chinese martial power. A combination of "Li" (muscular power) and "Qi."

Jin Bu 進步

Means "to step forward."

Jin Shao-Feng 金紹峰

Master Yang Jwing-Ming's White Crane grandmaster.

Jing (Jin) 勁

Chinese martial power. A combination of "Li" (muscular power) and "Qi."

Jiquan (H-1) 極泉

An acupuncture cavity belonging to the Heart channel.

Jiuwei (C0-15) 鳩尾

An acupuncture cavity belonging to the Conceptional vessel.

Jou Tsung Hwa 周宗樺

A well known Taijiquan master in America.

Judo 柔道

A style of Japanese martial arts similar to wrestling.

Jujitsu 柔術道

A style of Japanese martial arts which uses theories similar to Chinese Taijiquan and Qin Na.

Kan 坎

One of the Eight Trigrams.

Kao 靠

Means "to lean or to press against."

Kao Tao 高濤

Master Yang Jwing-Ming's first Taijiquan master.

Kong Qi 空氣

Air.

Kun 坤

One of the Eight Trigrams.

Kung Fu (Gongfu) 功夫

Means "energy-time." Anything which will take time and energy to learn or to accomplish is called Kung Fu.

Li 離
One of the Eight Trigrams.

Li Mao-Ching 李茂清
Master Yang Jwing-Ming's Long Fist master.

Liang 梁
A dynasty in Chinese history (502-557 A.D.)

Liang Dexing (Jeffrey D. S, Liang) 梁德馨
Master Liang Shou-Yu's uncle, currently residing in Seattle, Washington.

Liang Shou-Yu 梁守渝
A well known Chinese martial arts and Qigong master. Currently resides in Vancouver, Canada.

Liang Wu 梁武
An emperor of the Chinese Liang dynasty.

Lie 挒
Means "to rend" or "to split."

Lie Jin 挒勁
The martial power of "rend."

Lien Bu Chuan 連步拳
One of the Long Fist barehand sequences.

Lingtai (Gv-10) 靈台
An acupuncture cavity belonging to the Governing vessel.

Liu He Ba Fa 六合八法
One of the Chinese internal martial arts, its techniques are combined from Taijiquan, Xingyi, and Baguazhang.

Lu 攦
Means "to rollback."

Mai 脈
Means "vessel" or "Qi channel."

Mu 木
Wood. One of the Five Elements.

Na 拿
Means "to hold" or "to grab."

Na Xue 拿穴
Means "to grab the cavity."

Na Xue 拿血
Means "to grab the blood vessel."

Naohu (Gv-17) 腦戶
An acupuncture cavity belonging to the Governing vessel.

Nanking Central Guoshu Institute 南京中央國術館
A national martial arts institute organized by the Chinese government in 1928.

Neiguan (P-6) 內關
An acupuncture cavity belonging to the Pericardium channel.

Pao Chui 炮捶
The second routine of Chen Style Taijiquan.

Peng 掤
Means "to ward off."

Peng Jin 掤勁
The martial power of warding off.

Peng Kai 掤開
Means "to ward off" something or someone so to open.

Qi (Chi) 氣
Chinese term for universal energy. A current popular model is that the Qi circulating in the human body is bio-electric in nature.

Qi Chen Dan Tian 氣沉丹田
"Sink the Qi to the Lower Dan Tian." The name of a Taijiquan posture.

Qi Mai 氣脈
Means "Qi channels."

Qian 乾
One of the Eight Trigrams.

Qian Kao 前靠
Means "to lean" or "to press" forward.

Qigong (Chi Kung) 氣功
The Gongfu of Qi, which means the study of Qi.

Qihai (Co-6) 氣海
An acupuncture cavity belonging to the Conceptional vessel.

Qimen (Li-14) 期門
An acupuncture cavity belonging to the Liver channel.

Qin (Chin) 擒
Means 'to catch" or "to seize."

Qin Na (Chin Na) 擒拿
Literally means "grab control." A component of Chinese martial arts which emphasizes grabbing techniques, to control your opponent's joints, in conjunction with attacking certain acupuncture cavities.

Qin Xiong 擒兇
To catch the murderer.

Quchi (LI-11) 曲池
Name of an acupuncture cavity. It belongs to the Large Intestine channel.

Ren Mai 任脈
Conceptional Vessel. One of the Eight Extraordinary Vessels.

Riyue (GB-24) 日月
An acupuncture cavity belonging to the Gall Bladder channel.

Rugen (S-18) 乳根
An acupuncture cavity belonging to the Stomach channel.

Ruzhong (S-17) 乳中
An acupuncture cavity belonging to the Stomach channel.

Sai (Chai) 釵
A kind of hairpin for ancient Chinese women. Later, it was derived into a kind of southern Chinese weapon.

San Shi Qi Shi 三十七勢
Means "thirty-seven postures." Yang Style Taijiquan contains thirty-seven postures.

Shang Kao 上靠
Means "to lean" or "to press" upward.

Shangen (M-HN-4) 山根
An acupuncture cavity. A special point.

Shaohai (H-3) 少海
Name of an acupuncture cavity. It belongs to the Heart channel.

Shaolin 少林
Young woods. Name of Shaolin Temple.

Shaolin Temple 少林寺
A monastery located in Henan province, China. The Shaolin Temple is well known because of its martial arts training.

Shi San Shi 十三勢
Means "Thirteen Postures." Taijiquan is also called "Thirteen Postures." It is simply because Taijiquan is built upon eight Jin patterns and five strategic movements.

Shuai 摔
Means "to throw." An abbreviation of "Shuai Jiao" (wrestling).

Shuai Jiao 摔交
Chinese wrestling. Part of Chinese martial arts.

Song 宋
A dynasty in Chinese history (960-1206 A.D.)

Shui 水
Water. One of the Five Elements.

Sun 孫
A last name of a Chinese family.

Sun Lu-Tang 孫祿堂
A well known Chinese martial artist

Tai Chi Chuan (Taijiquan) 太極拳
A Chinese internal martial style which based on the theory of Taiji (grand ultimate).

Taiji 太極
Means "grand ultimate." It is this force which generates two poles, Yin and Yang.

Taiji Huan Yuan 太極還原
"Return Taiji to its origin." The name of a Taijiquan posture.

Taiji Qi Shi 太極起勢

"Taiji beginning." The name of a Taijiquan posture.

Taijiquan (Tai Chi Chuan) 太極拳

A Chinese internal martial style which based on the theory of Taiji (grand ultimate).

Taipei 台北

The capital city of Taiwan located in the north of Taiwan.

Taipei Xian 台北縣

The county in the north of Taiwan.

Taiwan 台灣

An island to the south-east of mainland China. Also known as "Formosa."

Taiwan University 台灣大學

A well known university located on the north Taiwan.

Taiyang (M-HN-9) 太陽

Name of an acupuncture cavity. A special point.

Taizuquan 太祖拳

A style of Chinese external martial arts.

Tamkang 淡江

Name of a University in Taiwan.

Tamkang College Guoshu Club 淡江國術社

A Chinese martial arts club founded by Dr. Yang when he was studying in Tamkang College.

Ti 踢

Means "to kick."

Ti 提

Means "to lift."

Tiantu (Co-22) 天突

Name of an acupuncture cavity. It belongs to the Conception vessel.

Tianzong (SI-11) 天宗

Name of an acupuncture cavity. It belongs to the Small Intestine channel.

Ting Jin 聽勁

Listening Jin. A special training which uses the skin to feel the opponent's energy and from this feeling further to understand his intention.

Tu 土

Earth. One of the Five Elements.

Tui Bu 退步

Means "to step backward." Retreat.

Tui Kao 腿靠

Means "to lean against" or "to press against" with the leg.

Tui Na 推拿

Means "to push and grab." A category of Chinese massages for healing and injury treatment.

Tun Kao 臀靠

Means "to lean againt" or "to press against" with the hip.

Wai Dan Chi Kung (Wai Dan Qigong) 外丹氣功
External Elixir Qigong. In Wai Dan Qigong, a practitioner will generate Qi to the limbs, and then allow the Qi flow inward to nourish the internal organs.

Wang Shu-Tian 王樹田
A well known Chinese martial arts master.

Wilson Chen 陳威伸
Master Yang Jwing-Ming's friend.

Wu 吳
The last name of a Chinese family.

Wuji 無極
Means "no extremity."

Wushu 武術
Literally, "martial techniques."

Wuyi 武藝
Literally, "martial arts."

Xi Kao 膝靠
Means "to lean againt" or "to press against" with the knee.

Xia Kao 下靠
Means to "press downward."

Xiao Jiu Tian 小九天
Small Nine Heaven. A Qigong style created around 550 A.D.

Xiao Lu 小攦
Small rollback.

Xiao Quan 小圈
Means "small circle."

Xin 心
Means "heart." Xin means the mind generated from emotional disturbance.

Xingyi 形意
An abbreviation of Xingyiquan.

Xingyiquan (Hsing Yi Chuan) 形意拳
One of the best known Chinese internal martial styles created by Marshal Yue Fei during Chinese Song dynasty (1103-1142 A.D.).

Xinzhu Xian 新竹縣
Birthplace of Dr. Yang Jwing-Ming in Taiwan.

Xiong Kao 胸靠
Means "to lean againt" or "to press against" with the chest.

Xue Mai 血脈
Means "blood vessels."

Xun 巽
One of the Eight Trigrams.

Yang 陽
Too sufficient. One of the two poles. The other is Yin.

Yang Jwing-Ming 楊俊敏
　　Author of this book.

Yang Mei-Ling 楊美玲
　　Master Yang Jwing-Ming's wife.

Yang Style 楊氏
　　The style created by the Yang family.

Yi 意
　　Wisdom mind. The mind generated from wise judgment.

Yifeng (TB-17) 翳風
　　Name of an acupuncture cavity. It belongs to the Triple Burner channel.

Yin 陰
　　Deficient. One of the two poles. The other is Yang.

Yin Jin 引勁
　　The Jin (martial power) of leading.

Yin Qi Gui Yuan 引氣歸原
　　"Lead the Qi to return its origin." The name of a Taijiquan posture.

Yingchuang (S-16) 膺窗
　　Name of an acupuncture cavity. It belongs to the Stomach channel.

You Pan 右盼
　　Means "beware of the right."

Yuanye (GB-22) 淵腋
　　Name of an acupuncture cavity. It belongs to the Gall Bladder channel.

Yun Shou 雲手
　　"Wave hands in clouds." Name of a Taijiquan posture.

Zhang Zhao-Tong 張兆東
　　A well known Chinese marital artist.

Zhen 震
　　One of the Eight Trigrams.

Zhong 中
　　Centering.

Zhong Ding 中定
　　To firm the center.

Zhong Quan 中圈
　　Middle circle.

Zhongwan (Co-12) 中脘
　　Name of an acupuncture cavity. It belongs to the Conceptional vessel.

Zhou 肘
　　Elbow.

Zhua 抓
　　Means "to grasp" or "to grab."

Zhua Jin 抓筋

Means "to grab the tendons."

Zhua Xue 抓穴

Means "to grab the cavity."

Zhuan 轉

Means "to turn around" or " to twist."

Zi Wu Liu Zhu 子午流注

Zi refers to the period around midnight (11:00 PM - 1:00 AM), and Wu refers to midday (11:00 AM - 1:00 PM). Jiu Zhu means the flowing tendency. Therefore: a schedule of the Qi circulation showing which channel has the predominant Qi flow at any particular time, and where the predominant Qi flow is in the Conception and Governing vessels.

Zuo 左

Left.

Zuo Gu 左顧

Look to the left or beware of the left.

Zuo Wan 坐腕

Settle down the wrist.

■ Index ■

Books & Videos from YMAA

YMAA Publication Center Book Series

YMAA Publication Center Children's Book Series

YMAA Publication Center Videotape Series

YMAA Publication Center 楊氏武藝協會

38 Hyde Park Avenue • Jamaica Plain, MA 02130
1-800-669-8892 • email: ymaa@aol.com